MW00655688

"You all have the ability to influence, and you all have your brand . . . who you are and what others say about you. The authors do a very practical and valuable job of exploring what is at the foundation of these two things . . . *CLARITY*. Be sure to read this one to get the insight, ideas, and inspiration to take your influence and brand to the next level."

—**Danny Bader**, keynote speaker and bestselling author of *Back to Life: The Path of Resilience* and *Taking The Sh*t Out of the Show: 7 Short Stories to Navigate Life's Challenges*

"Clear communication is as effective as it is hard to master. *The Clarity Advantage* is an excellent book that uses real-world stories to demonstrate why clear communication is crucial and provides coaching tips to help you succeed. It is a must-read for anyone looking to improve their communication skills and boost their influence."

—**Eivind Slaaen**, head of People & Culture Development, Hilti Corporation

"*The Clarity Advantage* provides insightful tips for both leaders and followers to ponder as they connect with one another. It challenges us to pause before making common communication missteps. Tobin and Peterson did a terrific job illuminating some of our tendencies to react before realizing the impact of our words."

—**Katie Rosenbusch**, PhD, professor at George Mason University and org development consultant

"Clear, concise advice in the form of relatable vignettes coupled with actionable coaching tips that can deliver immediate impact. I recommend this book for anyone looking to level up their communication tool kit."

—**Cady Wolf**, founder & CEO, A23 Advisors

"We would all like to have more influence in our organizations and our lives. But too often we derail our best efforts, getting distracted, failing to communicate skillfully, or just plain not thinking about the people we lead or the information we share. In this thoughtful book, Tobin and Peterson address this issue head-on making the keys to greater influence clear through practical examples, clear insights, and a gift for uncovering the foibles that make us human and limit our ability to lead people in a direction that matters. If you are looking to get your act together, be a better leader, and make more of a difference, this book is a great place to start."

—**Alan Gregerman**, founder of VENTURE WORKS Inc. and bestselling author of *Surrounded by Geniuses and The Necessity of Strangers*

"To be an effective leader, you've got to be an effective communicator. As a CEO whose firm is focused on media and public speaking for leaders in a multitude of disciplines, this book contains valuable information for our instructors to share with our clients."

—**Julie Parker**, president & CEO of Julie Parker Communications

"Infused with pro-level coaching tips, *The Clarity Advantage* is a playbook for anyone wanting to understand the world of professional work. Tobin and Peterson's easy-to-understand rules, coaching tips, and no-nonsense approach to upskilling your leadership game will captivate everyone from Generation X to Z and provide the essentials every great leader needs for continued growth and influence."

—**Shelley Kemp**, SHRM-SCP, HR business partner, Memphis Grizzlies; certified mindfulness coach, author, speaker for Pivot Life Global

"Full of tips for us to gain influence and as importantly connect more deeply with those with whom we work, live with and love, I will be referring to this book frequently to my one-on-one and team coaching clients. It is filled with relatable stories and actionable steps to have the impact you want!"

—**Lori Zukin**, PhD, executive and team coach

THE CLARITY ADVANTAGE

THE CLARITY ADVANTAGE

Overcome the Ten Communication Pitfalls and Boost Your Influence

TIMOTHY J. TOBIN *and* ROGER S. PETERSON

ROWMAN & LITTLEFIELD

Lanham • Boulder • New York • London

Published by Rowman & Littlefield
An imprint of The Rowman & Littlefield Publishing Group, Inc.
4501 Forbes Boulevard, Suite 200, Lanham, Maryland 20706
www.rowman.com

86-90 Paul Street, London EC2A 4NE

Copyright © 2024 by Timothy J. Tobin and Roger S. Peterson

All rights reserved. No part of this book may be reproduced in any form or by any electronic or mechanical means, including information storage and retrieval systems, without written permission from the publisher, except by a reviewer who may quote passages in a review.

British Library Cataloguing in Publication Information Available

Library of Congress Cataloging-in-Publication Data

Names: Tobin, Timothy J., author. | Peterson, Roger S., 1945– author.
Title: The clarity advantage : overcome the ten communication pitfalls and boost your influence / Timothy J. Tobin and Roger S. Peterson.
Description: Lanham : Rowman & Littlefield, [2024] | Includes bibliographical references and index.
Identifiers: LCCN 2024002570 (print) | LCCN 2024002571 (ebook) | ISBN 9781538179024 (cloth) | ISBN 9781538179031 (ebook)
Subjects: LCSH: Leadership. | Communication in management. | Interpersonal communication.
Classification: LCC HD57.7 .T628 2024 (print) | LCC HD57.7 (ebook) | DDC 658.4/092—dc23/eng/20240215
LC record available at https://lccn.loc.gov/2024002570
LC ebook record available at https://lccn.loc.gov/2024002571

∞™ The paper used in this publication meets the minimum requirements of American National Standard for Information Sciences—Permanence of Paper for Printed Library Materials, ANSI/NISO Z39.48-1992.

Contents

PART II
Stepping Around the Pitfalls . . . for More Enduring Influence

Introduction

The key to successful leadership today is influence, not authority.
—MANAGEMENT GURU KEN BLANCHARD

Something about the title of this book grabbed you. We suspect you just had to find out what those pitfalls and pathways toward influence are.

Here's the **gist of the book:** Our book is about the distractions people exhibit in their interaction with colleagues, blowing their ability to lead regardless of title. It can become a vicious cycle. Distractions impact clarity, and lack of clarity impacts credibility. We've all been there.

Our book includes scores of **slice-of-life stories** of folks who fell into these distracting pitfalls. These vignettes illustrate how their colleagues reacted . . . *often negatively*. You may well stop in a middle of a vignette and say, "Geez, I do that!"

Our book is loaded with **coaching tips**. If you want to improve *your* clarity of communication to bolster *your* credibility and *your* influence, we're here for you. In short, we can be your personal coach to help you build your clout.

We cover **ten common pitfalls** in part I. We communicate in so many ways—in meetings, emails, texting, or just quick conversations. And our exposure is compounded by our numerous online conversations, especially with colleagues in other countries. Too often, we find ourselves moving fast, with so many mounting deadlines and expectations that we don't even have time to think or to plan our communications. Without awareness and planning, the chance of stumbling into one of the pitfalls increases. We're here to help you know what to look out for.

We offer **five solid pathways** in part II to step around the pitfalls, to help you hold your colleagues' attention and enhance your influence.

Heads up: Still doubt you need this? Well, take our short quiz:

- Have you ever been in a meeting where everyone is contributing to the conversation, *except you*?
- Has anyone ever asked, "Ah, could you please rephrase that for us?"
- Has anyone ever asked you to provide missing details or suggested that your comment or message was unclear?
- Did anyone ever say your emails have come across as abrupt? (And then comes texting, which loses all aspects of voice tone and nonverbal communication.)
- Has anyone challenged you on how you interpret facts and data?
- Has anyone suggested your comments all seem to betray a bias of some sort?
- Has anyone questioned your credibility? If so, your influence is stuck.

If you answered yes *to even one of these questions*, our book is here for you.

The Four Cs: This book is all about mastering the Four Cs, so your influence with colleagues in any organization can make the difference you want:

- Critical thinking
- Clarity of communication
- Credibility
- Clout

We have a broad definition of critical thinking. It's not just about assessing what is factual and what is not, or what is right versus what's wrong. It's also how you think ahead about how you will communicate in a particular situation, or how you plan to present yourself in meetings with others. It's also about realizing that the way you think and communicate may differ from that of others. And now with artificial intelligence (AI), we must also think critically about images we see in social media.

Clear communication seems compromised all around us. If colleagues cannot understand what you say—*or, worse, don't believe you*—your influence is significantly limited. We will cover the stumbles along the way toward achieving clarity in several pitfall chapters.

Credibility goes bye-bye if critical thinking and clarity are absent. So does your clout, your influence on the job, in professional associations, with friends—you name it.

All of these issues are real, whether you have a managerial title or not. Perhaps absorbing all we offer may finally lead to that kind of title; at the very least, it will certainly lead to greater clarity and credibility.

Yes! It's about your "brand." Think of this as a personal marketing campaign to enhance your influence brand, with all of the product improvements and packaging you will learn on these pages. Pathway 5 introduces the concept of your aspirational personal brand (APB). Oh. Start compiling your personal branding notebook.

Don't miss the appendices: We have also included three valuable, practical appendices for your continuing reference; don't skip them!

- The first appendix is **the Crystal Rule**, a ten-step guide to clarity. Simply put, the Crystal Rule is about communicating with others and how *they* would want to be communicated with.
- The second appendix is a quick guide to **critical thinking skills** by an expert colleague of ours.
- The last appendix is a **short guide to problem-solving**, a tool everyone can use to boost credibility and influence.

Getting more curious? Check out our table of contents. You may well be surprised where, and how often, you can be misunderstood . . . or dismissed.

—Tim and Roger

Part I

Ten Pitfalls to Clarity, Credibility . . . and Your Clout

Pitfall #1: Speed Sprawls

When Haste Wastes Time, Clarity, Credibility . . . and Influence

The speed of communications is wondrous to behold.
It is also true that speed can multiply the distribution
of information that we know to be untrue.

—EDWARD R. MURROW

Edward R. Murrow was an American broadcast journalist who established his acclaim during his coverage of World War II. Murrow saw it coming. The "it," of course, is speed, and the desire for real-time information, which he delivered through a series of live broadcasts during the war. He covered war-torn London and became a television news pioneer.

But Murrow died before the Internet. Before email. Before texting. Before social media—and the influence wielded by all of these communication methods. Access to information has changed dramatically since then. What would Murrow say now about the effect of speed on factual communication? He wasn't the sort to hit "send" without considering all the factors.

With so much information available, you must be able to discern facts from feelings and opinions—not only in others' communication, but in yours as well. Too often, either in haste to get a message out, or for more sinister reasons, the line between fact and opinion is blurred. This can only result in a distraction from your credibility. (We discuss distractions a great deal in this book.)

We are not here to argue the merits of speed of information in general. Our combined experience spanning decades suggests there are times when getting information out quickly versus having it be perfectly stated is essential. Speed sometimes allows you to control the message, and if handled correctly, to minimize rumors.

It also allows you to do the other, very important part of the communication equation, and that is to listen. We advocate keeping people informed, but for the sake of your credibility, if you opt for speed, be sure to emphasize transparency regarding what you do know versus what you don't. If you always wait until you have complete and accurate information, people may have heard incomplete or inaccurate parts of a message from elsewhere.

There are other times when speed over accuracy of information can be detrimental to how the message is received—as well as damaging to your credibility. For example, a CEO we worked with had to make the difficult decision to lay off some of her staff. The layoff discussions were completed in a single day, and the CEO quickly held an all-hands meeting afterward to promise the rest of the company that there would be no more layoffs. Unfortunately, the economic factors didn't improve, and a short time later she had to conduct additional layoffs. Although the intentions of her initial message were genuine, she communicated before she understood the nature of the environment, and her credibility ultimately suffered. In this case, it was appropriate for the CEO to communicate with her staff when she did, but she should have provided more clarity and transparency about the uncertainty in the environment. Additionally, it was not to her benefit to make commitments given the level of uncertainty involved.

Communication can be challenging. It requires thought and careful planning. In fact, we would argue that when it comes to communication, the faster you want to get a message out, the more thought and planning is required. Is your message clear? Are you conveying what you intend to convey? And are you delivering it in the most appropriate way for it to be received correctly and acted upon if necessary?

COACHING TIP: Clearly define the objectives of your intended message and determine whether the words, tone, timing, and delivery support those objectives.

There is not a simple one-size-fits-all approach to communication. There are nuances, with multiple factors. We review them here, and we incorporate multiple vignettes so you can see them in action. Think about how you would handle a similar scenario. What would you do? And more importantly, what can you *learn* from these vignettes? (To further facilitate learning, we will include Coaching Tips throughout for quick reference.)

The Gist

In this first chapter, let's be clear about what this book asserts: To have influence with others (colleagues, family, and other acquaintances), you must be credible. Makes sense, right? After all, credibility is about being trusted and believable. There is a saying that it takes one hundred acts to build trust and only one to tear it down. That is especially true of how you communicate. But to be credible, you must communicate clearly and accurately. That means without ambiguity. The problem arises when we convey our thoughts too quickly, and ambiguity results.

So, first order: Is your message clearly conveyed?

Second: Is your message conveying facts, partial facts, or opinions? Make that clear from the outset. Communication should not be a guessing game. If you treat it as such, you risk your credibility being questioned.

But to communicate clearly, critical thinking is necessary. Objective thinking acknowledges facts and evaluates issues without preconceived notions or biases. Aristotle once said, "It is the mark of an educated mind to be able to entertain a thought without accepting it."

Have you ever dashed off an email or text and later regretted it? Everyone has done this at least once! Haste can happen with verbal or electronic communication. The issue here is the quickness as much as, *if not more than*, the content. Haste is when you rush to get a message out and lose the point or the clarity of the message. Speed is more deliberate—an effort to get information out quickly before rumor can spread, but still with an emphasis on accuracy.

Remember this: Speed requires consideration so you can maintain your credibility—and influence. But haste is the enemy of critical thinking. In some instances, haste may also be the enemy of clarity and credibility.

Most communication regrets involve speed—that is, not taking the time to craft the message you intend, or to think about how it is delivered or received. So, we encourage you to consider the following questions throughout this chapter and in your own practice: When is speed of communication important? And what impact will the speed of communication have on how the message lands?

Scene #1

One leader we coached, Deborah, was very well liked and respected by her team. She connected well with them, and they were engaged. However, after several weeks of a project being stalled out, without much thought or planning, Deborah hastily began Monday's weekly update meeting by chastising the team for not making progress.

They were working hard but had faced some unprecedented challenges that Deborah hadn't considered. She didn't have all the facts. And worse, she didn't give her message much thought. Not surprisingly, it landed with a thud. She spent the next week apologizing to the team as a whole and to everyone individually. Her credibility as a leader never fully recovered.

COACHING TIP: Be wise—don't chastise . . . at least not in public. If you must provide critical feedback, do so individually, in private. Feel free to give praise in public or private, as the situation calls for.

This chapter, Pitfall #1, is about managing speed in balance with critical thinking. Critical thinking is a quality compromised by hasty communication in a growing era of factual sloppiness. This was exacerbated with the evolution of the twenty-four-hour news cycle. It became increasingly important to get a news story out quickly, knowing that any of the outstanding or inaccurate facts could be filled in or corrected later. In other words, the lines have become blurred. It's important to remember that reality exists, regardless of how you feel emotionally about the issue. Call it the BHWY Reality: Be honest with yourself.

Scene #2

Richard is the international sales manager for Acme Company. He has representatives in the United Kingdom, Australia, South Africa, Japan, and India, a staff spread across several time zones and each a local national. Sales are not meeting the quarter's projections, something Richard did not anticipate. He's frantic. His email to his reps follows:

> *I don't know what you are all spending your time on, but I suspect your focus is on the wrong things. In lieu of the quarter projections, I want your call sheets returned ASAP. We have an incredible product line that has earned fulsome praise from management and the VCs. Those VCs are unforgiving. Are you pitching the new service suite? If not, it's a joke. It's not even funny. I can't wait to see those call sheets. I want them ASAP.*

Richard's email surely would not portray him in any way other than frantic, so it worked in that sense. The email, dashed off with little forethought, hardly added to his credibility. But there are other problems. As for communication, Richard made six big errors aside from suffering a speed sprawl. Can you spot them? If not, be sure to read Pitfalls #2, 3, and 4.

Although Richard's email may have been the quickest form of communication, it was not the most effective. It landed with a thud. The team felt dejected, demotivated, and even angry. In fact, rather than boost productivity and get the team moving, it had the opposite effect. Most of the team spent the next few hours discussing Richard's email rather than focusing on the work.

COACHING TIP: Never send anything via electronic communication that will elicit emotional responses. Have those conversations face-to-face.

Let us take a quick little detour on the topic here. We know what you might be thinking. What about the multiple videoconferencing platforms available today? There are too many to list here, and the vendor landscape will continue to evolve, so we will speak broadly about real-time video conversations. Although there are benefits to having such technology at our disposal, it should not completely replace face-to-face communications.

Let's be real: In this global and hybrid work environment we operate in, it is unlikely that you are going to fly across the country or even drive across town to have a face-to-face conversation on some topic. We're not suggesting that you do that. What we are suggesting is that there is a time and place for various communication methods, and you should not simply choose an approach because it's easy or fast—or because it allows you to avoid an uncomfortable conversation while looking at the other person.

Real-time videoconference platforms such as Zoom and Skype can be a great alternative to face-to-face conversations. However, keep in mind that they have their limitations. For example, you may not be able to observe all the body language cues. Additionally, it is possible for one of the participants to be distracted or multitasking during a videoconference.

Harnessing the Power of Critical Thinking

Critical thinking is the process of balancing your hunches with your questions and using your questions to uncover the hidden nuances of an issue. Hunches, or intuition, often grow through experience. It's a "Been there, done that—and learned from it" approach. This can also be described as a hypothesis-driven approach. It allows you to focus quickly on a few essential possibilities. Once you master that, speed can be better managed and more carefully considered. We will give you some guidance on critical communication later in this chapter. Also, in the appendix, you will find a resource to help get you started—a hypothesis-driven approach to problem-solving.

> *The fundamental cause of trouble in the world today is that the stupid are cocksure while the intelligent are full of doubt.*
>
> —PHILOSOPHER AND MATHEMATICIAN BERTRAND RUSSELL

What would Russell say today about what social media has done to hasty communication?

A pocket guide to critical thinking. Other pitfalls in this book will deal with aspects of critical thinking, such as the chapter on logical fallacies. But given the importance of critical thinking to your clarity and credibility, here is a minimum baker's-dozen list of essentials to serve as a foundation:

- Be curious in all aspects of communication—those you receive and those you issue.
- Know your biases and keep them under control. (Yes, you do have some.)
- Preconceived notions cannot possibly fit every issue.
- Look for nuance. As much as we all love simplicity, not all issues are simple.
- Give up the notion that there's a simple yes/no answer to every issue.
- Give up the notion that there's a simple right/wrong answer to every issue.
- An approach or proposal does not necessarily have to be accepted in its entirety. Parts, one at a time, might work better.
- Past practice should always be questioned as possibly obsolete practice. Be suspicious.
- Consider the source. Do they have a track record of credibility? Do they have an agenda?
- Always ask, "Where's the evidence?"
- Always ask, "What will work and what won't work?"

- Always ask, "Is the short-term fix really better than a long-term fix?"
- In law firms, several partners typically take up the case against the client to flesh out what the opponent's lawyers will likely do in court. In short, become a good debater.

A journalist's essential critical questions. Long ago, the field of journalism went through cloudy times, historically called "yellow journalism." It then reformed itself with professional schools of journalism at several universities. Reporters are trained to ask these six simple questions about any issue or crisis before filing their stories:

- What?
- Who?
- When?
- Where?
- Why?
- How?

You don't have to be a journalist to memorize these questions and use them for your own communications. Answering these basics often conveys the necessary information and can help you avoid bias. Einstein said it well: "The important thing is not to stop questioning. Curiosity has its own reason for existing."

The Powerful Practice of Questioning

Good questions help to clarify. Someone known for asking good questions has earned credibility. That colleague who asks lots of questions is likely to ask the same questions others are too timid to offer. But that colleague may also be asking questions no one else has considered.

It is not about the quantity of questions. It's more important that the right questions are asked. Asking the right questions requires critical thinking. Think about incorporating this phrase: "Help me understand . . ." followed by how or why. (Note: In our Additional Resources at the end of this chapter, we have included an excellent encyclopedia of questions across many workplace situations.)

COACHING TIP: Encourage thoughtful questions prior to, during, and after you deliver a message. Although it adds time, it also fosters clarity.

Be especially attentive to questions coming from a new colleague. They bring to your organization a neutral mind not limited by their own expertise. They may well be posing something powerful. In fact, you should encourage new colleagues to ask questions. Similarly, you should seek alternative viewpoints when trying to solve a complex problem. For example, if you are trying to solve a complex operational problem, consider including a team member with a different functional background, such as finance or marketing.

Scene #3

A church's longtime founding leader, George, calls a meeting of the congregation's planning committee. It's time to plan the next major outreach event, called The Festival, to which congregants invite friends in hopes they will decide to join the church. The leisurely format includes an array of treats interspersed with tabletop displays that focus on established programs, such as children's activities, picnics, Bible study, and special services. George has always led the way with this format. He started most of the activities. At the planning meeting, several members mention that newer churches offer refreshments at the weekly service and have sports clubs, such as a tennis team. "No, what we have has worked for decades," George asserts. "I started all this many years ago when we opened." Committee members look down or glance furtively at each other. After the meeting, several chat in the parking lot. George goes to his car with his authority intact.

What advice would you give to George?

COACHING TIP: Leverage experience (yours and others') to generate ideas and hypotheses. This will allow you to focus valuable time and resources on the most likely and influential alternatives.

The outsider advantage. Someone new to an organization has not yet absorbed all of the culture, its habits, and its knee-jerk reactions and consistencies. They may say things that strike at a sacred cow somewhere, or may just bring up an angle that has never been broached. Sometimes the outsider will pursue this line of reasoning until an insider admits the outsider's question spotlights a point well made.

COACHING TIP: Incorporate into your communication the four most powerful words a leader can use: *What do you think?*

Had George actively sought input from the committee, here are some questions the outsider might have asked:

- Why do you do this every year? What's the payoff?
- How do we know this is working? How do we measure this?
- What is the long-term consequence if we don't do this anymore?
- What's the worst thing that could happen if we change course?
- What if X has some admitted downsides; can we put it into the long term to improve it?

Speed is not only the enemy of critical thinking, but it can also result in unanticipated consequences, as we've seen through these vignettes. Deborah did not set out to break her team's trust, nor did Richard intend to demotivate his staff. And George did not intentionally set out to minimize his congregation's contributions. But, whether intended or not, they each got negative results. Each team member likely felt diminished and less engaged, and each leader lost some of their credibility in the process.

This can be addressed before it even occurs. Here are some questions to consider and questions to ask before sending an important communication:

- Can it wait until tomorrow while I think about it? What's the rush? (And beating rush-hour traffic is a poor excuse.)
- How will the audience perceive my wording?
- When are they likely to read it, and with what level of attentiveness?
- How will your sharpest employees, colleagues, customers—or boss—react?
- How will your weakest employees, colleagues, customers react? And your boss?
- What is your intended outcome of sending this message now?
- What would be the reaction if your message was posted on the front page of a newspaper? (Of course, we hope this doesn't happen; our point is to get you to think about what the reaction might be if others saw your message and tried to interpret your tone.)

COACHING TIP: Hit pause, not send. Let your message sit in your drafts folder for a few minutes, hours, or even overnight before hitting "send." If, after some time away, you would still deliver the same message the same way, then proceed. Otherwise, edit accordingly.

Scene #4

A new assistant pastor arrives at George's church. Susan is younger than her popular, retiring predecessor. She's much younger than George. After weeks of introductions, quiet inquiries, and just plain eyeing the surrounding landscape, another planning meeting is called. The meeting opens quietly as the coffee is poured and the pastries are grabbed. "I've spent some time, as you all know, getting up to speed," Susan says with a broad, nonthreatening smile. "You've built a very nice congregation, which won me over, after all." Then this outsider innocently asks these questions:

- What is the average age of the congregants?
- How many children now attend versus, say, thirty years ago?
- Why have some people left for other churches?
- Whom are you seeking to attract with the church festival—what demographic?
- What are the objectives of the event?
- What from the past has worked particularly well at meeting this objective? What has detracted from it?
- Does anyone have any other ways for how we might achieve the objectives?

Everyone looked to George. No comment. Susan wasn't seeking to challenge anyone, including George. She just wanted to clarify the local situation, given that it was called a planning meeting. During past planning meetings, no one had thought to consider these questions.

COACHING TIP: To foster productivity and minimize miscommunication, align with key participants and leaders on meeting expectations and objectives prior to having a meeting.

Form an outsiders' club. Gaining multiple perspectives on issues is valuable. Consider forming a monthly breakfast group of people in your profession. No competitors. Just people with the same title as yours, sharing work challenges, asking questions, and offering insights. This should be viewed as a peer-mentoring approach that allows you to raise a difficult issue and gain insights from people who may have, or had, the same issue or problem. H. L. Mencken hit the nail on the head: "To every complex problem there is a simple answer, and it is wrong."

And Back to Your Communications

We all acquired an education to better face life's issues and to solve problems, both personal and within our organizations. Solving problems in contemporary society, with worldwide communications and worldwide diversity, has never been more complicated—especially due to the speed of communication.

Nothing is simple anymore. The wrong message can reach everywhere, immediately, with good and bad consequences. Be a master of questions. Avoid being a superficial champion of simplistic answers. It's all about how others perceive you. It's how you build your credibility and your influence—your clout.

Four free and helpful tools. What follows are some tips to guide you in managing communications and the speed you use:

1. **Your sweet spot.** What is your writing/communication sweet spot? What time of day (e.g., before colleagues arrive in the office)? What place (e.g., at home by the fire)? When and where can you more comfortably plan out critical communications for, say, a week? Co-author Roger often must get away from the keyboard and just go outside or sit by the fire with classical music playing, armed with nothing but a yellow pad and a nice fountain pen. (Yes, a pen. We once used them a lot.) Cognitive psychologists have shown such get-away-from-it-all actions are truly mind-stretching and blow open the door to creative breakthroughs. Call it communication yoga! Promise yourself you will try it.
2. **Your writing buddy.** A second pair of eyes is always helpful, someone who might see your words in a very different light and provide another perspective. Your buddy could be a spouse/partner or a trusted colleague. Don't always pick someone with whom you work, because they are in the same work culture.
3. **Your deadly file.** If you have been pummeled by resistance and flak from any previous emails or texts, keep them in your email archive file. Look for consistent complaints, such as vagueness, terseness, or even tartness, misused humor, biases, discriminatory language, judgmental tone, veiled threats. Some of these things may be your old habits of communication. We have all accumulated a deadly file. Time to get rid of old habits?

4. **And the productive pause of benign neglect.** If some communication can wait a day, wait a day. Writers routinely do this to give themselves a chance to revise things that appear vague upon second reading. See what some hours of benign neglect reveal that went over your head when you first wrote it. Combine this with your sweet spot and see real change.

To be persuasive we must be believable; to be believable
we must be credible; to be credible we must be truthful.

—EDWARD R. MURROW

COACHING TIP: Find a writing buddy. Consider having someone you trust review a critical, time-sensitive communication before sending.

When is speed justifiable? You may be saying "Hey, this isn't realistic! It's a fast-paced organization. It's either the quick or the dead!" Fair enough. So, when is it acceptable to dash off something quickly? When is it inadvisable? You'll get to experience this in greater depth in Pathway #1 in part II of this book. However, here are some justifications for your quick reference. Speed is justifiable:

- to stop a major disconnect with a customer;
- to stop someone from an immediate course of action due to policy change;
- to avoid significant risk to the company or its stakeholders, and/or to prevent a major legal problem from occurring, the solution to follow comfortably later; and
- to alert the recipient they are needed elsewhere right now.

I didn't have time to write a short letter,
so I wrote a long one instead.

—NOVELIST AND HUMORIST MARK TWAIN

The implication behind Twain's quote is that getting to the point concisely takes time, thought, and effort. Rambling is so much easier.

We have so many methods of communication at our disposal now. Be thoughtful in which one you choose and how you utilize each tool. Just as not every household fix requires a hammer, not all communication requires an email or text. Since those media have become so commonplace, however, you should be prepared when you have to use either of those options.

Composing an urgent email or text requires a sense of brevity so that the message isn't lost in wordiness or tone. Although you want to keep your email short and simple, do not overlook the pleasantries consistent with your organization's culture. Think critically. For text messages, don't go over ten words. For emails, follow the four-finger rule: Don't send anything longer than the width of your four fingers when held up to your computer screen. Try to avoid prepositional phrases, adverbs, and even adjectives. In short, get to the point, and always consider the recipient's physical situation and time of day. For example, what if it's a message about a customer or colleague with whom the recipient is having lunch at that moment? The recipient must read the message fast without appearing rude.

COACHING TIP: Keep your written communication short—ten words or so for texts, and follow the four-finger rule for emails.

In an era in which texting is king, remember an old-fashioned form of communication: the telephone call. In short, consider all aspects of time and timing. Don't risk clarity and credibility, and thus, your influence.

Summary of Coaching Tips

- Clearly define the objectives of your intended message and determine whether the words, tone, timing, and delivery support those objectives.
- Be wise, and don't chastise—at least not in public. If you must provide critical feedback, do so individually in private. Give praise in public or private, as the situation calls for.
- Never send anything via electronic communication that will elicit emotional responses. Have those conversations face-to-face, whether it's in a Zoom or Skype call, or by telephone, in that order of preference.
- Encourage thoughtful questions prior to, during, and after you deliver a message. Although it adds time, it also fosters clarity.
- Leverage experience (yours and others') to generate ideas and hypotheses. This will allow you to focus valuable time and resources on the most likely and influential alternatives.
- Incorporate into your communication the four most powerful words a leader can use: *What do you think*?

- Hit pause, not send. Let your message sit in your drafts folder for a few minutes, hours, or even overnight before hitting "send." If, after some time away, you would still deliver the same message the same way, then proceed. Otherwise, edit accordingly.
- To foster productivity and minimize miscommunication, align with key participants and leaders on meeting expectations and objectives prior to having a meeting.
- Find a writing buddy. Consider having someone you trust review a critical, time-sensitive communication before sending.
- Keep your written communication short—ten or so words for texts, and follow the four-finger rule for emails.

Summary of Pitfall #1

Some of you may have dismissed this chapter as wishful thinking, or naive. We admit our current work style embraces speed. "Gotta be quick. . . . Can't slow down for a minute. . . . Must keep up. . . . Do it now, and clean up the mess later."

We have all worked in fast-paced organizations with complex tasks and multiple competing priorities. Both your authors have been in such industries and organizations, including high tech and advertising. We tried in this chapter to provide practical guidance you can use to manage communication and critical thinking. Throughout this chapter on Pitfall #1, we want to help you avoid rushing to failure.

Those who would suggest this is wishful thinking or naive help make the case for exactly why this is a pitfall you must step around, or risk your credibility taking a plunge. Speedy communication too often happens without considering the costs. Too often, the focus is on checking that box. Hit "send" now. Forgo the consequences. What we assert is that under no circumstances should we confuse lazy, terse, or inaccurate with speed. You can be thoughtful and quick. When a situation calls for speed, your goal is not fast *or* thoughtful; it's fast *and* thoughtful.

Another way to look at the issue of speed is to consider how much time it takes to clean up the mess from a single message gone wrong, or the downstream engagement and productivity lost from hastily firing off a message. When it comes to great leadership or great communication, don't confuse speed or quantity with quality.

Moving you along. The next chapter, Pitfall #2, focuses on words. No, not spelling. Not grammar. Rather, the focus is on sloppiness, incorrect usage, and wordiness that can rob the user of credibility. And just to warn you—we've all used some of the words and phrases, including you. Got your attention?

Additional Resources

Each pitfall is written to pique your interest. For further guidance on communications and critical thinking that suffer from haste, and more on the fine art of asking good questions, check out these classics. (Actually, buy them for your personal library.)

- *Don't Believe Everything You Think: The 6 Basic Mistakes We Make in Thinking* by Thomas Kida (New York: Prometheus Books, 2006).
- *Questions That Work: How to Ask Questions That Will Help You Succeed in Any Business Situation* by Andrew Finlayson (New York: AMACOM Books, 2001).
- *Invisible Solutions: 25 Lenses That Reframe and Help Solve Difficult Business Problems* by Stephen Shapiro (Herndon, VA: Amplify Publishing, 2020).
- *The Intelligence Trap: Why Smart People Make Dumb Mistakes* by David Robson (New York: W. W. Norton & Company, 2019).
- *The Constitution of Knowledge: A Defense of Truth* by Jonathan Rauch (Washington, DC: Brookings Institution Press, 2021).

Pitfall #2: Word Wanderings

Wrong Words, Weak Words, and Wordy Phrases Can Blow Your Credibility

It's not what you say, it's what people hear.
—POLITICAL CONSULTANT DR. FRANK LUNTZ

That quote is the subtitle of Luntz's book, cited below in our Additional Resources. His clients are politicians who often get a foot stuck in their mouth. This chapter will help you avoid the same distasteful problem.

Inside a Washington hearing. During the 2006 confirmation hearings for Justice Samuel Alito, a prominent academic testified to the Senate Judiciary Committee. When asked about Alito's impartiality, he stated, "I have no reason to think that Judge Alito begins with a strong dispositional inclination to only favor governmental power over individual rights."[1]

You now know, readers, why we titled this pitfall "Word Wanderings." Any high school English teacher would have edited that statement in a writing assignment. What was wrong with simply saying "I don't think Judge Alito favors government power over individual rights"? Isn't the rephrased version more to the point? The original statement may be grammatically correct, but this pitfall is not about grammar. It is about precision and clarity.

Word choice can say much about you. Are they the right words? Do they make sense? What message do they convey to the audience? It is essential that you know your audience. But an even bigger warning: Don't allow your unclear wording to be a distraction. Distractions are pitfalls to credibility.

The purpose of communication is to convey a clear message and connect with your audience. *That* is where your credibility comes from.

The wordy thank-you. Let's bring it down to another level. How often have you heard a guest speaker at a casual luncheon, stepping to the podium after polite applause, say "I want to take this opportunity to thank you for your invitation to speak to you." Unless it is a formal conference, it is simpler to say, "Thanks for inviting me." Why all the words?

COACHING TIP: Imagine every word you use costs you a dollar and you are on a tight budget.

Influence is a function of credibility. Credibility is a function of clarity. Clarity is a function of preciseness, not wordiness. Put another way, you want colleagues to say "Right. Of course," not "Huh?"

The wordiness in advertising can be comical. A jewelry store ran a radio spot with a happy customer describing how the store psychologically held his hand through the process of buying a ring for his intended: "Buying a diamond was the most intimidating thing I have done in my life to this point so far." What's wrong with simply saying "Buying a diamond is intimidating" and pitch the duplicating phrases? We do hope he found his spouse less intimidating.

One of America's most successful authors was Ernest Hemingway. Aside from his novels, he was known for his direct, concise writing. Mark Twain once commented that had he more time, he would have written a shorter note. Twain's point: Get to it! Don't load your point with unnecessary verbiage. This is particularly relevant in a business setting. Long is not always wrong, but wordy is. So, the reminder here is that being concise may take longer. If you are writing a novel, you will have more freedom to choose your style, but in business, plan your message accordingly, or risk losing clarity and credibility.

Do not say a little in many words but a great deal in a few.

—GREEK PHILOSOPHER AND MATHEMATICIAN PYTHAGORAS

The Gist

This chapter, Pitfall #2, is about the relationship between the clarity of your communications and your credibility. Credibility counts in what you say and *how* you say it. Be clear and direct, not wordy and scattered. An ungrammatical message is not the only issue. So is an air of superiority, hints of sexism, and superfluous phrases. Incorrect words and phrases are also distracting. How you talk and write makes an impression on people. Can you relate to your audience for each communication?

Here's the reality: Your clout and your influence can be hampered if someone can't understand you, or if what you say is so cluttered that it prompts eye-rolling. Do you want people to spend time trying to decipher your message or acting upon it? The harder your message is to decipher, the more likely it is to be misinterpreted.

Improving Your Messaging

This chapter helps you deliver clearer, more credible messaging by spotlighting common errors. Distracting errors. You may become startled, but we will try to make it a little fun on your pathway toward more clarity.

Scene #1

Ah, good. The last meeting of the week, scheduled for 4:00 p.m. on a Friday. The fifteen participants have settled into their seats, wondering how quickly this will end so their weekend can start. Luckily, the leader opens by saying "In lieu of the time, let's dispense with personal introductions." She confused the phrase *in lieu of*, which means "instead of," with *in light of*. For some of the attendees, that language mistake has distracted them from the topics to be covered in the meeting.

Remember sales manager Richard in the previous chapter, Pitfall #1? He made the same mistake, one likely conspicuous to his British colleagues. He made other mistakes, like the ones we will outline in this chapter.

Scene #2

One emerging leader we worked with, Steve, had the opportunity to present an important departmental report to the managing director of his company. The presentation was going well. After he made his recommendations, he stated, "Irregardless of which direction we take, there are good opportunities ahead for this department."

Steve made a few more comments. When he was done, the managing director leaned across the desk and said, "I like your work here, Steve, but 'irregardless' is not a word." That was not the only grammatical distraction the top boss noticed. Steve's credibility took a hit. Why? The error hints—fairly or unfairly—of inadequate education.

Phrases that get stuck in our heads. We all have strings of words that seem to pop out regularly when more thoughtful comments would be clearer and more credible. These are phrases we should have ceased using years ago, phrases that are just bad habits.

Scene #3

Imagine you are in a two-lane street, and everything comes to a stop. Horns up front are blaring. After tedious minutes, you roll down your window and ask the guy in the next car if he can see what's holding things up. His comment, "It's a nightmare. It's a joke . . . it's not even funny." How can those three states of mind fit seamlessly together? Well, impulsively—if those three phrases are often his top-of-mind responses and he doesn't think about what he is saying. If someone takes you aside and says that you use the same empty phrases over and over, thank that colleagues and ask which phrases. And try to stop using them.

When it comes to your business communication, sometimes you will be called upon to communicate in the moment and won't have the luxury of planning your message. There are two coaching tips associated with this.

COACHING TIP: Plan for moments that may require you to communicate a quick, concise message. Think of it as your elevator speech—that five-second summary always at the ready—and keep in mind the audience.

COACHING TIP: When you are put on the spot and have not planned your message, consider this phrase: "Let me get back to you." It's better to take some time, gather your thoughts, and plan your message rather than blurting out something that will backfire on you.

Co-author Roger was once in a naval air squadron. Instead of just saying they landed the plane, the pilots loved to twinkle an eye and substitute an expression everyone could see coming: "When I finally set my bird down on the blue marble . . ." We all had to smile. Each time we heard it. No matter how often. Just remember such endlessly repeated expressions get old fast.

Be observant of any such phrases you routinely use. They take the place of true messaging and compromise your credibility. And remember those other English speakers in our increasingly international lives. Here are some you have likely heard:

- We need to get all our ducks in a row.
- That's Greek to me.
- Take it with a grain of salt.
- You need to push the envelope a little more.
- Well, that's a line in the sand.
- At the end of the day . . .
- I'm a little out of pocket . . .
- For all intents and purposes, we are done.
- Not on my watch!
- She needs to toe the line.
- We need this done ASAP.
- We need to socialize this idea.
- Let's address the elephant in the room.
- And while we are on animal phrases, we need to be the eight-hundred-pound gorilla in our marketplace.

Question: Will all English speakers—no, will all of your colleagues across the globe—understand these American clichés? Dialect differs greatly across America and especially across the world's English speakers. Note: Don't skip Pitfall #3 on dialect downers.

Big important people also suffer from wordiness. Oh yes. Here are just a few:

- Diplomatic language is the source of endless study. When communicating with people from different cultures, words matter more because of the potential for conflict and misunderstanding. Summaries and communiqués are eyeballed by scores of advisors. But Donald Trump was casual about his meeting with North Korean leader Kim Jong Un. In one of the most flippant statements ever uttered by a president, he referred to his exchanges with Kim as being like "love letters." His choice of words surely dropped jaws in embassies and foreign ministries around the world. Political linguist George Orwell once said, "*The great enemy of clear language is insincerity.*"
- Hillary Clinton, when asked about her husband's surgery, said, "I am confident he will be fine once he finishes his recovery period." How about "He will be fine once he recovers."
- President George W. Bush once said, "I am really anxious to meet the prime minister." We all hoped Bush's anxiety did not show when they

finally met. To be anxious is to be worried or reluctant. He meant eager. The PM likely had quite a laugh over the language lapse from across the pond.

And members of the media make mistakes, too! Here are some curious examples of not thinking ahead of time, or just not editing before going to press or going on the air.

Dictionary alert. We know you keep a dictionary handy. However, be mindful that contemporary usage dictionaries, for example, may well suggest that the words "anxious" and "eager" are interchangeable. A college dictionary may list slang expressions and jargon as permissible. *Standard English, however, is different.* If you regularly communicate with other English speakers, especially those in Great Britain, Ireland, or India, do not rely on such dictionaries. It's best to have some version of the Oxford English Dictionary handy. Why? It's all about your clarity. It's all about avoiding linguistic distractions to your credibility, and thus, your influence.

- An interviewee once said, "Movie stars need the paparazzi desperately, to some extent." Well, which is it? Do they desperately need those pesky cameras in their face, or only to some extent? One or the other.
- A newspaper once reported, "Senator Johnson makes his first public appearance since his brain hemorrhage Thursday in Sioux Falls." What a fast recovery! But that severe illness did not happen the prior Thursday. His appearance was the recent Thursday that followed a long and critical recovery. Newspapers are increasingly plagued by poorly written headlines because newspaper staff reductions first hit copyeditors who used to write the heads. And it's gotten worse.
- A magazine once published "Spanish cuisine is a gourmand's new favorite food." A gourmet knows and appreciates fine food. So does a gourmand. But a gourmand often overeats and may be seen as sloppy. Don't tell someone they are a gourmand.
- A news service once stated "The full picture isn't revealed until the very end, in a revelation that reveals the poignant truth to be found in vulnerability." The only thing this reveals is the sloppiness of repetitive writing.
- A writer once commented, "European leaders marked Reagan's death with unusually fulsome praise." The formal meaning of *fulsome* is "disgusting; in bad taste." But it has come to mean "full" or "flattering."

Same word; two different meanings. Here is a simple solution in an Internet-connected world of multiple languages, not just multiple English dialects: Don't use the word *fulsome*. You won't impress anyone by misusing that term.

- "The soldier was accused of taking naked pictures of female soldiers." The soldiers were naked, not the photographs. *This is basic grammar.*
- "The attack appears to have been obviously well planned." Ahhh, which was it? It was either obviously well planned or merely appeared to be so. Can you see how imprecise and unclear such reporting can be?
- "It might work, but it won't be a slam-dunk home run." Suggestion: Pick and choose sports metaphors wisely. Not all countries play the same sports. Better yet, don't use any. Note: Pitfall #3 discusses such sports metaphors. Not every English speaker uses them.
- Sometimes if reporters cannot get closure on what the subjects in a story are doing, they will report that the subjects are "taking a wait-and-see attitude." In your daily interactions, how often do you sit down to just wait and see? We don't live in that kind of world.

Blurted bombshells—or when a speed sprawl splatters. Raise your hands, readers, if you've never blurted out something you wished you could take back. Silence. One hand . . . now two. Okay, yes, we've all done it.

However, remember this: Communication is irreversible. Once you write or say something, it's out there. You can regret it, apologize for it, wish you hadn't said it, or say you didn't mean it, but make no mistake—it's out there. How many times have you read about someone famous who tweeted something they later regretted?

Think about how much time is spent on damage control for some messages. Wouldn't that time have been better spent on planning your message? At least then you would have a more thoughtful message out there and your credibility would not have taken a hit.

During the 2016 campaign, Hillary Clinton referred to Trump's followers as a "basket of deplorables." You could just imagine the T-shirts rolling off the presses with "I'm a proud deplorable!" printed on the front. Her clarity was not an issue. But what about her credibility? And her clout? Granted, presidential campaigning is exhausting for any candidate. Remember: Fatigue is fodder for foibles. As presidential candidate and UN ambassador Adlai Stevenson once said, "Man does not live by words alone, despite the fact that sometimes he has to eat them."

If politicians and others with a platform can make mistakes, surely anyone can. Imagine: It's the end of a long, tiring day. You want to beat the traffic and get home, but you feel compelled to get in one last, quick email or text to several people. As we said in Pitfall #1, monitor your haste against the barometer of clarity. Texting something negative is like blurting out something verbally. Maybe worse. Anything put online is permanent and can be widely shared.

Don't make colleagues search for your meaning. Clarity is essential in an international business environment with many English dialects and non-English speakers. We have all seen product promotions filled with business hyperbole. How well do they translate?

Company mission statements are great examples. "Our goal is to leverage our state-of-the art customer service to expand into new international markets using aggressive sales techniques while refining our product line to suit new customer needs."

How do words such as *aggressive* and *leverage* translate? Will anyone spend the time to decipher their meaning? Or will the statement itself be dismissed for being opaque?

Overused words that have lost clarity—and power. The public media and our personal communication are cluttered with words whose meaning has changed and become powerless. Here are a few you might consider dropping to enhance your clarity and your credibility:

- *Awesome*. You are in a diner getting a quick lunch. A very friendly server asks for your order. "Ah, I guess I'll just have one of your BLTs and some chips," to which the server replies, "Awesome! Coming up." Dear reader, a BLT is not awe-inspiring; it is not awesome. Nor is a humble hamburger. Seeing your first child being born is awe-inspiring. A rainbow after a long, noisy storm is awesome. Seeing *A Chorus Line* in New York is awe-inspiring. If you do indeed eat a BLT you find awesome, please email us the novel ingredients and where we might share in the awe, so long as it isn't an excessively long road trip for lunch. Of course, at this point, the word *awesome* has been mangled by overuse, and its original meaning is mostly lost.
- *Incredible*. "What an incredible hamburger that was." What is not to be believed? It had a meat patty, a pickle, a bun—as usual—but what is *not* believable, we ask? The word *incredible* does not mean outstanding,

great, or superb. It means not believable. Remember *all* your audiences, including speakers struggling with English.

- *ASAP.* What is the deadline here? EST at COB? And what about those ten other time zones ahead of yours? Our European colleagues find ASAP a tad tart. Remember how Richard in Pitfall #1 said this? How is anyone to respond? Note: Be cautious with all abbreviations.
- *Factoid.* Another word worthy of burial. It can mean a piece of unreliable information, or it can mean a trivial piece of information. Do you really want to choose? Simple: Don't use it.

These words have been emptied of their true meaning and should be avoided in business communication. They can be a distraction at best and impact your credibility at worst. It is best to eschew such trite words and go for what you mean.

Words used incorrectly—and which often mean the opposite of what you think. This list will surely include some surprises for you:

- *Peruse* means "to read carefully and completely." It does not mean "to skim." We suggest you peruse this book—not skim it—to find out how often your credibility is compromised by the misuse of words . . . even if well-educated people use the words incorrectly.
- *Penultimate.* Someone might say Tavern on the Green in Manhattan is the penultimate dining experience. We suspect the chefs there would disagree—or should. *Pen* means "second to last," followed by *ultimate*, which means "last, or final," not "superior." If you are near Central Park, the penultimate place for lunch might be that hot-dog cart across the street.
- *Disinterested.* Highly misused, this word does not mean someone isn't interested in something. It means "impartial" or "objective," as in "A jury is rightly composed of twelve disinterested observers willing to listen to both sides."
- *Enormity* is different from *enormous.* "The enormity of the battle scene was its awful, bloody tangle of bodies." Enormity does not refer to size; enormous does. The enormity of a situation was how awful it was.
- *Literally.* "He was so upset he literally hit the ceiling!" We do hope he did not leave a mark on the ceiling or cut his scalp. *Literally* means "word for word." It's not a filler for flippant exaggeration. To people

who know better, this misuse of language can become a mark on the user's forehead that is hard to ignore. A distraction. In some ways, this entire book is about avoiding distractions to your clarity, credibility, and clout.

- *In lieu of*: This phrase means "instead of," not "in light of."
- *Partner, partnering*: Be careful when using these terms. When you say you are partnering with someone, it implies a contractual arrangement. Company lawyers wince at the misuse of this word.
- *Ensure* vs. *insure*: Unless you are in the insurance business, avoid the word *insure*. It means "to protect or indemnify." Telling a customer your product "will *insure* their company performance" will give your company attorney a headache.

As mentioned so often in this book, we live in a wide world of English speakers with a range of dialects. Our public communications are instantaneous and hard to recover, and our clarity and clout can suffer if we aren't careful with our wording.

Wandering phrases. We have a needless tendency to cobble words together that mean the same thing. Here are some common examples:

- *Consensus of opinion*. A *consensus* means what all have agreed upon. To add *opinion* is wasted space, time, and breath.
- *Mutual cooperation*. To cooperate is a mutual endeavor. This phrase is like saying a "cooperative cooperation."
- *End result*. A result is what happens at the end of something. No clarification needed beyond that.
- *At this point in time*. How is this better than saying "now"?
- *Very unique*. *Unique*, based on the Latin, meaning "one," says it all. One of a kind. If something is unique, it cannot become very one-of-a-kind. He is a very studious person. If he is studious, what does the word very add?
- *Despite the fact that*. The word *despite* says it all. Get rid of the fluff.
- *Hold a meeting*. How can you "hold" a meeting? You can host a meeting, in which case you simply say, "Let's meet."
- *We are very client-focused here*. Really? Can you name a product or service provider that is *not* client-focused? Is any company only a *little* client-focused? Answer: Only those no longer in business.

Words and phrases that can make you sound . . . well, uncertain. Or weak. Weak words are vague. Used occasionally, these words don't compromise clarity or credibility. But not so if frequently used.

- "Oh, my bad!" Please. Just say "Excuse me" or "I'm sorry," unless you want to sound like a teenager. And only use "I'm sorry" sparingly and genuinely.
- "We have executed a paradigm shift in our business." Readers, you might see a paradigm shift once, maybe twice, in your career. Other shifts may not be positive ones.
- "I am a little out of pocket today." Not prepared?
- "To tell you the truth . . ." No, lie to me, please.
- "To be honest with you . . ." Oh, sometimes you *do* lie to me?
- "I'm not sure, but . . ." or "I'm not positive, but . . ."
- "I hope that's okay . . ."
- "I will try to do it . . ."
- "I think it will work . . ."
- "I guess . . ."
- "Sorry to bother you . . ." or "I hate to bother you . . ."
- "I need . . ."
- "I hope . . ."
- "I suppose . . ."
- "Perhaps . . ."

COACHING TIP: Incorporate stronger words into your communication. Strong words are clear and specific. They are action-oriented. They influence others and trigger a response. Examples of strong, direct verbs include *describe*, *analyze*, and *explain*, to name a few. Too many to list here, so we suggest a quick Google search of Power Words to incorporate into your messages.

Mansplaining—sexist words and phrases. No one wants to sacrifice credibility with half their colleagues. But we guys have often done that because of an obscure clump of defensive neurons deep inside our heads that can dismiss what our female colleagues ask or state.

Some phrases follow, but first, a scene from our own experiences.

One of us once worked with a man who had a Harvard MBA. Whenever a female colleague entered his office, he would barely glance over, asking, "Hi, hon . . . what do you need?" This was thirty years ago, and times have changed. But some language habits die hard. Are you using these phrases with women?

- You don't understand.
- Why is this confusing? It's clear to the rest of us.
- You need to be more cooperative.
- She's too talkative.
- You need to listen more.
- When you get more experience, it will become clearer.
- Let me explain this to you.
- I think what (woman's name) is trying to say is . . .

Sometimes this extends beyond using a word or phrase to include behaviors. Mansplaining occurs when a man takes time out of a message to "explain" something in a condescending way to a woman. The man may not intend to be condescending, but the mere act of explaining is condescending. Whether it is overt or subtle or intentional or not, it negatively affects the men's credibility rather than the women's.

Shorter advice, especially in your international settings: If you would not say it to a man or for a man, do not say it to a woman or for a woman. (Some guys need an app on their phones that senses these transgressions.) Alfred, Lord Tennyson once warned us. "Words, like nature, half reveal and half conceal the soul within."

COACHING TIP: Never say, write, email, or text anything you wouldn't want to hear repeated or see forwarded elsewhere. Similarly, never put anything in an email that you wouldn't want forwarded to a broader audience.

Don't be a distraction. It is inadvisable to endlessly talk about a favorite pastime for which colleagues have long since shown no interest, to the point of smiling and walking away from you. Commenting on how boring things are at work would be clear and even credible, but not likely to build your clout. In a meeting, just be content that not everything you have to say is electric. Doing so is not a clout builder. One of us once worked with a manager who rarely spoke up in meetings, but, when he did, his comments were always electric and always influenced the CEO, prompting others in the meeting to wish they had said it first.

How to Say It at Work

This section extends beyond what you would or wouldn't say at work to *how* you would say it. We recognize that every organizational culture is different, and that some ways of delivering a message might be more acceptable in some organizations than others. However, as a rule, it is important to treat others the way you would want to be treated. Be respectful in how you deliver your message.

Scene #4

Kate is a senior executive in a large global organization. A more junior leader, Ted, was assigned an important project. After reviewing his work, she sat down with him and praised his effort. They began talking about deadlines and delivery, but then Kate asked Ted if he had considered two other factors. Ted thought her points were excellent. After another day working on the project, he presented the summary to Kate once again, to her admiration. "Good work," she said. Ted thanked her for the suggestions.

She could have been critical and unsupportive. It's often all in the packaging—in this case, words and tone.

Words that do not exist (except in compromised dictionaries) or just have better alternatives. These words sound oh-so-right, but they are oh-so-wrong, and will not enhance your credibility with many English speakers:

- *Irregardless.* As noted earlier in this chapter, few nonwords in our language so negatively slap a label on users' foreheads as this mutation does. The correct words are "regardless" or "irrespective."
- *Reoccur.* The correct word is *recur.*
- *Accidently.* The correct word is *accidentally.*
- *Disassociate.* The correct word is *dissociate.*
- *Incent.* Use *motivate* instead, a good word. Other English speakers may use this more traditional word, which is widely understood and easily translated.
- *Calendarize.* Avoid snickers and smirks. Avoid turning nimble nouns into vacuous verbs.
- *Contextualize.* What did we just say!

- *Holistic.* Ask several people, individually, to define this term. You will be surprised at the differences. It may be in some dictionaries, but it is sufficiently vague and should be avoided.
- *Vet.* Try finding this "verb" in any dictionary you would dare to keep nearby. How will other English speakers understand? Just say *verify*. Easily understood, right?

Word authority. You may find the words listed above in your dictionary. If so, you are likely referring to a contemporary usage or collegiate dictionary. It's time for a change, such as the Compact Oxford English Dictionary. *Be international.*

The art of evasive wording. Enron was an American energy, commodities, and services company founded in the mid-1980s. It was once a big player in the energy world. They were named *Fortune* magazine's most innovative American company for six consecutive years. Here is an excerpt from its last letter to shareholders:

> *We have metamorphosed from an asset-based pipeline and power-generating company to a marketing and logistics company whose biggest assets are its well-established business approach and its innovative people.*

Sometimes it's easy to hide behind words; sometimes doing so can be illegal. The principals behind this jargon-filled missive were convicted of securities fraud in the early 2000s.

> *A great many people think that polysyllables are a sign of intelligence.*
>
> —TELEVISION JOURNALIST BARBARA WALTERS

Structural things to avoid. Throughout this chapter, we have urged brevity and clarity. Here are some guidelines.

- Twenty words in a sentence is too long. Just about any sentence can be shortened.
- Any sentence with three prepositional phrases is hard for the typical reader to follow. If the reader is someone for whom English is a second language, the problem is worse.

- Beware of multiple negations: "Today the Supreme Court overturned a district court's ruling against a state law that forbade schools from banning books about slavery." Just break it up.

Summary of Coaching Tips

- Imagine every word you use costs you one dollar, and you're on a tight budget.
- Plan for moments that may require you to communicate a message. Think of it as your elevator pitch, and keep your audience in mind.
- When you are put on the spot and have not planned your message, consider this phrase: *Let me get back to you.*
- When writing, emailing, or texting, be sure to proofread your work before sending. Autocorrect is not always your friend.
- Get to your point quickly and clearly.
- Don't bury the lede (sometimes rendered "lead," which in journalism refers to not hiding the most important and relevant part of the story).
- Incorporate stronger words into your communication.
- Never say—or write, email, or text—anything that you wouldn't want to see in print.
- Never put anything in an email that you wouldn't want forwarded to a broader audience.
- Communicate respectfully.

Summary of Pitfall #2

Always remember: Good writing is evidence of a logical and persuasive mind that commands attention and respect. Clarity and credibility lead to respect and influence—enhanced clout.

Moving you along. Our next chapter, Pitfall #3, is about dialect differences. We have many places in North America where English usage and words differ. Then there is the rest of the world. Complicate that with hastily sent emails and texts, and you face lots of wasted time clarifying your communications. Have we sparked your curiosity? You will be surprised!

Additional Resources

- *Magic Words: What to Say to Get Your Way* by Dr. Jonah Berger (New York: Harper Business, 2023).

- *Words That Work: It's Not What You Say, It's What People Hear* by Dr. Frank Luntz (New York: Hyperion Books, 2007). Luntz is a Republican consultant and pollster. He shows how words matter and how they build credibility in campaigns. A must-read and a must-have for your library collection.
- *Smart Brevity: The Power of Saying More with Less* by Jim VandeHei, Mike Allen, and Roy Schwartz (New York: Workman Publishing, 2022).
- *Why Business People Speak Like Idiots: A Bullfighter's Guide* by Brian Fugere, Chelsea Hardaway, and Jon Warshawsky (New York: Free Press, 2005). This book is hilarious and revealing, and we list it in other chapters, too.

Note

1. Senate Judiciary Committee confirmation hearings for Samuel Alito, transcript, *New York Times*, January 12, 2006.

Pitfall #3: Dialect Downers and Cultural Clashes

Subtle Distractions to Your Influence

England and America are two countries
separated by a common language.
—PLAYWRIGHT GEORGE BERNARD SHAW

What's dialect? It's the flavor of English you learned growing up, the words and phrases unique to that region. It's always a surprise to encounter people who don't use the same words and phrases. They grew up elsewhere. Nothing wrong with dialect; we all speak some dialect of English. Just recognize that your dialect could be distracting to others. This could create a pitfall to avoid in becoming clear, credible, and influential.

Dialects are also buried inside cultures. We have many subcultures in America, too; we do not all think and speak alike. Rural America can be a surprise for city visitors, and vice versa. And sometimes our naive cultural presumptions can cause cultural clashes. It's called ethnocentrism—the attitude that how you see things must be just how other cultures see things. In intercultural encounters, being an ethnocentric culprit will distract from your credibility.

We will not cover every dialectal nuance in this chapter; instead, we will spotlight many words and phrases. Just think of this as a sampler to motivate a broader search. If you want to learn more, and have fun doing so, check out the Additional Resources section at the end of the chapter.

Scene #1

Sometimes the dialectal differences can be amusing. It's summer sales meeting time at XYZ, Inc. Four sales reps decide to lunch together at a place with a nice, shaded outdoor dining area with music. The waiter was slow with the menu, so John asked what everyone wanted that could be quick, and good. "I want a sub and a coke," he said. Jill said she was itching for a hoagie and a tonic. Frank said, "I hope they have grinders—that would be good with a soda." Juanita just hopes for a simple Italian sandwich and a glass of nectar.

We do hope the server is used to waiting on a diverse crowd. All of those orders were the same thing, simply using different American dialect words. In America, a soft drink is variously called pop or soda or nectar, and often just coke, including in Atlanta, where Coke is a brand name.

As the three talked, accents were front and center. Juanita was a New Yorker. Jill was from Philadelphia. John is a Californian. Frank hailed from New England. "So why is California so crazy?" Juanita asked John, who was a tad startled by her in-your-face style. Frank and Jill traded their worst moments visiting each other's turf. Then the food arrived, and they all seemed to realize that working in the same company provided the necessary collegiality to compensate for it all.

Accents can become distractions, but we all have one. Be aware that this pitfall focuses on dialect-based words and phrases and their meaning, not the accents used to say words. Nonetheless, too many people suffer from the temptation to judge people by their accent. A Northerner reacts upon hearing a Southern accent, just as a Southerner reacts when hearing a Brooklyn accent. It's an impulse we almost can't help.

Scene #2

One of us was at a sales meeting in San Francisco. Jamie was a new colleague straight out of Dallas. We were waiting in line to check into our hotel, and Jamie approached the very formal, unsmiling, and barely verbal—let's say arrogant—registration clerk. As Jamie got his key and walked away, he turned and blurted out in a loud voice, "Oh, hey! If mah toemater [read, tomato] calls me, you be sure to let me know!" The clerk's mouth dropped.

Then we all went to lunch. After ordering iced tea, Jamie grabbed the waitress's arm and said, "Ya be sure ta gimme lots of ahze [read, ice]." The waitress was quite offended, thinking Jamie had said "ass." We quickly schooled her on Texas accents. By the way, his "toemater" was his girlfriend. Use it with care.

While we are still talking lunch, be aware that in some Southern locales, asking a waitress for some sugar can be heard (perceived) as asking for a kiss. And let's say someone invites you to dinner. Be aware that in some dialects of American English, "dinner" means "lunch"; "supper" is always the evening meal. As a Californian, co-author Roger has never once heard the word *supper* used for the evening repast. Culture at work here, not just dialect.

COACHING TIP: If you don't understand what was said due to accent or dialectal meaning, politely seek clarity from the communicator. It is better to clarify than misinterpret.

The Gist

The intention of this chapter is to make sure you are aware of dialectal and cultural differences. Some things don't translate well from region to region, and especially from language to language. This pitfall is a cultural conversation that covers words, phrases, and even some behaviors to be aware of. (Note: We will also cover nonverbal cultural hazards in Pitfall #9.) Without this knowledge, you could be misunderstood. This can become a distraction for others and compromises both clarity and credibility. Our message here is simple: Be aware, plan, and ensure that the meaning of your message is understood by the intended audience.

Dialect differences emerge everywhere, including regional dialects in America. Long ago, co-author Roger and his wife Rita took their two-year-old back to visit relatives in Wooster, Ohio. Rita's father picked up Heidi and asked, "Do you mind me? Do you mind me?" Roger blanked. What could a two-year-old mind think about Grandpa holding her? Rita explained. In the dialect of northeast Ohio, to ask "Do you mind me?" is the same as asking "Do you remember me?" Roger added that one to his Dialect Survival Guide. (Reader, you might start keeping one yourself.)

But what does this have to do with your influence on peers? An important concept here is perception. As marketing guru Tom Peters once said, "Perception is all there is."

Using a dialect localism in someone else's "local" can be a distraction. For example, in Texas, someone who looks frazzled might be greeted with "You look like you've been rode hard and put away wet." Someplace else, that dialect phrase would likely prompt "Huh?" and a stare.

Many of the examples we provide spotlight differences between British English and American English. You may be thinking this pitfall is not as relevant to you, since you don't have any upcoming international business travel planned. Travel? These days, Zoom is travel.

Other dialect differences exist across generational divides as well as regional geographies. Say the wrong word in a different culture and you toss a huge distraction into your message. Not exactly a recipe for clout.

The words and phrases you choose will determine whether your intended message is received or it gets lost because you didn't plan well. Not only will your message be lost, but you will also appear disconnected and uninformed. It's about being a socially and culturally aware person. Rather than simply avoiding the inappropriate words, use the culturally appropriate ones with your audience. Your message will then be delivered directly and clearly without distractions.

You may be wondering, "How can I possibly know who is in a mixed audience and all the possible dialect differences that I may encounter?" The reality: It's difficult. It begins with knowing who will be in your audience. Then, as part of your presentation, be sure to have someone—preferably someone familiar with the group—review your message. We spoke earlier about acquiring a writing buddy. Your job is to learn the local language.

Scene #3

We often hear expressions that permeate our workplace. Sometimes it's the phrase itself; sometimes it's how it is expressed.

ABC Company has openings for several exempt professional positions. Chuck, the COO, is particularly keen to things an interviewee says that have become red flags for him, phrases that are a view into their soul, and likely, the relationships they will form with their colleagues.

Austin arrived for his interview to become marketing chief. After chatting amiably, Chuck asked about his management style. "Well, Chuck, my attitude with direct reports is it's my way or the highway." Red flag.

Two days later, Phyllis arrived. Her résumé as a sales manager was tops with several previous companies. "So, what are you looking for now, Phyllis?" Chuck asks. "I am looking for a place where I am the one in charge of sales, not the talking heads in HR or Marketing or the CFO." Red flag.

Maybe it's Chuck's biases, but both of these people came across as possible problems for him. Dialect can include workplace phrases that bounce around the Internet and social media and gain misplaced popularity.

Note: We cover the buzzwords, jargon, and idioms of the business world in Pitfall #4. Many examples may well cross into dialectal differences as well. For example, many terms in the auto industry surely are used throughout Michigan's other industries. Terms used in Silicon Valley may migrate to other industry cultures as well.

COACHING TIP: Since we cannot cover every dialect situation you may encounter, it's important that you do your homework when presenting to an audience with a dialect different from yours.

As you read on, we hope some of the examples bring a smile to your face. Better a smile here than one at your expense, when you are trying to convey an important message. Keep this in mind: Whatever dialect you use is just fine, but be mindful of its distraction elsewhere.

The world of English is a wide world of dialects. English may well be the language of worldwide commerce and the Internet. While not the only language spoken in India, it is the predominant language of educated Indians. Students in China begin learning English in the early grades. However, even with the expanded prevalence of the English language, different meanings of words and phrases exist. It would be wise to not assume that just because someone speaks English, everything you say is clear to them.

A history of cross-pollination in English. The English language covers much of the globe, but it's important to be aware of how many other words have been added to English. Latin and Greek are easily 70 percent of English. French contributed hundreds, thousands, of words. Spanish added much. Do we have English words for rodeo, salsa, taco, bonanza, patio, ranch, breeze, cafeteria, or chocolate? No. All are Spanish in origin. The words sugar, coffee, algebra, alcohol, zero, candy, and tariff? All Arabic in origin. Get the worldly picture?

Imagine you are in a business setting. You are making a presentation to a diverse audience, and you've given little or no thought to your wording, and how it may have a different meaning for your audience. You say something that has an alternative meaning, and the audience becomes startled. At the very least, it's a distraction that overshadows your message. At most, you are sending an unintended message: Your lack of awareness is seen as a lack of preparation. Credibility? They might be saying to themselves,

"Didn't she know what that word means here?" Not the impression you hoped to leave with your audience. If clarity, credibility, and influence are important to you, remember: It's all about marketing, including yourself.

But English evolves . . . doesn't it? It surely does. Thus, even more reason to make sure changes in the language are not clouding your clarity and credibility. If necessary, reread Pitfall #2 on word wanderings.

The United Kingdom comprises four nations. Dialectal differences abound. Understanding this is essential to our online world of video calls across many time zones, as well as at our many international trade shows. It is easy to say or do something that might not be a distraction in the UK but can be a big distraction abroad.

Scene #4

One of us was in England for a trade show. He was having lunch with his British public relations firm. This was in the 1990s, when American men often wore suspenders rather than a belt. He happened to use the word *suspenders* during the chat, prompting the British woman at the table to turn red with embarrassment. Her male colleague smiled and gently told him that suspenders are what holds women's underwear in place. He gently suggested using the British word *braces*. No offense intended! But they surely must have had a head-shaking laugh back at their office.

It doesn't end there. Americans wear pants, but *pants* in Britain means women's underwear. Their word for men's pants is *trousers*. Public embarrassment can be a powerful way to learn any lesson. However, we are hoping this book can help you avoid this learning method by planning and reviewing ahead of time to prevent any potential stumbles.

Alas, it can get even more embarrassing. If you, the reader, travel to Britain with a waist pouch commonly called a fanny pack here, use the terms *waist pouch* or *bum bag* in conversation. In Britain, the word *fanny* is an obscenity. And while we are down below there, avoid the word *moist* in Britain, because moistness refers solely to the pelvic area. You might also say *door handle* rather than *doorknob*, because *knob* is British slang for "genitals." Wishing to praise a British colleague for his or her energy, don't say "He's got lots of spunk," as that word is also vulgar in Britain.

We suspect we probably now have your full attention—and curiosity.

You don't want anything to compromise your credibility and influence with peers. In Britain, if you propose something, you want your peers there to say, "Bob's your uncle!" That's good. It's an expression that means they think you are on the right track. Now that's credibility and influence.

Hotel floors in Britain and elsewhere are not labeled as they are here. The first floor in Britain is what we call the second floor. And if you are in a business meeting there, your British colleagues hear "Let's table that item" as "Let's discuss this *now.*" In America, *tabling* means to postpone.

The issue is not different words and phrases, per se. It is also about communicating clearly without using words or phrases that are big turn-offs to others, both other English speakers and other language groups.

Read further and see why. Your mouth may drop.

Some British sensitivities: You should be aware that some people in the United Kingdom do not think of themselves as part of Europe. We do; they don't. Scots do not consider themselves English, nor do inhabitants of Northern Ireland or Wales. No matter how much you love to hear them talk, do not tell them how much you love their accent. To them, we are the ones with the accent, and some American accents are hilarious to the Brits.

Regardless of how often you've heard the expressions in old movies, do not engage the British with "Cheers, mate!" Same with the words *buddy*, *bro*, or *governor*, which they consider condescending. When you do something wrong, the proper reply is "I am sorry," not "Excuse me," and never "My bad." And when first introduced, never say "What's happenin'?" That is American slang at its worst.

Scene #5

James is a new director for the nascent European operations for his American technology company. He is really looking forward to being in Glasgow, Scotland, for a presentation with a system integrator that could be a good fit for expanding business in the UK and the Continent. As the room fills with the principals, James feels confident about the fit, but is somewhat anxious about coming across as an overconfident or aloof American.

As he steps to the front of the room, he exclaims, "Hey, what's happenin'? Good to see y'all." Polite smiles. "It's great to get out of the States right now—kinda crazy—and I'm jazzed to be here in Europe and to have the chance to do business with you Brits."

Those seated in front of him look down or glance around the conference table.

"I want to show you this morning how we can greatly expand yours and our business and really move the needle. I know you have a lot on your plate right now, but have you had a chance to review our proposal?"

Dead silence.

The chief officer says, "Yes, we have discussed your proposal, and thank you for sending it on such short notice."

James quickly replies, "Hey, no problem. I hope you can see we have our ducks in a row."

A couple questions come up, to which James replies. The session ends with no decision, prompting James to ask, "Can we calendarize the next meeting with you?"

As you read the vignette above, where did James go wrong? Take a minute and circle, underline, or make a mental note of the words, phrases, or tone that negatively influenced James's clarity and credibility. You will quickly find that regardless of what his intention was going in, the execution was not what he'd imagined.

This little story is one example of dialectal differences gone wrong and the associated implications. James's presentation became more distraction than clarity, forcing his audience to dig for the clarity. It had an immediate effect on his personal brand and how he was perceived by the group with whom he sought to connect. And unfortunately, his message became an afterthought.

As you reflect on this vignette, here is some additional guidance to consider when preparing your communications.

Expressions to avoid. Here are some expressions that confuse or irritate non-Americans:

- Let's shoot the breeze.
- He's second-guessing us.
- That's for the birds.
- I plead the Fifth.
- Is she in the loop?
- Will that move the needle?
- Well, take it with a grain of salt, or Read his suggestion, but with a grain of salt.

- What's on your plate right now?
- Wow . . . he's really off the reservation!
- Using *ask* as a noun for the word *question*.
- Using *spend* as a noun for the word *cost*.
- "No problem" instead of "You're welcome."
- Open the kimono.
- Going forward.
- What is actionable now?
- Give us a heads-up first, or Let's give them a heads-up.
- Saying "No, I'm good" for "No, thank you."
- We need to talk!
- Can I get a . . . ?
- It's a holistic solution.

This list is certainly not exhaustive. What are some ways you could expand this list? The best way is to ask a local. You can begin broadly by asking whether there are words or phrases you should avoid while interacting with the audience. That approach can be difficult, because the person giving you feedback will likely not think of every possible word or phrase. Alternatively, you can share a draft of your message with a local or someone familiar with that dialect to identify words or phrases to modify. Then, it will be up to you to stick to the script.

Give up those sports metaphors. The British use the term *football* for *soccer*. Neither baseball nor basketball are preferred delights of a British afternoon. We Americans use too many sports metaphors, which is a good example of ethnocentrism. The implication: Your message gets lost, and your credibility suffers.

Here are sporty expressions to avoid with any non-Americans:

- He's a Monday-morning quarterback.
- She's behind the eight ball.
- He needs to step up to the plate!
- It's time for a full-court press.
- Are we covering all the bases?
- How's our bench strength in marketing?
- Can she carry the ball for us?

Red Flag Cultural Distractions and Your Reactions; Or, Do You Want to Close the Deal?

To put things up close and nearby, never tell a Canadian, "Oh, you're all just like Americans." Deal-breaker. Canadians are proud of their heritage. Who is the head of state in Canada? The King of Great Britain? Get the picture? When in Scotland, never call a Scot an Englishman. They may be in the United Kingdom, but they are so not-English.

Here are some key areas you should acknowledge when doing business outside the USA. We cite two good books in Additional Resources, but do search for others before any trip abroad.

Conversation stoppers. If you are surprised to learn that Canadians dislike being perceived as just like Americans, you need to read up on much bigger issues, especially in Asia and the Middle East.

- Gifting: Many societies have rituals about gift exchanges. For one, always give and receive gifts with both hands, and never the left hand alone.
- Negotiations and deals: Rituals abound as to who says what and who leads. Cultures vary, and there are too many to cite here. Making toasts at dinners includes more rituals and rules, including who pours when, and who takes the first sip.
- And the nose on your face? Blowing your nose while dining with Japanese or Korean colleagues will become a distraction unlike any other. It's disgusting to them. They will talk about you for days. Best rule of thumb: Excuse yourself to the restroom, water closet, loo, privy—or whatever your guest calls it—and take care of it there.
- Food at dinners: Develop an iron stomach. Insects and reptiles are common courses in Asian societies. One of us had a colleague doing business in South Asia. Negotiations were proceeding, and soon, it was dinnertime. The large table had a conspicuous hole in the middle. The waiter strapped a small monkey through the hole from beneath, leaving the little guy's head exposed. The waiter then wacked the top of the monkey's skull off. Everyone applauded, grabbed chopsticks, and dove right in. Fresh monkey brains! (By the way, our colleague closed the deal, but downed a full bottle of the pink stuff that night at his hotel.)
- Dinner manners: Your grandmother has nothing on the table manners of some societies. Had our colleague refused to sample the monkey

brains, that distraction would have been seen as rude. (Pouring soy sauce on rice, for example, is a distraction to be avoided in Japan. It's true!)

- Colors: Be sensitive to colors, especially if gifting flowers to a host. White is the color of death in some societies, so handing white flowers to a host is a big distraction from your credibility. Certain flowers are also symbols to be avoided. One would think flowers, any flowers, are safe. Be careful. Roses suggest romantic interest in much of Europe. Dahlias symbolize death in Spain. Marigolds and carnations are funereal in Sweden and Poland. For more examples, check out Mark McCrum's book in Additional Resources. And be prepared before you go abroad.
- Numerals: Some societies have a problem with certain numerals. Some perceive odd numbers as unlucky, while others see even numbers the same way.
- Tipping: Americans tip, but tipping in some cultures, such as Japan and Iceland, is insulting, while in Italy, a tip is expected, in addition to the service charge.

Scene #6

Another no-no: Don't ask colleagues in the UK what the King does all day long. British royalty is extremely important to many of them. This vignette gives you a sense for how a question like that can backfire.

Julie and Frank, two product managers for Acme, are planning a trip to Europe. The first stop is London, and then on to Berlin and Geneva. They have heard horror stories of how Americans make many verbal gaffes with people across the Pond. They don't want to blow it. Consequently, they retained a marketing professor from the local state university who is a British national.

"My main advice is, don't be presumptuous about anything, and don't question local habits and customs," he warned. As the casual lunch and light small talk progressed, the professor leaned across the table and sternly asked Julie and Frank an odd question. "Tell me something: Why do you still have fifty states? Goodness, fifty states is sooooo not modern, and makes unity so difficult."

Truly startled by such an off-the-wall criticism in an otherwise pleasant luncheon, Julie and Frank did not know what to say. The professor did. "You see what I mean?"

Now, do you?

Avoiding slights in Asia and the Middle East. As with the British, never ask the Japanese why they have an emperor. Their royalty and its traditions are much revered.

You'll need to think beyond just the words you use, considering behaviors that can send a message as well. Be aware on your first trip to South Korea not to smile at strangers on the street. It is considered way too familiar.

In Japan, do not be late for an appointment; doing so is considered ruder than it is in the United States. So is talking loudly, even on a public street. When introduced to someone in Japan, always repeat their name but never address them by their first or family name. Always use the last name followed by the polite *san*, which equates to the formal "Mister."

It goes beyond dialect. Never use your left hand for just about anything in the Middle East or Asia. Insulting? No, very disgusting. Can you guess why?

We will expand on all-important nonverbal communications in Pitfall #9, Body Botches. You may be quite surprised.

Summary of Coaching Tips

There is much to think about when it comes to dialect and cultural differences. To avoid being misunderstood—or worse, to unintentionally insult people—here's a summary of our coaching tips to consider as you plan your communication.

- If you don't understand what was said due to accent or dialectal meaning, politely seek clarity from the communicator.
- Be aware and plan ahead. Get to know who will be in your audience. Are you communicating outside of your common geographical area? Could the audience be a multinational group?
- Keep your messages simple and straightforward. Only use metaphors that you are certain will resonate. You never want to be stopped to explain a metaphor, as it will distract from your message, and your credibility.
- Ask a local colleague to review your presentation and talking points. You may not always have this luxury, but if you do, it will help to refine your message and decrease the likelihood that you might stumble with a dialectal difference.

Summary of Pitfall #3

We are increasingly in contact with people from other cultures who speak other languages, whether it's regional differences within your home country or differences across continents. The definition of ethnocentrism is naively believing that your cultural and linguistic habits are just like everyone else's. Some culturally inappropriate words and behaviors may be overlooked, but at what cost? How does dialect unfamiliarity impact your credibility?

Following World War II, many Americans touring Europe thought of themselves as entitled saviors. It led to the expression "ugly Americans." Now with online communication and frequent international travel, anyone wishing to build a clear and credible perception of influence must know how to handle different cultures. And what not to do. Or say.

Moving you along. We should be concerned about dialect in other regions, and especially other countries; but what about words and phrases *inside our professions*? Idioms, euphemisms, and plain old buzzwords are like an insider language. Sometimes they are meant to hide something. Sometimes they are meant to just be sort of cute. But if others cannot understand your insider idioms, you will have no clarity with them. No clarity, no credibility. No credibility, no clout. Read on to Pitfall #4.

Additional Resources

- Check out these pages of dialect maps, including where you grew up. *Speaking American: How Y'all, Youse, and You Guys Talk: A Visual Guide* by Josh Katz (Boston: Mariner Books, 2020).
- John McWhorter is a very visible linguistics expert often quoted in major media. If the evolution of English has become a keen interest for you, read his *The Tower of Babel: A Natural History of Language* (New York: Times Books / Henry Holt & Company, 2001).
- Two young British citizens have a YouTube channel called *Those Two Brits*. Joel and Lia are instructive and very entertaining about our language differences. Laugh . . . and learn.
- If you are planning a long trip to the UK, you must bring this thorough guide to British English: *Blimey, I'm Knackered! An American's Survival Guide to British English* by Marshall Hall and Mark Cowle (Las Vegas, NV: Imbrifex Books, 2021).
- Not going to Britain? Here is another helpful guide. *Going Dutch in Beijing: How to Behave Properly When Far Away from Home* by Mark McCrum (New York: Henry Holt & Company, 2008).

Pitfall #4: Insider Idioms

How Euphemisms, Buzzwords, and Jargon Sound to Others

Incomprehensible jargon is the hallmark of a profession.

—FORMER YALE UNIVERSITY PRESIDENT KINGMAN BREWSTER

We chose the above quote because it has some truth to it. The "incomprehensible jargon" extends beyond the professional level to include organizations and even teams. And when you include acronyms with the insider idioms, you've got your own language. Unfortunately, others may need a translator.

Sure, the jargon may include commonly understood English words, but the meaning behind those words and phrases are only relevant to a select few. It's a classic insider/outsider approach meant to distinguish who's in and who's out. The unique language represents a proverbial secret handshake, and it strengthens bonds.

How many times have you joined a new team or organization only to spend your first several weeks trying to figure out what the heck people are saying? What is the meaning behind certain words or phrases? You may begin by recognizing that this is a new language ("Hmmm, that's different") followed by questioning it ("What does that mean?"), but it's not long before you are using it yourself. Once you do, you're in. You are officially part of that group.

Some would argue that this is the hallmark of any culture, be it a society, profession, or corporation. The idioms represent a group's unique way of communicating and connecting with one another.

But to the outsider, it sounds like gibberish. Trying to use those words and phrases outside of the intended community will cause puzzled looks, curious head tilts, and questions. You may as well be speaking a foreign language. Your message will be lost, and you risk your credibility being impacted.

We don't suggest shying away from such bonding jargon; however, we do recommend using it within the context for which it is intended: to communicate and connect within said community. Know your audience.

Separate from these idioms are buzzwords. Like idioms, they can be used to strengthen and engage a group. However, buzzwords can also take on a negative perception depending on the audience and the word or phrase. Examples of business buzzwords include *core competency*, *unpack*, *ballpark*, *synergy*, *quick win*, *bandwagon*, *alignment*, *ping*, and *move the needle*, to name a few. There are many others, and they change over time.

You may have even heard about (or participated in) Buzzword Bingo at a meeting or conference. Yes, it's a real game. You can even buy premade cards or build your own online. If you are delivering a message to an audience that isn't playing Buzzword Bingo, it's fair to say you are mastering distractions. You can also assume your message has been lost.

Many of us have gotten caught up in using business buzzwords. As noted earlier, they can represent and strengthen a culture. They are not all bad. However, overusing or misusing them *is* bad and negatively impacts your credibility. Our advice is to avoid buzzwords, or if they must be used, to do so sparingly.

A great cartoon in *The New Yorker* shows a group seated at a business meeting. The leader exclaims, "I want us to get in on the ground floor of the next bandwagon!" After a few minutes, anyone in that imaginary business meeting could jump up and shout "Bingo!"

Scene #1

Phil is the regional manager for a company that developed a communication system for small medical practices. Today he is calling on a practice with two locations in different zip codes and different area codes. He is meeting with Dr. Adams, the founder, who has not always been eager to make big capital purchases. Dr. Adams brings up some problems with the existing system. Phil states, "That can't happen because our system is integrated end to end. It's a holistic approach."

Dr. Adams is used to professional terminology, so his ears perk up. "Define *holistic*. And what do you mean by 'end to end'?"

Phil squirms. Later that day, Phil emails the doctor. "Our system insures that failure won't happen."

What advice would you give to Phil for his next meeting with Dr. Adams? How about his next sales call?

The premise of our book is the importance of clarity for your credibility. Phil's need to email the doctor shows a lack of clarity, and it affected his credibility with Dr. Adams. It's like two people speaking different languages and trying to negotiate. *Holistic* and *end to end* are buzzwords that are imprecise and vague. They could potentially mean something different for each person.

The other issue is that Phil made a claim that could get his company in big trouble. He said his system "insures" that the doctor's problems won't happen. Big no-no. He meant to say *ensure*. To use *insure* means to indemnify, and that could end in a lawsuit if the doctor's two practices run into the same problems with Phil's "holistic" approach.

Words matter. Do you want to be taken seriously by everyone? Can you chance not being perceived as a critical thinker who communicates without ambiguity and is perceived as credible? That's influence.

COACHING TIP: Avoid buzzwords and phrases that represent sweeping generalizations.

The Gist

Pitfall #2 focuses on how words wander, how they are misused, how they bump into each other, and how some speakers think they will appear smarter by adding syllables to words and phrases. Pitfall #3 focuses on how language and words differ across many maps.

This pitfall, #4, is about things we say, sometimes innocently, sometimes not, because we don't want to describe something directly—the way it really is. Alternatively, we may use words and phrases to make something sound more grandiose than it actually is. This is the definition of hyperbole, and that exaggeration or embellishment can come back to bite you.

COACHING TIP: Stay away from hyperbole in your messages.

Idioms and euphemisms are a common way to talk about things we want to dance around. Users somehow think doing so sounds, well, cute. But such statements prompt listeners to ask: "Okay. What does that mean? Define it for me." They may smirk and look aside. Then you are caught in your own word jungle. That's surely not clarity, and it surely does not enhance your credibility or clout.

The Key Issue for Readers

Do you want to be taken seriously? If so, read on to see how others—smart people, all—prompt listeners to roll their eyes.

Scene #2

Renee was an ambitious mid-level manager at a manufacturing company. She was regarded by her peers, colleagues, and immediate supervisor as someone who knew the business well. She cultivated this perception by the way she spoke about business challenges, opportunities, and solutions. She spoke about drilling down to take deep dives on issues, having a holistic approach, creating synergies, and bandwidth challenges. In her immediate circle, people were impressed, and she was viewed as a credible leader. Her role was elevated, and she soon found herself regularly interacting with the company's directors. She had arrived.

Renee wanted to impress them, so she increased the usage of business buzzwords, jargon, and hyperbolic language in her conversations and presentations with this new leadership group. There were multiple conversations among the directors behind closed doors where they asked each other, "What is Renee even talking about?" The directors just wanted straight talk so they could make informed decisions. Renee was perceived by many in this new group as trying too hard to impress; she was aiming for style over substance, and even *she* didn't know what she was talking about. Not a great brand, and certainly a significant ding to her credibility. While Renee had valuable insights, the leaders never got a chance to observe them because they were overshadowed by her jargon. She was getting in her own way.

What coaching would you provide to Renee? How can you avoid a similar path?

The lesson in the vignette above is that you can impress people more with your clarity than you can with lofty jargon.

Televised idioms. Americans love their euphemisms. In the early days of television, the word *constipation* was banned, so drugmakers invented the word *irregularity* to replace it. Viewers got the point and went to the store with less embarrassment. The word *toilet* was also banned from early broadcasts. *Restroom* sounded better, even though everyone knew few people enter restrooms to slumber. Some still ask where the women's bathroom is, though no bathtub can be found there. And broadcast companies never show reruns; rather, they offer "encore presentations."

Television still struggles to explain things in roundabout terms. In a famous incident during a Super Bowl, Janet Jackson was said to have suffered a wardrobe malfunction. The announcer proclaimed it a "wardrobe malfunction," a term that entered watercooler conversations the next morning.

More recently, during the COVID-19 pandemic, there has been much advocacy for social distancing, both a euphemism and an oxymoron. Most people think of "social" as being together with people, so as this phrase joined our lexicon, there was some uncertainty at first. Now, social distancing is part of the norm.

Readers, are you beginning to nod in agreement, realizing that euphemisms you use may also sound a tad strange to colleagues outside of your profession or trade? Some phrases may alert a curious, intuitive mind that something is being hidden. Aside from the lack of clarity, your credibility takes a hit, and thus, your influence. This chapter serves as an eye-opener, a chance to review how you communicate—not just with colleagues, but with clients.

Not convinced yet? Let's investigate inner idioms and some more professional domains.

Used! Used? In decades past, the Cadillac was the symbol of automotive envy in America, long before the BMW, the Lexus, the Benz. So used-car dealers would not dare demean the lofty brand by saying "We've got some good deals on used Caddies here." Goodness no. They were "previously owned Cadillac motorcars." *Used* sounded . . . well, soiled. Stained. Some old Caddies were even "certified pre-owned," although what was actually certified was left to buyer discretion. How dare anyone demean a Cadillac?

Removable metal domiciles on wheels were once called "coaches." That didn't sound right, so "coaches" became "trailers." That led to "mobile homes" located in "parks," whose residents typically chose to stay rather than become mobile. Having suffered many slights, such parks sought to upgrade their image entirely. They were now "mobile estates." As the adage goes, your home is your castle . . .

Those lawyers. Each profession develops jargon and buzzwords that go beyond what are called "terms of art." For example, in the legal profession the phrase *double jeopardy* is a term of art. But courtroom jargon includes the phrase *rocks in a box*. Not a term of art, nor likely a term of endearment. It's lawyers' jargon for the pool of potential jury members.

"Are you listing?" Euphemisms can become code words, the esoterica that replace winks and sly signals. In real estate, if the buying agent wants to know how soft the seller's price is, the agent might ask the seller's agent, "Are the sellers motivated?" This is a clear signal to the buyer's agent to go for a lower price, because the sellers may be especially eager—even anxious—to sell and get out. Here are some other real estate code words:

- Charming, lots of character: Old. Get a house inspection.
- Great potential: The place is a mess.
- Close to shopping: High traffic, busy area.
- Quiet, secluded: Expect a long commute to anything.

Public education. K–12 education has enough jargon, buzzwords, and euphemisms to fill its own book, not to mention their ubiquitous acronyms. Here is a sampling that must prompt parents to seek a principal's explanation:

- Collaborative learning: Put students in a group and encourage them to figure out the concept on their own, with each other. Teacher? Are you nearby?
- Chunking: Break large concepts into smaller ones to make it easier. Chunks—get it?
- Scaffolding: This most recent concept has become the darling used to replace many terms. Students once learned in steps. Layers. Then building blocks. Then chunks. No, now concepts are subject to scaffolding to make things sound, well, new. Parents, take notes at back-to-school night!

Bits 'n' bytes. No other enterprise has contributed more euphemisms and jargon than the high-tech/computer area. One of us once worked for a semiconductor manufacturer. It took a few tries before learning that the office slang *bandwidth* meant "one's available time," not FM frequency. Then came the novel use of the word *space*. No, that's not a cubicle in the gopher farm. For example, "We are focusing on the market for chips in kitchen appliance space." What was wrong with the old, reliable concept of "market niche" was not apparent.

Other high-tech terms abound:

- *Paradigm shift.* You still in the same business, or did you escape to something else?
- *User-friendly.* Regardless of how complicated your product is, better claim it's user-friendly, or you'll need a paradigm shift for sure.
- *Fully integrated, end to end.* Does this mean the product is finished . . . finally?
- *Killer app.* Presumably this is a positive term.
- *Best of breed.* Says who?
- *Category buster.* Ditto.
- *Next-generation.* We repeat ourselves.
- *What's the spend on that?* Translation: What did it cost?
- *What was the prospect's toughest ask?* Translation: What was their toughest question?

Jobs and careers. It used to be the personnel department. Now it's human resources. But some companies now use the title "chief people officer." If someone believes they are working beneath their abilities, they claim to be underemployed. And if not employed, we are "between jobs," not unemployed.

Marketing is sometimes called customer outreach. A manager in marketing might be called the firm's brand ambassador. Leave it to marketers to be creative.

Why are such words so useful and so commonplace? A euphemism can help deflect unwanted questions . . . sometimes. It can replace a word or phrase to be avoided. Maybe the original is a tad embarrassing. It might be unpleasant. Slightly offensive. A tad icky, maybe? Replacing the targeted word or phrase makes the conversation less distracted. That's until an inquisitive mind speaks up.

We want to draw your attention back to something we said earlier: Words matter. Words have meaning. They send a message. They can help connect people or divide them. They can engage them or turn them away.

Although some of the previous examples may seem trivial on the surface, they are real and meaningful, and they reflect changing perceptions. We are not here to argue the merits of whether these meanings *should* change. The reality is that the meaning and impact associated with words *do* change over time. Our job when communicating with clarity is to be aware of those changes and the effect we have on others with the words we use.

Scene #3

Rodney was the department head in his organization. He considered himself "old school," and was very open about his belief that, in his terms, "The world has gotten too damn soft and sensitive." He thought everything had gotten "too politically correct." Rodney was not supportive of having to be overly conscientious of his word choice. As a result, on multiple occasions, he offended people. Rodney was coached often, but he refused to adapt. He was eventually coached out of the organization (euphemism for being fired).

COACHING TIP: Don't use words and phrases flippantly or casually. Think about both your intended message and the audience. Does your choice of words help to clarify your message? Or do you use them to impress or confuse? How will the recipients feel? Practice empathy and put yourself in their shoes.

Did we say careers? How about job interviews, too! Chuck hired and managed many people across the publishing and the technology industries, and had a list of euphemisms that could shut down an applicant fast. Whenever an interviewee said "I'm looking for a challenge," Chuck politely thanked them for coming in. Likewise, whenever Chuck himself was being interviewed for a job, he was not impressed by the tough-guy attitude. "Our workday begins at five a.m., and you'll be running hard as soon as the door hits you from behind." Nope. Not Chuck's kind of employer—and Chuck was a former marine.

Be *oh so careful* with language. Some euphemisms are designed to make a point for sociopolitical purposes. The term *politically correct* is an example. Who decides what is correct in a democratic society? (Note: Additional Resources at the end of this chapter cites a speech on euphemisms that George Carlin delivered in Washington, DC, the prime spot for political jargon. It is very instructive.) Here are some good examples:

- *Pro-life.* The anti-abortion cry.
- *Pro-choice.* The flag waved by legal abortion advocates.
- We don't have prisons; we have *correctional institutions.*
- No one is poor any longer; rather, they are *economically disadvantaged.*
- *Inner-city.* Replaced the word *ghetto*; this term is also likely to change.
- *Revenue excesses.* What nonprofits rush to use instead of the awful word *profits.*

- *Alternative facts.* Used when you disagree with cut-and-dried information, or just want to be "creative with the truth."

> *I can, however, try to move forward in a manner that is consistent with the values to which I subscribed before slipping my moorings.*
>
> —FORMER CIA DIRECTOR DAVID PETRAEUS, AFTER ADMITTING HIS AFFAIR

COACHING TIP: If in doubt about a new phrase or description, run it by your writing buddy or the breakfast group we suggested you form.

Summary of Coaching Tips

- Avoid buzzwords; if they must be used, do so sparingly.
- Avoid buzzwords and phrases that represent sweeping generalizations.
- Stay away from hyperbole in your messages.
- Don't use words and phrases flippantly or casually. Think about both your intended message and the audience. Does your choice of words help to clarify your message? Or are they used to impress or confuse? How will the recipients feel? Practice empathy and put yourself in their shoes.
- As you plan your message, be clear and succinct on what your objectives are. What do you want the recipients to walk away with? Make sure those points are stated clearly and concisely, and avoid surrounding those points with jargon or buzzwords.

Summary of Pitfall #4

Your objective with communication should be clarity and connection. There is a time and place for insider idioms. On the positive side, it helps to build cultures. However, when used inappropriately, your message gets lost and you risk your credibility being negatively impacted.

You can be guarded and proprietary, or you can be open and clear—it's *your* choice—but remember, we're talking about *their* perception of your clarity and credibility. Frankly, it is very much a career choice: Be influential, or be ineffectual.

For those of you who already incorporate jargon, buzzwords, and euphemisms inappropriately, you will need to create a heightened self-awareness and build new communication habits. This may be easier said than done, because some people may not even know the extent to which they use such language ineffectively, and the impact it has. Those people have a communication blind spot which will require a greater level of effort to adjust. Whether you are aware of this as a weakness or it is a blind spot, a writing coach coupled with your open mind can help you to quickly avoid this communication pitfall and tip effective communication in your favor.

Moving you along. While we admit that jargon and euphemisms are rather innocent—merely creatures of fervent (or feverish) minds—other things are not. We all have biases, and there are many from which to choose. We all have consistent attitudes about things—until we find out consistency is not always good. On to Pitfall #5.

Additional Resources

- George Carlin was one of the sharpest observers of critical thinking, clarity, and credibility. Listen to his luncheon address to the National Press Club in Washington on May 13, 1999. His focus: euphemisms. You can find it easily on YouTube.
- *Why Business People Speak Like Idiots: A Bullfighter's Guide* by Brian Fugere, Chelsea Hardaway, and Jon Warshawsky (New York: Free Press, 2005). We list this in Pitfall #2 as well. It's a fun book to read, and quite instructive.
- *The Buzzword Dictionary: 1,000 Phrases Translated from Pompous to English* by John Walston (Oak Park, IL: Marion Press, 2006).
- *What Got You Here Won't Get You There: How Successful People Become Even More Successful* by Marshall Goldsmith (London: Profile Books, 2008).

Pitfall #5: Inner Isms

Recognizing Your Hidden Biases and Your Precious Consistencies

When people show you who they are, believe them the first time.
—POET MAYA ANGELOU

Angelou is right: First impressions linger. Some can be a big distraction to credibility.

You might ask how personal biases about things can affect someone's clarity, credibility, and clout. "If I don't like someone because of ____ [fill in the blank], I keep my mouth shut. If I keep it to myself, what's the problem?"

Fair question. Simply put, beliefs influence actions. In the example above, not liking someone contributed to silence and then to action, such as putting someone down or talking behind their back. Those actions can affect how you are perceived. They distract from credibility. To understand what we mean, read on.

Scene #1

Executive coach Cara Hale Alter (whose valuable book is cited in Additional Resources, below) describes a situation that perfectly fits the phrase "hidden biases" in this chapter's title. She had a female attorney as a client. The attorney arrived early to the deposition conference room and went about making herself a cup of coffee. When the opposing counsel walked in, he assumed she was just an office support staffer. He sat down nearby with his client and began a confidential but very audible overview of his defense strategy. The female attorney listened closely as she slowly stirred her coffee, making strategic mental notes.

What fun it was for her to take her seat at the table across from counsel a few minutes later. She introduced herself to the attorney, now suddenly ashen with a "lawyer in the headlights" expression on his face. He surely felt the sting of his hidden bias about what he thought was her lower station in employment.

Let's assume the male attorney was, up to that point, a master of lawyerly clarity and credibility. But as Cara's female client shared her story with many colleagues, especially female ones, each retelling took the male attorney's reputation down a notch. Certainly this was the case with female colleagues. The male attorney had given away his strategy, thereby giving his opponent an advantage in the courtroom—and in credibility.

Actions, and assumptions, contribute to or detract from credibility. Sometimes biases are hidden, and sometimes they are overt. The hidden ones are unconscious bias the holder barely admits having. The overt ones are considered conscious bias, and they surface in ways that blow your credibility even more. In either case, they can cloud judgment, influence communication, and drive decision-making, thereby impacting your credibility. Credibility builds clout. No credibility, no clout.

And those precious consistencies about demeanor, style, or management? You've always been told to be consistent rather than switch approaches on things. Consistency is a virtue, right? Are we recommending you abandon such a habit? May the first reader without biases or dubious consistencies of communication move on to the next pitfall. Or do we have your attention? Let's see.

Scene #2

One of us once worked in college textbook publishing. Nathan was one of the editors, but he was unique in his upbeat, back-slapping manner. Even on the phone, you could feel his arm around your shoulder, patting away. Never grim, always the optimist. At sales meetings, seasoned salespeople would ask if his upcoming new textbook covered this concept or that theory. "For sure, for sure!" was his consistent mantra, often multiple times in a single presentation. Eventually, as his sponsored textbooks were published but earned only spotty success, Mr. For Sure earned another nickname: Slippery Nathan. His consistent manner was perceived as untrustworthy. He eventually left the company.

The Gist

This pitfall moves you from words and phrases covered in the prior pitfalls to something we all have: attitudes, biases, and our potentially faulty consistencies. They can become distractions to your clarity, and thus, your credibility. We address biases you may not realize are negative perceptions in the minds of others; hence, the term "blind spots."

You have likely been told to always be consistent. Predictable. But what happens when your consistencies are faulty? Unfortunately, many people who seek to be influential are holding on to precious consistencies that slap a big label on their foreheads, and they don't even realize it. Poet Ralph Waldo Emerson spotted it well. "A foolish consistency is the hobgoblin of little minds, adored by little statesmen and philosophers and divines."

Why do we label all this as a pitfall?

Because such behaviors result from unclear thinking that in turn ruins influence. Colleagues can't perceive credibility if they are distracted and can't get that distraction out of their minds. As with Nathan above, there goes your message.

As you will see throughout this chapter, it may not take much to lose credibility with your intended audience. It could be as simple as a single sentence. And once your point of view has been expressed—right or wrong, fact or opinion—there is no turning back. It's out there, a distraction colleagues will find difficult to forget and easy to discuss.

Remember, it may take a hundred acts to build trust, but only one to tear it down. Too often, if someone questions one aspect of your message, they soon begin to question everything you say. It quickly becomes a fragile house of cards.

We are not coaching you to be neutral in every aspect of your communication. We are suggesting that you *be aware of your biases.* With that knowledge in mind, know your audience and the impact that certain words, phrases, and points of view may have on those receiving your message.

COACHING TIP: Uncovering and eliminating biases all begins with self-awareness. Conduct activities that improve your self-awareness, such as maintaining a daily journal, identifying your values, and exploring your initial emotional reactions to situations. Reflecting on your beliefs, actions, and responses is the most powerful, but you can also consider reflecting on others' actions and statements.

What can be done to increase self-awareness? Once you become aware of your biases, how can you overcome them? Read on to find out.

One of the worries about a presidency is that everybody tells you yes. Nobody helps you figure out where your blind spots are.
—CBS NEWS JOURNALIST JOHN DICKERSON

The Dickerson quote is not limited to presidents. It applies to any manager who seeks to lead with influence, not with title. If presidents have blind spots, how about others, such as you?

Where Do Biases Come From?

Biases don't always have to be extreme or negative to have a negative impact. Personal biases are built over time and through experience. Some biases represent gross, often inaccurate, generalizations about other people or situations. They may develop through your personal experience or be passed down from others through their stories and statements.

In many cases, because the biases can be deeply rooted, they also are blind spots for the individual. Often associated with unconscious biases, blind spots are those behavioral areas that an individual is not aware of, nor are they aware of the impact they can have on their credibility.

Toward self-awareness. Just because you believe something does not make it true. You have seen us call out the need to differentiate between facts, feelings, and opinions when communicating. (Note: We will do that especially in Pitfall #6 and Pitfall #8.)

When it comes to biases, what fuels a certain bias often comes down to blurring the lines between opinions and facts. With biases, you feel certain of something. You may have experienced something personally or repeatedly enough that you believe it is fact. You may not be willing to see outside the bias, and it will likely affect how you communicate about said topic, as well as the decisions you make. However, that belief is merely an opinion. If you cannot differentiate between fact and opinion, you will not likely be moved from your opinion, and your credibility can suffer as a result.

COACHING TIP: Focus on facts over feelings and opinions.

Laws matter, but it's not just about laws. Biases can lead to discrimination, and we all know employment discrimination is illegal. Nonetheless, we all still make judgments about people. (If you want a thorough scientific overview of human resource management practices and associated laws, we recommend the Dessler book highlighted in the Additional Resources section at the end of the chapter.) As we continue, the primary focus of this chapter is on the impact that biases have on your communication and your credibility.

In the past couple of decades, many employees in their fifties and sixties have sensed that they were being sidelined or offered early retirement because of a lack of technical Internet skills. Compared to new hires in their twenties and thirties, this may have been true. (Or it may be a faulty generalization.) Many such layoffs were not due simply to perceived skill deficiencies but also because of higher salaries. Many of these employees received early-morning calls from a termination contractor announcing they were cut off from the communication system.

A biased view based on age is not just about faulty generalizations regarding older workers. Some people generalize that younger workers lack effective communication skills because they were brought up using social media with its 140-character, emoji-filled communications.

Beyond an individual's or an organization's credibility, there are many risks associated with this blanket (and biased) approach to talent decisions. First and foremost is the liability exposure to lawsuits. Additionally, there are opportunity risks associated with using such biases as the basis for decision-making.

What happens to institutional knowledge? Or the missed opportunity costs? How about the false positives—those talent decisions that are simply wrong? The basis for decisions should link to the needs of the business and the individual's qualifications to do their job.

That's not our opinion; it's the law. And it's not just about laws that can be circumvented. It's about deep-seated attitudes and how they impact your interactions with others.

Types of Biases and Some Common Blind Spots

Are the people you are communicating with just like you? Or are they unlike you in some ways? We may have biases that fit each circumstance.

What makes biases particularly complex is that there are many types you can encounter in the workplace. Our focus continues to be on how you may utilize these biases to communicate differently with someone.

However, many other talent management decisions can be impacted by such biases.

Below are some common types of biases and blind spots we've all encountered. You may find yourself cringing at a few of these. We hope you say, "Well, I don't believe that." We hope that is the case, but we also hope you recognize that other people *do* hold some of these biases. The position we stand behind is that all of these biases are faulty, many are illegal, and all diminish your credibility.

Affinity bias. This is a bias *for* certain people. It occurs when people gravitate and show preference toward people with whom they share some connection. Connections themselves are good, but making preferential decisions or communicating more positively about those people over others is bad.

Scene #3

Alex is a fan of the Dave Matthews Band. He enjoys all the songs and going to the live concerts. Marty is one of Alex's direct reports who also likes the band. They often spend time talking about the concerts and songs at the exclusion of others. Other team members feel left out and believe Alex spends more time with Marty and shows him preferential treatment.

What advice would you give to Alex?

Remote worker bias. Some people hold an unconscious bias against colleagues who are working remotely. Some have called it the "face-time bias" or a "situational bias." The notion here is that you become used to colleagues in nearby cubes and offices, those "reliable and committed workers" compared to "those remote workers we never see." The other consequence of "face-time bias" is that remote workers can subconsciously feel left out, which compromises team spirit.

Scene #4

Sara has called a meeting in the conference room for eleven a.m. Her staff are assembled and ready to go. Everyone looks around to acknowledge familiar faces. Suddenly Bill says, "Hey, what about Jesse—did he get the notice?" Jesse has been working remotely for two years. Then Betty pops up and said, "Hey, the folks in London are eight hours ahead of time. They are ready to board the transit and go home." They had forgotten about Jesse. Out of sight, out of mind. And time-zone bias can cause real resentment.

Attribution bias. Like the situational bias above, attribution bias has a greater focus on one's behavior. Jeff is often late for work. The general perception of Jeff is that he is "unfocused and unmotivated." However, upon a deeper understanding, it turns out that Jeff is a single father with competing child-care obligations in the morning.

Chitchat bias. To cultivate bonds, women might say "I like your shoes." Some men might see this as silly or even unprofessional, although they think nothing of starting off with "Hey, how'bout those Bears yesterday—you see that?" What's the difference?

Scene #5

As a staff meeting starts, Betty asks Georgette, "So how are your kids doing with ballet lessons?" Georgette smiles at the friendly inquiry and is about to answer when Bob jumps in. "Okay, folks, time to move on. I see everyone made it in spite of that accident on the freeway. Anyone see it happen?" Who is wasting time, and who is being concerned? Depends on your unconscious chitchat bias. When does cutting off small talk send an unconscious message? Additionally, keep in mind that some small talk is about making personal connections that can serve you well in future communication.

Gender bias. It may take another generation for men to perceive female colleagues as, well, full colleagues. If an educated lawyer unconsciously thinks a woman fixing coffee in a conference room is a nonexempt staffer, it would take significant reorientation to change his subliminal assumptions. Reread the section on mansplaining in Pitfall #4.

Educational institution bias. "Let's only hire Ivy League MBAs." One of us once had a San Francisco client who thought otherwise. "Give me an MBA from Golden Gate University over Cal or Stanford anytime. They are more practical."

Religious bias. "She's a Mormon [Catholic, Muslim, atheist]. How can I expect her to be logical and reasonable if she believes that stuff?" An MBA from Yale is still an MBA from Yale, regardless of religious affiliation.

Professional blind spot. One of us once worked with a CFO who thought marketing was suspect because it was not "measurable." Marketing people often dismiss salespeople as parochial and laser-focused. It took some time to get an essential point across: Salespeople focus on the trees; marketing people focus on the forest. And that makes a good team with balanced perspective.

Sex and age. Sales managers are reluctant to hire single women in their twenties fearing they will have children, resulting in maternity leave.

Regional blind spots. We all have perceptions of different regions, and we attach those perceptions to applicants from those areas.

- "He's qualified, but geez, do you wanna have to deal with that Alabama accent all the time?"
- "She's from LA! She will never be happy in the Bay Area."
- "A New Yorker? No, too pushy. It's in their blood."

Experience baggage. Matching experience to job descriptions can be faulty unless we challenge our assumptions. Have you ever said things like:

- "Yeah, but she comes from Acme. They have ways of doing things that aren't compatible with our ways."
- "He has an MBA, but what was he doing working for a nonprofit? That says something about his priorities."

Physical bias. This is also known as appearance bias, and is most associated with a person's height, weight, or physical looks. "All other things being equal, always hire salespeople who are at least six feet tall."

Hiring bias. Hiring managers understandably recall the last person they interviewed more than the previous candidates. One exception is often the first person they interviewed. Obviously, the first person met the criteria well enough to be granted an interview. "Wow, get her in here before someone else hires her." First and last only? What are the opportunity costs there?

Academic orientation. Some may call these professional orientations, but they are still biases.

- "We are all clinical psychologists here in this practice. Always have been. So why are you so big on hiring a humanistic psychologist? How would we handle that when it comes to assigning patients?" Doesn't it depend on the patient's needs?

- "You can't have a University of Chicago PhD in economics working in this government agency! It's a recipe for ongoing problems with the legislature's liberals."

The big one—confirmation bias. Social psychologists have become the dominant observers of the social sciences. They seem to isolate lots of our dysfunctional behavior as social animals. We have all seen many people hold to a belief or attitude and be unwilling to consider countervailing evidence; instead, they reinforce their beliefs by seeking only that information which confirms their position. Hence, confirmation bias.

In a setting of multiple perspectives and professional outlooks, suffering from confirmation bias will destroy your credibility. Don't chain yourself to any one position, on any issue. Admit that circumstances can change. Otherwise, you will earn little influence because observers will always be reminded of your inflexible attitude or bias on that other issue.

COACHING TIP: Consider attending bias training.

And the Consequences

Think of someone who has displayed these blind spots. Did it not color your perception of their credibility? How credible and influential were they in other matters? Or did your perception of them carry over to other issues? Biases demonstrate not just faulty thinking but also narrow thinking.

The outsider as devil's advocate. "Why don't we hire someone with experience in our technology? Her experience is so outside of the field. Look how much time it will take to train her." This, of course, ignores the reality that an outsider can ask questions and raise issues that insiders may have forgotten to ask as the market changed around them. An outsider can be a devil's advocate. This means briefly taking the opposite position from colleagues to make them think more critically and more clearly about the issues at hand. You can win good points for credibility by doing this at planning meetings.

Big law firms often do this. Some partners go off to a nearby conference room to imagine they are representing the opposing side. They outline what they would do if they were the opposing attorneys. Then the two teams pretend they are in the courtroom, and it becomes important planning for the firm.

You can also develop what Dr. Adam Grant (see his book in Additional Resources below) calls a "challenge network" in your organization. (In Pitfall #1 we suggested starting a breakfast group of noncompeting colleagues doing the same job as yours with whom you can bounce around ideas.)

COACHING TIP: Seek input from alternative perspectives (e.g., your writing buddy or your mentor).

Taking the Tobin/Peterson bias walk. Don't stumble into the bias pitfall. Ponder these questions. It's not too late to spend some quality time in your quiet place and be honest with yourself.

- Have you ever listened to someone and said to yourself, "Wow, what a blind spot." If so, how did you label that person's blind spot?
- Consequently, did you ever discuss the comment with them to see how and why the person thinks that way?
- Do you typically form first impressions of people?
- What are your typical triggers when encountering new colleagues, both good and bad?
- Do you sometimes allow one negative factor to color your perception of a person?
- Do those triggers tend to persist in your mind throughout all subsequent encounters?
- Were you surprised that someone you first liked later triggered one of your biases?
- Can you list the reasons why you have typically not hired people, other than job experience? Any patterns?
- When you decide someone is not a candidate for personal friendship, have those same factors also become the reason you would not hire them?
- Have you ever been privately asked, following a meeting, "Why do you think that way?"
- Has anyone ever asked if you are an optimist or a pessimist? If so, did you respond, "Why do you ask?"
- Do you see yourself as an optimist or a pessimist?
- Does all of this prompt you to ask trusted colleagues what their perceptions are of you, positive and negative?

- Think of a past blind spot or consistent attitude that you have dropped. What new perspective, fact, or situation prompted you to change your position?

Perception is all there is.

—MARKETING GURU TOM PETERS

Peters is correct about personal perceptions, as well as product or company perceptions. If colleagues perceive you as inflexible and blinded by your attitudes, you can forget about credibility or clout. Actor Alan Alda spotlighted the issue well: "Begin challenging your own assumptions. Your assumptions are your windows on the world. Scrub them off every once in a while, or the light won't come in."

Summary of Coaching Tips

- Conduct activities that improve your self-awareness, such as maintaining a daily journal, identifying your values, and exploring your initial emotional reactions to situations.
- Reflecting on your beliefs, actions, and responses is the most powerful, but you can also consider reflecting on others' actions and statements.
- Focus on facts over feelings and opinions.
- Consider attending bias training.
- Seek input from alternative perspectives like your writing buddy or mentor.

It's important for a leader to hear about his blind spots on a regular basis so working on them is periodically top of mind.

—VENTURE CAPITALIST SCOTT WEISS

Summary of Pitfall #5

So far in this book we have outlined words and attitudes that color people's perceptions of colleagues, including your own. Much can detract from your credibility with so many biases, whether they are conscious or unconscious. Your ability to communicate effectively around these biases begins with self-awareness. We encourage you to embrace our coaching tips to help you build self-awareness and ultimately reflect an unbiased view in your communications.

Moving you along. Next comes Pitfall #6, which applies what we have covered so far to a controversial topic that just hangs in the air these days: What is a fact, and how do you recognize and acknowledge facts versus opinions? Mark Twain warned us all years ago when he said, "It's not what you don't know that kills you. It's what you know for sure that ain't true." When it comes to clarity of thought, clarity of communications, and the asset of credibility, this is where clout or influence can blossom to make you a respected leader. (Warning: This does not include "alternative facts.")

Additional Resources

- *The Credibility Code: How to Project Confidence & Competence When It Matters Most* by Cara Hale Alter (San Francisco: Meritus Books, 2012). Cara Hale Alter is an executive coach whose seminars are well worth attending. Go to www.speechskills.com.
- *Think Again: The Power of Knowing What You Don't Know* by Adam Grant, PhD (New York: Viking, 2021).
- *The End of Bias: A Beginning* by Jessica Nordell (New York: Metropolitan Books / Holt, 2021).
- *The Constitution of Knowledge: A Defense of Truth* by Jonathan Rauch (Washington, DC: Brookings Institution Press, 2021).
- *Human Resource Management* (15th ed.) by Gary Dessler (Upper Saddle River, NJ: Pearson, 2016).

Pitfall #6: Fact Foibles

How to Tell When Facts Fail—or Fall Flat

Get your facts first, and then you can distort them as much as you please.

—MARK TWAIN

We live in a wonderful information age. Publishing was once limited to paper and ink. Now with the Internet, online publishing and social media platforms have burst open the doors to access. Anyone with cash and a cause can become a publisher.

Another example comes from the advent of the twenty-four-hour news cycle. Being the first to report breaking news, which used to be based in facts derived from diligent research, is a media winner. But as we learned with Pitfall #1, with speed comes certain trade-offs, such as factual accuracy. Who among us takes the time to research the accuracy of news stories, especially those from social media or cable sites? Without any accountability, how would we know?

So, speed wins. And we, the consumer of information, lose. But ideally, when something smells wrong, we begin to question the accuracy of information.

And therein lay big problems: Factual clarity in a sea of murky information and opinion. Verifiability concerns. Uncertain expertise. Dubious credibility. Whose influence can be followed?

It's not just the traditional news and social media. All of this applies to memos, telephone calls, Zoom meetings, emails, and texting. By anyone. We are inundated by communications compared to just a decade or so ago. People read quickly, often too quickly, and thus incompletely. (Note: Just as we said in Pitfall #1 about the risks of hitting "send" too hastily.)

The variety and sources of information can quickly become an echo chamber—an environment where folks encounter only information or opinions that resemble their own. It is the opposite of critical thinking. And it is particularly dangerous for the unknowing, because it slyly serves to validate one's own beliefs, ultimately resulting in believing as fact what was once merely opinion. Hence, it is even more important to engage our critical thinking, so our communications are clear and credible to assure that our influence will be accepted. (Note: Don't miss our item on critical thinking in appendix B.)

In short, it is far easier these days to compromise your credibility than it was for, say, your parents. When is a fact true, and when does it cease to make sense? Welcome to Pitfall #6.

The Gist

We all make decisions about what to accept as comfortably within our domain of knowledge, but when we naively assume some level of knowledge outside our domain, we can become conspicuous. Our communications may be more a distraction than food for thought. We may be perceived by colleagues as lacking in critical thinking skills. Unclear.

When we get flippant with facts, it flops in our face. There goes credibility and clout. Pitfall #6 may be the toughest chapter for many readers because we challenge you on two sides of the clarity coin. On one side, you must consider the sources of information that you receive. We are not trying to create paranoia or doubt about every bit of information. To the contrary, we want you to be good *consumers* of information. On the other side of the coin, we want you to be good *stewards* of information. In other words, pay attention to your beliefs—and yes, biases (see Pitfall #5)—and whether you are passing them off as facts.

Just be open to this question: When is a fact true, and when does a cherished fact or rule become false—or obsolete?

How can you tell the difference between facts, feelings, and opinions? Each has an important place in how we interact with others. Knowing whether you are communicating facts, feelings, or opinions influences how your message is received and ultimately affects your credibility. Furthermore, in the workplace, the greater your clarity with what type of message you are communicating, the better the decision-making can be.

Facts are objective pieces of information that can be proven to be true or false with multiple pieces of reliable data. Your goal when communicating facts is to inform, not persuade. The better, more objective, and factual the information, the higher the quality of decisions you will make. Taking a balanced approach to objective information allows us to look at the facts from multiple angles. It allows us to form our own conclusions independent of others' opinions. This is the essence of critical thinking. Rather than being told how to think, you are encouraged to think for yourself.

COACHING TIP: As you are planning your message, challenge yourself to identify the objective information that makes something a fact.

Feelings are an emotional reaction state that allow us to develop and navigate relationships, make certain decisions, and connect to events and experiences. They can be based on intuition. There is a time and a place to express your feelings. For example, feelings when appropriately expressed can create stronger connections. They demonstrate authenticity and can reinforce empathy.

COACHING TIP: When expressing feelings in the workplace, take a balanced and situationally appropriate approach. Avoid becoming overly emotional and maintain a level emotional state.

Scene #1

Aaron was a vice president at a publicly traded tech firm. He was affable and optimistic. As he made his way from the elevators on the fourteenth floor to his corner office, he passed by his team of over forty professionals sitting in open cubicles. Each morning, Aaron would say with his booming voice, "It's going to be a great day, ladies and gentlemen. A great day."

While this positive message was generally appreciated and was only sometimes tuned out, it didn't matter what else was going on in the company. Aaron still said the same thing each morning. On two occasions, colleagues pulled him aside and suggested he become better informed about the company news and updates and tone down his canned positivity. The first time was when Javier pulled him aside the day after the announcement of a rather dismal earnings report. And the other was a couple of months later, when Beth confronted him on a Monday morning following several team layoffs the preceding week.

There is a time and a place for expressing feelings of optimism—or other feelings, for that matter. Unfortunately, Aaron missed the mark. He appeared oblivious to the team, and his enthusiasm was misplaced. The team picked up on this and began to question his credibility.

Aaron continued his morning message. Behind his back, when something didn't go well, the associates would sarcastically say, "But don't worry, because it's a great day." It wasn't long before more people started tuning Aaron out, and a growing number of associates could not take him seriously on a variety of topics.

Communicating feelings goes beyond words. We often communicate feelings through a variety of expressions and other nonverbal cues. You'll learn much more about this in Pitfall #9, but we'll touch on this briefly here as well.

Opinions are subjective pieces of information that you have come to believe are true. When people think you are trying to pass off your beliefs or opinions as facts—whether intentionally or not—your credibility is out the window. The perception is that you are trying to trick your audience or that you have an agenda. At the heart of sharing your opinions is the wish to persuade.

COACHING TIP: When someone is communicating an opinion you don't agree with, use the phrase "Help me understand . . ." to better appreciate their point of view.

The Four Distinct Levels of Knowing Something—*and We See All Four Every Day*

1. Knowing you know something *for sure*. Example: Accountants are confident they know accounting and how to do it. They have the training and the license, and they have happy clients.
2. Being comfortable knowing you *don't* know something. Example: An accountant has no problem saying they know nothing about astrophysics. They have no problem admitting this and listening to a scientific discussion on astrophysics (maybe).
3. *Thinking* you know something. Example: An accountant thinks they know something about investment strategy and advice, but does not have the training, fiduciary certification, or state license an investment broker has. They may well have some good leads. Nonetheless, it is wise to check their suggestions with a fiduciary broker.
4. *Not knowing* you don't know something—but acting like you do! Example: An accountant with no military experience insists the

> president should send troops to X place or order bombing there. Worse, the accountant urges his/her clients to invest heavily in munitions companies' stocks. This is the most dangerous form of "knowing." Long ago, Confucius summed it up: "To know what you know and what you do not know, that is true knowledge."

This last—regrettable—level of knowing has an academic term gaining considerable attention lately: the Dunning–Kruger effect. As you can guess, it is the mentality of someone absolutely convinced of their expertise on some topic while others around them are turning their heads away and smiling. It is a cognitive bias if people overestimate their knowledge or ability in some specific area. This results from inadequate self-awareness that blinds them from accurately assessing their own skills. Even more striking is the tendency for someone lacking competence or expertise in something to be aglow in overconfidence about their ability.

It's common. Chances are we have all done this, even regarding something small and unimportant.

Scene #2

One of us served in a naval air squadron and worked in the legal office. The legal office dealt with infractions and discipline, among other things. One afternoon an enlisted man with no formal education but with many years of service stopped by and pontificated on his deep knowledge of an aspect of military justice. We all listened politely, including the legal officer, who could easily have dismissed the man and told him to return to his workstation. Once the man had left and was out of sight, the three of us in the office burst into laughter. The label naval folks attach to this man's pontification is "sea lawyer." Pundit and social commentator George Carlin nailed it: "Some people have no idea what they're doing, and a lot of them are really good at it."

Whole organizations sometimes suffer, without knowing it, by following some long-held rule or position. Unwritten rules or cherished notions of reality can doom organizations because no one wants to say, "The emperor has no clothes." Without an established challenge network or an outsider who can ask *Why?*, an organization can roll right into a pitfall of blindness.

Scene #3

Organizations often fall in love with a presumption that becomes a rule no one thinks to challenge. Polaroid was, for decades, a much-loved consumer company. The Polaroid Land Camera spit out a printed picture as soon as you pressed the button; no need to take your roll of film to a processing center and wait for days. But then digital camera technology became a reality. Nonetheless, some members of Polaroid management held close to their bosoms the notion that everyone would still want a hard-copy photo once they'd snapped the image. It was an unchallenged rule, and it paved the way to Polaroid's demise.

Decades later the BlackBerry was almost a cult object for email reception, but the company lost its chance for a big piece of the consumer market. Consumers fell in love with apps, something BlackBerry did not want to offer, and touchscreen technology became a hit. The bigger idea was that smartphones weren't restricted to just voice and email. They were handheld computers and entertainment centers, not to mention cameras. Perception is all there is, said Tom Peters.

Devotion to unspoken rules limits imagination and what-if questions. Where were the outsiders' questions, the challenge network, the devil's advocates? Imagine the influence you can have by simply asking "Why do we still do it this way?" Clout. Risky, yes, but credible, nonetheless.

A note on feedback. Giving or receiving feedback naturally elicits emotions. The emotion stems from what is said, how it is said, and where or when it is said. When giving feedback, it is critical to differentiate facts from feelings and opinions. The purpose of feedback is to help develop people and motivate them to reach their goals. It requires an artful balance of tact, finesse, honesty, and—you guessed it—clarity. When done well, feedback reinforces positive behavior and refocuses the wrong habits to improve performance and results.

Feedback can include opinions, but to be effective, it must be backed up with specific and objective examples of performance. Furthermore, it's just as important—perhaps even more so—to *listen* when giving feedback. Seek input on the feedback and solutions. This is very much a coaching approach to leadership, and it allows the recipient to be a participant and take greater ownership and accountability for any follow-up actions.

COACHING TIP: When giving feedback to a colleague or direct report, be factual and provide multiple specific examples to illustrate key points.

Scene #4

Jordan looks at her calendar for the week, and she's excited to see she has a performance review discussion with her boss Steve on Tuesday morning. She has been an associate consultant with her company for almost a year and has worked on multiple projects during that time, each with a different project manager. She appreciates that each project leader met with her periodically to provide her with constructive feedback about her performance.

Judy was one of the leaders who said Jordan is valued for the ideas she brings to the project, and she always gets her tasks done on time, which is an asset to the team. Judy also provided several examples. Another project manager, Elizabeth, agreed, stating that Jordan's timeliness on project deliverables has allowed the team to save money and finish the project ahead of schedule.

This would be Jordan's first opportunity to meet with Steve. She knows how important Steve's feedback is to her growth, development, and progression with the company. Steve opens their meeting by saying how glad he is that Jordan is part of the team, but then quickly transitions to providing very vague and general feedback. He says he thinks she needs to work harder on projects. When she asks for specifics, he uses another colleague as an example of how to work harder—"Be more like Sandy," he says. He continues the feedback session by talking about what he thinks it takes to succeed in the company, and then closes with some advice: "If you want to succeed here, be on time and keep your nose to the grindstone."

Jordan doesn't even know what all of this means. She has no clarity from her conversation with Steve. She feels blindsided, dejected, and confused. On top of that, since Steve's feedback doesn't match the more specific and objective feedback she's received throughout the year, she's uncertain what to do next or how exactly to improve. And as for Steve, his credibility as a leader has taken a hit.

What should Steve have done differently?

Scene #5

Tom works for a regional learning technology consulting company. He is the project lead for a multimillion-dollar project that has high visibility with leaders across the company. The core team is comprised of ten subject-matter-expert contributors who are assigned this project in addition to their other key responsibilities. The project has become increasingly off schedule. During previous delays, the team has been able to identify opportunities to get back on track during their weekly team meetings.

Now, nearly ten months into what is planned to be a twelve-month project, Tom confronts the group during a regularly scheduled team update. He begins the meeting in an atypical way, with elevated voice and visible frustration. He is uncharacteristically animated and lets the team know in no uncertain terms that they are missing deadlines, and that he and other executives are disappointed in the project status. He berates two of the sub-team leads, Annika and Max, for not being more proactive, and comments on their inability to keep the team focused.

People look around in disbelief. Sure, the project has struggled, but much of it is outside of their control. They had used previous project update meetings to help get back on track, but this one ends with a thud. The entire working team is dejected. Tom had let his feelings get the best of him, and he took it out on Annika, Max, and the rest of the team.

Later that afternoon, Tom realizes he was out of line. Over the next couple of days, he seeks out each team member, beginning with Annika and Max, to apologize. Unfortunately, Tom's outburst proves to be counterproductive to the project, resulting in lower morale, missed opportunities to problem-solve, and further delays. It becomes a negative turning point for the project.

Eventually the project is completed eight weeks after the deadline. Tom's credibility as a leader never fully recovers—not only because of the missed deadline and cost overruns, but because of the way he lost the team.

What can be learned from Tom's experience?

COACHING TIP: When giving feedback, criticize in private; give praise in public or private, as the situation calls for.

Why vs. how. You encounter a friend who is quite opinionated about an issue. It could be something at work or a broader policy issue in government. If you ask why they are so concerned, they bring up many reasons supporting the veracity of their opinion.

Then you ask your friend how their position should be implemented. How would it work?

Suddenly all the confirmation bias cools, and you begin to hear several *maybes* or what-ifs and other hedges on your friend's certainty. You may have given them the space to become their own devil's advocate and avoid the Dunning–Kruger effect. They survive and learn, but you have gained credibility in their eyes, as well. You are now perceived as someone whose thought processes can critically dissect an issue and bring clarity to controversy. Clout.

COACHING TIP: Avoid personal attacks in your communication.

Becoming a devil's advocate. Imagine someone has a proposal in your organization. Your intuition tells you something doesn't add up. Something does not make sense. Exposing the logical deficiency could raise your credibility and your influence. What to do? Here's a possible checklist to use.

- Is this proposal tied to some unwritten rule everyone unconsciously follows? We discussed this in earlier pitfalls. As organizations age, they seem to develop deep-seated attachments to how they think and how they do things. Classic stories of this backfiring: Polaroid, BlackBerry.
- Do you sense any conflicting words or phrases that hint at something wrong?
- Do you suspect a hidden agenda? Do you sense the suggestion has a motive behind it that the advocates are not acknowledging?
- Who benefits from the proposal or idea, and why?
- Who's vulnerable? What staff members could be affected?
- Identify the end goal sought. Suggest one or two other approaches that will attain the same end.

I have six honest servants; they've taught me all I know. Their names are what, why, and who, and when and where and how.

—NOVELIST ROBERT LOUIS STEVENSON

Playing devil's advocate comes down to asking questions, and there's an art to it. It's important to be genuinely inquisitive as opposed to confrontational. The latter puts people in a defensive position and can quickly spiral negatively. One potentially disarming way to initiate a conversation in a devil's advocate role is to state it up front. For example, consider starting with "Let me play devil's advocate for a minute." This approach provides greater transparency about how or why you are asking questions. If you prefer an even softer approach, you can phrase it as a question. "Do you mind if I play devil's advocate for a minute?"

COACHING TIP: It's okay to respectfully disagree with someone else's opinion that differs from yours. The operative word is *respectfully*. Stay open-minded to hearing them out.

Fact words or opinion words. What follows are fact words compared to opinion words. If you find you are using more words on the opinion side, it's time to reevaluate your position and your reasoning with colleagues.

- Fact words:
  - Certified
  - Confirmed
  - Verified
  - Stated
  - Quoted
  - Corroborated
- Opinion words and phrases:
  - Best, worst
  - Most important, least important
  - Think
  - Somewhat
  - Feel
  - I believe
  - Argue
  - Claim
  - Virtually, almost
  - Can be, could be
  - In my point of view/perspective
  - Acts like
  - Always, never, must
  - Should, should not
  - Implied, denied
  - In my opinion
  - Suggested

COACHING TIP: As a leader, it's great to ask about others' opinions—especially those with knowledge of a situation. Asking colleagues and team members what they think about a particular topic or situation helps to understand issues, generate ideas, establish buy-in and connections, and make informed decisions.

How Facts Escape or Morph in Our Thinking

Dr. Thomas Kida summarizes our thinking issue in six basic mistakes. (See his great book listed in our Additional Resources below; better yet, get the book.) He cites many robust examples to shine the light on his list, but here's a quick summary:

1. *We prefer stories to statistics.* We can access all kinds of studies, but one anecdotal comment from someone, especially an influential person, can change your mind.
2. *We seek to confirm.* Other pitfall chapters discuss confirmation bias. We all do it.
3. *We rarely acknowledge chance or coincidence.* In short, don't go to casinos. You can't figure out the next roll.
4. *We often misperceive the world.* We have used the quote "Perception is all there is" many times in this book. We also too often perceive what we want to perceive.
5. *We oversimplify.* We all do this. Twice in one week comes news of a two-car crash on Highway 9. In any metro area, there may have been other two-car crashes, but, geez, stay away from Highway 9 this month. Must be its frequent drivers!
6. *We have faulty memories.* Looking back, how often have you reconstructed some pleasant event from, say, high school, but no one at the last reunion can remember it?

Beware of vague words. Some questions, upon closer examination, are tricky. Try this one: When was the United States established?

Well, most people, remembering that family picnic in July, would say July 4, 1776. But the verb *established* is a bit vague. American colonies declared independence on July 4, 1776, but many participants did not sign the Declaration until several weeks later. More importantly, the Constitution (replacing the flawed Articles of Confederation) was not offered for adoption until September 17, 1787. It required nine states to become law. Colony number nine signed on June 21, 1788. (Four states came into the union later.) That is when the United States became *one* country, because the Revolutionary War was fought with *thirteen* begged-and-borrowed colonial militias, many of which did not want to fight beyond their own borders.

So, define the word *established.* Words, like facts, are tricky things. Vagueness is inherently unclear and surely doesn't boost credibility or clout.

Here are some vague words to avoid—or at least, be mindful and careful when using them:

- may
- some
- third party/ies
- time to time
- generally
- various
- appropriate
- reasonably
- usually
- may be
- periodically
- impact
- next level
- a few
- enough
- things
- stuff
- good
- like
- whenever
- whatever

When is vagueness acceptable? Sometimes we cannot be precise, and might even avoid committing to exact information. For example, when a situation lacks certainty, it is better to admit it and be general. Here is an example in action: It's December, and you are being asked to provide an update on your work and development plans for the following year. It may backfire on you to have specific dates, nor is it helpful if you just say "By next December 31" and risk looking unprepared.

The idea is to provide your best guess as to when people, such as your boss, can expect certain items to be completed. You may opt for a specific date, and we recommend that approach if you are certain of it. Alternatives, though, would be providing the month or even the quarter when the work item is expected to be complete. As you get new information or the time frame gets closer, you should refine to a greater degree of specificity.

This is situational and varies by organization, so it pays to know your audience. The intent of using vague words is not to be sneaky or manipulative, but rather to manage expectations.

Summary of Coaching Tips

- As you are planning your message, challenge yourself to identify the objective information that makes something a fact.
- When expressing feelings in the workplace, take a balanced and situationally appropriate approach. Avoid becoming overly emotional and maintain a level emotional state.
- When someone is communicating an opinion you don't agree with, use the phrase "Help me understand . . ." to better appreciate their point of view.
- When giving feedback to a colleague or direct report, be factual and provide multiple specific examples to illustrate key points.
- When giving feedback, criticize in private; give praise in public or private, as the situation calls for.
- Avoid personal attacks in your communication.
- It's okay to respectfully disagree with someone else's opinion that differs from yours. The operative word is *respectfully*. Stay open-minded about hearing them out.
- Ask informed colleagues and team members "What do you think?" about issues and challenging situations they have familiarity with.

You are what you think . . . geez, that's frightening.

—COMEDIAN LILY TOMLIN

Summary of Pitfall #6

Repeating information as facts when they are not is a certain way of blowing your clarity, credibility, and clout. It's like slapping a sign on your forehead that says "Don't believe me all the time!" Almost as damaging is passing information along that has not been verified. Remember what Abe Lincoln supposedly said: "You can fool all the people some of the time, and some of the people all of the time, but you can't fool all the people all of the time."

Moving you along. Pitfall #7 moves you from facts versus opinion into numbers and data, often the easier way to deceive people—or to be deceived yourself. This isn't good for either clarity or credibility, so, let's learn to use data for influence the right way by being aware of the classic mistakes. It's all about clout. Read on.

Additional Resources

- *Don't Believe Everything You Think: The 6 Basic Mistakes We Make in Thinking* by Thomas Kida (Amherst, NY: Prometheus Books, 2006).
- *Originals: How Non-Conformists Move the World* by Adam Grant (New York: Viking, 2016).
- *The Leadership Challenge: How to Make Extraordinary Things Happen in Organizations*, 6th ed., by James Kouzes and Barry Posner (Hoboken, NJ: Jossey-Bass, 2017).
- *The Constitution of Knowledge: A Defense of Truth* by Jonathan Rauch (Washington, DC: Brookings Institution Press, 2021).
- As mentioned, anyone with a cause and the cash can publish whatever they wish. This begs the need for careful media consumption. Here is a website devoted to this need: https://medialiteracynow.org.

Pitfall #7: Fumbling Fallacies

The Slippery Slope of Sloppy Logic

You better cut the pizza in four pieces because
I'm not hungry enough to eat six.

—YOGI BERRA

When sound reasoning stumbles. Everything Yogi ever said still prompts a smile. Evergreen humor. But in our everyday lives, at work and elsewhere, colleagues' trust is lost if our thinking loses clarity. Yogi's quote above is an example of the **fallacy of composition**—in other words, when you confuse the parts and the whole. Logic of thought is as important as the logic of mathematics. More on that later in the book.

So just what is logic? Simply stated, a logical argument is one in which the premises support the conclusions. But we are human, and humans can be emotional and hasty. People can communicate facts, feelings, and opinions, yet sometimes those get blurred or twisted. We often react too quickly rather than ponder more reasonable options. It comes across as fuzzy thinking rather than clear thinking. Do it consistently, and you lose credibility.

Everyday examples of fuzzy logic are called fallacies. Funny thing about fallacies. At first, they all sound reasonable. And that's the problem: Fallacies can survive the moment. But then colleagues take another moment to think about your statement: "Say what?"

The word *fallacy* is based on the Greek word for "deceive." Therein lies a sad aspect of communication: Some people use fallacies to deceive. Whether intentionally deceptive or not, try maintaining your credibility and influence with a bad habit like that.

Fallacies number in the hundreds. Although they are quite fun to study, they can be frustrating and misleading in practice. We introduce several common fallacies here so you can avoid them as a communicator and have your antenna up for others who try to pass them off as fact.

Twelve Common Scenes

We walk you into twelve situations we have all likely encountered. They are examples of the slippery thinking that compromises clarity and credibility. You may recognize some situations you have witnessed, maybe recently. Additionally, we show you how to recognize this type of thinking and communication in yourself and in others and coach you on what to do about it.

Scene #1

It's late on a Friday afternoon. A meeting is called about the future direction of the organization. Everyone is seated, but most are quietly plotting how to cut the meeting short so they can clear out for the weekend. Several ideas are casually mentioned and put on the whiteboard. Suddenly Bill comes up with an off-the-wall idea that awakens everyone into rapt attention. But on the way out, Sue grabs George's hand and says, "Hey, George, get real! Bill is an accountant. Everything to him is black or white, debit or credit. This is too deep for him."

Let's hope Sue becomes more charitable in future critiques. Sometimes great ideas come from people whose backgrounds, on paper, don't match the task at hand—*until you give them some creative space.* In fact, in some innovation circles, breadth of background and approach can stir new ways of thinking.

Sue's mistake is called the **ad hominem fallacy**—an attack on the person, the source, rather than the merits of the idea. She was radically generalizing. Such a fallacy is common in people's blind spots and biases. "Oh, Italians are so emotional." "She's a Republican, so naturally she thinks that's wrong." "He's a devout [religion name here], so how can you believe he thinks clearly on this kind of issue."

What makes this fallacy particularly bad is that generalizations can be flat-out wrong, and the audience may accept it nonetheless, or not hear any message at all. (See appendix A for the Crystal Rule.)

Scene #2

Over lunch with colleagues, the discussion turns to diet and vitamins and nutrition. Phil states that his neighbor, a nurse, claims that men in their forties need to get more niacin in their diets to maintain hormone levels. Phil's lunchmates perk up their ears.

The problem here is that nurses are not necessarily nutrition experts. Neither, frankly, are medical doctors. Comments that initially sound credible must be checked to see if the source is legitimately knowledgeable. This is especially so in the era of social media, where anyone can publish weak information or claim to be an expert. In fact, the individual may not claim to be an expert at all. There may simply be an assumption of credibility based on title. In some circles, these individuals falsely serve as credibility substitutes. Don't fall for the fallacy known as the **appeal to authority**. Titles can bestow authority the holder may not really have.

A common mistake occurs in business. Someone has been a successful salesperson. An opening in marketing occurs, so the firm promotes the sales superstar to marketing director. The issue here is that marketing is a body of knowledge no less than IT, human resources, finance, or engineering. Salespeople are supposed to focus on the trees, the individuals to close, but a marketing director is supposed to focus on the forest, the big picture. Big difference in perspective. So, the actions and statements of a new marketing director may carry the title's appeal of authority but not the right knowledge—or perspective. Same with nurses playing nutritionists. The implications can be detrimental, because expectations may be set, and actions may be taken based upon this information.

Similarly, there can be implied institutional authority, both positive and negative. Brenda went to Harvard; therefore, she is an assumed authority, whereas Doug went to a lesser-known college or had a nontraditional educational path. Therefore, his points of view may be questioned more. Your role is to allow individuals to stand on their own merits, positive or negative. Your impartial thinking affects your credibility—and frankly, theirs as well.

Scene #3

A company is deep in preparation for their annual trade show. The CEO insists on hosting a big cocktail party with mounds of shrimp in a center display. The marketing communications manager asks if other exhibitors also host such lavish events.

"Oh, yeah, lots of the big companies throw hospitality spreads, and we have always done it," asserted the CEO. The marcom manager claims little research supports the notion that attendees remember the next year what companies hosted such parties the prior year. After much give-and-take tainted with subtle warnings, the CEO agrees to forgo hosting the party at the trade show.

The following year, many attendees stopped by the company's booth and commented on how great last year's party was—*even though the company had not hosted any*. So much for the recall value of one hospitality party in a mezzanine crowded with others.

It's all about the fallacy called the **appeal to tradition**. In a rapidly changing business climate, past practice can become a passé practice. Organizations can suffer from being on autopilot as they try to keep up with everyday demands. It's a good idea to routinely wipe the assumptions clean and ask, "Why are we still doing that?" You can gain much credibility and influence merely by asking what data supports the notion that such an expense has demonstrable ROI (return on investment). Fresh perspectives can add value to ideas. It can be a delicate balance of trying not to fix what isn't broken while also exploring and testing new ideas. Remember: Clarity of thought builds influence.

Scene #4

Jill has been urging her church group to go door to door in a recently completed housing development to invite people for services, but also to collect donations to a local food bank. Others in the church leadership are hesitant, worried that a door-to-door campaign would be too intrusive. One after another, they all line up in opposition. Instead of presenting examples of how the tactic has worked for other nonprofits—and not wishing to tarnish her image—Jill gives up and says, "Well, maybe you're right. It's not worth the effort." Jill has succumbed to the fallacy called **the bandwagon effect**.

Employees new to an organization typically don't want to challenge colleagues right away. However, a thoughtfully presented premise might be well received. For example, what if Jill had suggested, in response to the others' reactions, that they might take two streets and see how effectively door-to-door works, then evaluate the effort against time spent. In other words, test the idea and gain new insights.

When hiring new employees, consider offering this suggestion to them: During their first sixty days, take note of any processes, programs, and practices that are either a) unique and amazing; or b) don't seem to make sense. The latter analysis can provide you with fresh, valuable insights that challenge the status quo.

You may wonder what this has to do with clarity and communications. With such a strategy for new hires, you will have clearly communicated your expectations, as well as implicitly communicated the type of team and culture you are building. So long as your actions match your words, you are communicating that you're open to new ideas.

Scene #5

George, a sales manager at a medium-size business, is under pressure to lower costs. He has decided the travel and entertainment budget for his forty-person sales staff needs tweaking. At lunch with two of his sales reps he pops the idea of no longer taking clients to dinner, while keeping "lunch entertainment" in the budget. He also floats the idea of the sales staff staying only in budget hotels/motels. His two direct reports at lunch seem agreeable. As a result, George decides to proceed with the changes.

Unfortunately, George's conclusion is based on a **biased sample** (also, too small of a sample), a common fallacy, and, to make things worse, he has reached a **hasty generalization**, both fallacies of logic. The two reports he quizzed may be new. Or they may already be using budget hotels. Or they may really prefer luncheon entertainment because it can be quicker and does not intrude on the evening's paperwork demands. Or, they may have been deferring to what they thought George wanted to hear rather than offering sound, thoughtful insight based on data or experience. What's more, George surely has other lines in his budget that might need reevaluating. Instead, he made a generalization based on responses from two people.

Scene #6

Two neighbors, Sam and Jack, want to take their wives to dinner tonight. They are debating which Italian restaurant in town is more authentic. Sam argues that the Roman Gladiator has the perfect lasagna, with three cheeses used by great chefs. Jack claims the Bountiful Boot makes its own fresh pasta, including the best ravioli in town, and has the best selection of Italian wines. The culinary debate continues among grins and the aura of authority. Then Jack says, "Hey, the parking is better at the Boot, and it's easier to get there off Main Street."

Jack has introduced an irrelevant argument with the goal of closing the deal with Sam to get the reservation phoned in. Jack raised what's called **the red herring fallacy**—a distraction. So much for the food.

Choosing a restaurant illogically is harmless. But Sam and Jack work together, too. One day they face a decision about naming a new product. The product has many attributes, which doesn't make the naming decision a slam dunk. Should the name focus on ROI, ease of training, new technology, or ease of use? Sam and Jack debate it for days until Jack mentions that the guys in R&D have called it Project XV for years and were now used to that name. Sam, being new to the company, goes along with it. Project XV it will be. The issue here is that R&D is not marketing. Product identity, a key marketing function, should appeal to customer needs. Hurt feelings in R&D are irrelevant. Jack threw a distraction at Sam, and that is what a red herring is. One of this book's authors once worked at a technology giant that frequently used development names for product names. That company no longer exists.

Scene #7

Helen, a product manager, goes to her boss in R&D and asks for more resources to get her product to at least 95 percent completion. Adrienne, the boss, sits back fast, with her mouth dropping even faster.

"Helen, if I give you more resources, Ken will ask for the same. And if I give in to Ken, Rachel will ask for more. And then the whole rest of the product department will be begging for more support!"

Adrienne anxiously envisions a "me too" surge of pleadings from the other product managers. She has fallen down **the slippery slope**, a common logical fallacy. Helen's product may be unique in its needs, whereas the other products are mature or less complicated. It may be a strategic priority of the company. What's more, perhaps the other product managers are quite confident and would never rush to expose managerial shortcomings when their products are known to be stable. Adrienne, get a grip. Stop slipping, or you may lose credibility and influence.

In most—if not all—organizations, resources are limited. Requests *should* be scrutinized. How will these requests, if fulfilled, contribute to the overall success of the department, or the entire organization? You should prepare in advance for such an argument. Being more prepared to defend your point of view, but also, all the reasons it may not be approved, can help you anticipate the dialogue and offer solutions. It's easy to say that your department or every other one could benefit from additional resources. However, there must be business filters in place when making such requests, and, ultimately, decisions. What is the business case, or business value of any such request? There's no guarantee your request will be approved, but, without those details, it's certainly less likely to be approved. A good tip: Create your own Q&A of likely reactions, as we suggest in Pitfall #1.

Scene #8

John and Vince are in the conference room waiting for Sally, the newly hired product manager, to present some suggestions for the coming year. Vince, unusually vocal that day, leans over and whispers to John, "Hey, don't believe a word she says. She worked for Acme in Denver. Their products are weird. And, geez, now she's with us!"

Well, Vince, it all depends on how sound your contacts and information really are. But in the interim, you've just committed a grave error: the fallacy of **poisoning the well** for John and everyone else at your company. Sally was hired with the same due diligence that resulted in your hiring, right? What would you say if Sally recruited a colleague from Acme to join your firm? If you pounced on that, you would be guilty of the fallacy of **guilt by association**.

Vince's poisoning the well may start as a simple, offhand comment. It could be that Vince is threatened by Sally, or maybe he's just trying to be funny. The real risk of the generalization associated with this fallacy is that perceptions can be formed quickly. Vince has planted a seed of information. Perhaps he plants a few more of the same seed, or John, taking Vince at his word, begins planting some of the same seeds. Before you know it, Sally's image, through no fact or fault of her own, has a negative reputation, her credibility potentially impacted. Or, if the company is fortunate, Sally goes on to shine in her performance. In this case, Vince's credibility and judgment are put into question.

Scene #9

Steve told the management team the software they will sell to accountants will be as successful as the software they sell to medical offices. "They both have clients."

Oh? Steve's simplistic comparison should prompt management to ask "Say what? How successful?" Steve's assertion is an analogy. An analogy typically suggests that if two things are similar in one respect, they are similar in other respects. In this case, Steve is using a **false analogy**.

In general, be suspicious of any analogies used to make predictions and comparisons, especially where business is concerned, because analogies are not the strongest, clearest, most credible arguments. Steve's credibility is not strengthened with such a statement.

Papayas and blueberries are both fruit, and corn and artichokes are both vegetables. But the recipes for consumption are different. Even if it's billing software, accountants do not deal with Medicare discounts and reporting, and physicians typically don't warn patients about the tax implications of certain invasive procedures. Salespeople—and anyone else—can blow their reputations with poorly conceived generalizations. The cure: Complete the due diligence required to know your audience and how to connect with them in more relevant ways.

Scene #10

Alice is CEO of a large company that has been losing employees following the COVID-19 pandemic. In a meeting with Henry, her human resources chief, Alice insists it's a salary issue, but she's worried about whether current revenue is sufficient to support raises, to retain workers.

Henry sees an opening. "How do you know it's a compensation issue?"

Alice says she knows her employees and what drives them: money.

Henry wants to hold a series of focus groups in each department.

"Oh, forget it," says Alice. "We can't take employees off the line right now!"

Henry regrettably relents.

Alice is seeing the issue in black-versus-white terms, i.e., only a pay raise will stop the attrition, and nothing else. We all know from the pandemic that employment issues are no longer that simple. Alice is falling for the fallacy of the **false dichotomy**, or **black-and-white thinking**.

We are in a complicated world where gray options outnumber the black-versus-white choices that can really cloud our objectivity, and our influence. Asking colleagues probing questions can shine a light on many workplace motivations, from flexible hours to problem relationships with other departments.

Scene #11

Paul was chosen to organize a special charity reception for his local civic group. The organization budgeted a substantial sum to support the event. It crashed. Attendance was unexpectedly low compared to similar events.

At the next board meeting, Paul is grilled about his promotional tactics. After listening impatiently, Paul says, "Keep in mind the successful spring fund-raiser that took in good revenue—don't forget about that." Well, Paul, that's not what your board colleagues are probing. They are focused on your charity event.

Paul has set up a **straw man argument**, a common fallacy used to distract colleagues' attention. He is hoping to deflect or redirect attention from the performance shortcomings and have the board focus on something more successful. Not a good credibility tactic. It may be a while before Paul is asked to manage another event. His brand is a tad tarnished now.

Scene #12

XYZ is a small, agile technology firm that sells a unique security product to large consumer goods manufacturers. The firm exhibits at two annual trade shows attended by the security managers of such companies. At both trade shows each year, they have a contest to attract visiting managers to their booth. The winner gets a weekend pass to a nice vacation getaway, all expenses paid. Their exhibit is very popular.

Three months after the most recent show, the firm closes two deals with the biggest consumer goods companies in the country. Reflecting on their success in the two sales, XYZ's team decides to budget even more for next year's weekend giveaways.

But the XYZ executives are suffering from the fallacy of **the questionable cause**. The winning attendees may have recommended XYZ's products to their big firms—*may* have—but the big firm's management gets many such pitches. The CEOs sign the checks, but the CEOs do not attend such trade shows, and thus know nothing of the weekend getaways. Correlation does not always mean causation, a common misunderstanding, especially with those who relish their past practices and traditions.

Warning signs: Nearly all incidents of a logical fallacy are prompted by speed. You quickly react to something someone else says, or you seek to head off what you think someone will say, and a fallacious comment spits out that might not have been said if you'd thought carefully about the situations and the facts.

So, how to protect yourself?

How to Avoid a Fallacy Fumble

To prevent your credibility and influence from being compromised, be aware of your thought processes in the following situations:

Fatigue: Unless it's an emergency and can't be delayed, avoid making any comments in a controversy if you are tired, like at the end of a tough day. Here's what to say: "Let's take a break on this one and reconnect tomorrow after we think about the issue. We don't have to decide today."

In a hurry: If you or the others have another pressing meeting, or you must make the day-care pickup on time, again, postpone the issue. Reality: You are distracted. "Let's revisit this when we're not so frazzled. How about tomorrow?"

Personal gain: You are part of an organization. Everyone knows each other. So don't make a comment that betrays that subliminal need to benefit yourself.

Blind spots: If the discussion involves something or someone that could reveal a personal blind spot, be extra careful of what you say. No one you work with has to know your blind spots because you unconsciously use an ad hominem fallacy. Better yet, get rid of that blind spot.

Incomplete knowledge: If you don't have all the facts or haven't learned the latest developments from across the organization, you best not say anything. Suggest everyone revisit the facts and decide tomorrow. Saying something that indicates you are ill-informed will blow your credibility and influence.

Summary of Coaching Tips

If these stories have led you to recall something you have communicated, you have several remedies, some of which further reinforce coaching tips we have mentioned earlier. We encourage you to jot down any additional lessons you have learned in addition to those below.

- When solving problems or innovating, seek alternative points of view. The novice or contrarian point of view can often provide productive input.
- When disagreeing with someone's point of view, focus on the issue rather than generalizing or making it personal.
- It's okay to constructively validate an expert's source of information. It's a delicate balance to question someone's expertise versus seeking clarity on how their expertise contributes to a point of view, so it is best to err on the side of being respectful. A phrase to consider in such instances is, "Help me understand . . ."
- Provide data to support hypotheses and recommendations.
- A business case that includes a description of the issue/topic, as well as the pros, cons, and recommendations tied to key aspects of the business, can help you to organize and clarify a point of view and its impact.
- Similarly, balance business decisions with sound data and intuition. Intuition is often based off of one's own experiences.
- When utilizing data and analytics, be sure the context and comparison is clear. For example, if you are comparing 2021 data with 2020 data, you may be able to show a large and favorable difference due to the unique environment presented by the pandemic. Same with 2022 data compared to 2021.
- Ask questions (or be open to them if you are the primary communicator). Questions can help us gather information, gain clarity, and make better decisions.

Summary of Pitfall #7

Logical fallacies are not as confusing as the damage done by numbers. Dumb correlations. Lying statistics. Too many business decisions are made using sloppy numbers. Worse, you can make numbers say whatever you want. If you think these fallacies dropped your jaw, prepare to take a long calming walk after reading the next chapter. The Crystal Rule may apply more to our numbers than it does to our words.

Moving you along. We can see fallacious, often silly, reasoning every day, especially on social media. But there is one area that's just as bad, if not worse: numbers and statistics. You can make numbers say whatever you want. That snack you bought at lunch is 90 percent salt-free? Check your blood pressure, because 10 percent salt is still heavy salt. On to Pitfall #8.

Additional Resources

- *Critical Thinking Skills for Dummies* by Martin Cohen (Hoboken, NJ: John Wiley & Sons, Ltd., 2015).

Pitfall #8: Dumb Data

How Misused Numbers Can Blow Your Credibility

There are three kinds of falsehoods. Lies, damned lies, and statistics.
—FORMER UK PRIME MINISTER BENJAMIN DISRAELI

Do not fear. We are not going deep into this topic. We surely don't want you to break out in a sweat the way you did in your college course in elementary statistics (which you probably called "elementary *sadistics*"). Here we present some basic warnings to keep you from losing your credibility and influence with colleagues, the mathematical way. We want you to understand the role and power of data in your communications.

When it comes to data, what do you want to be known for? Do you shy away and become overwhelmed by data? Do you overly rely on data without consideration of any contextual information? Do you manipulate data to suit your needs? Or do you take a more objective approach to data? How you answer these questions and how you approach data will impact your credibility, for better or for worse.

COACHING TIP: Embrace the role and power of data to drive decisions. Make it a priority to become fluent in the data and metrics that are important to your organization.

Whatever your comfort level is with data, as you continue to grow in your career, you will need to develop some expertise—and yes, comfort—with utilizing data to make decisions. Therein lies the power of data. Data should be used to make informed business decisions.

There's a saying in business: "You can't manage what you don't measure." The measuring allows you to see trends and peculiarities, which in turn allows you to adjust your course if needed. Without data, how would you know whether you're making progress, or how or when to modify?

You should also incorporate your expertise into decision-making. When you combine data and experience, you can generate ideas—or hypotheses. These hypotheses help you to focus your efforts on possible solutions. (For your reference, we have included an overview of the hypothesis-driven approach to problem-solving in appendix C.)

COACHING TIP: When presented with a business challenge or problem that you need to solve, generate two to three hypotheses for what may be causing the challenge. Focus efforts on proving or disproving those hypotheses to work toward solutions more quickly and effectively.

The Gist

Data can be subjective or objective. It can be qualitative or quantitative. It can come from internal or external sources. Simply put, subjective data incorporates your or others' opinions, whereas objective data is not influenced by opinion. Qualitative data are measures of types and may be represented as themes, symbols, or names, whereas quantitative data are measures of values and expressed as numbers. And finally, internal sources of data come from within your organization, whereas external data come from outside your organization, such as various competitor analyses and environmental sources.

Context matters. Numbers look oh-so-simple. Data by itself may not be significant or meaningful, but when given some context, it can tell a story. Tuesday, three accidents. Wednesday, two accidents on the same corner. Thursday, only one accident. What kind of accidents? Two issues always exist: What they count and how they compare. What is just as important is how the numbers are perceived and heard by uncritical observers. How will this story be told? Is it that there are six accidents in one week? Is that good or bad? If there were six accidents per week for an entire year, it's likely to get someone's attention, with action taken before the end of the year is reached. So yes, data plus context can drive action.

Perhaps someone will want to show that a new intervention—such as a stop sign, in this case—is working. The story they tell with the data may indicate that after the three accidents on Tuesday, a new stop sign was added to the intersection. There was over a 30 percent drop in accidents, followed by another 50 percent drop. Once again, context drives the relevance and meaning of the data.

The objective aspect of the data is that there were six accidents during the week in question. That's a fact. It is also a fact that there was one less accident per day on Wednesday and Thursday. Once we place a personal value on it, such as "That's a lot of accidents," it takes on a subjective quality.

Statistics are not facts in themselves; rather, they are interpretations, and some interpretations can compromise your credibility. You can fool your colleagues with numbers maybe once or twice. More importantly, don't fool yourself. Would you rather a colleague points out your data error, or do you prefer to keep your numbers straight on your own? If the latter, read on.

Scene #1

Brian wants to compare his firm's salaries with those of members of his breakfast group, made up of other human resources managers. It's a casual group of non-competitors, and they often meet to discuss common issues. Sally says her firm's average salary is around $68,000. Bill reports that his average is $93,000. Brian comes in at $107,000. They pause, sip coffee, and wonder about education levels and other averages. Is this their best breakfast meeting ever?

No, it's not. We hope their eggs were not as cold as their numbers.

Sally's firm is a landscaping business with many unskilled laborers. Bill's outfit is the local branch of a unionized retail chain. Brian works for a civil engineering firm. Two problems. The big one is this isn't even an apples-to-oranges comparison; it's more like apples to zucchini. Second, of what significance is the average salary of employees ranging from unskilled nonexempts to educated, credentialed professionals? For each of these HR people, how would they use the average salary point in their own firm, and for what purpose?

What if we looked at that same salary data and, rather than different labor types, the focus was on different levels of experience or geographical considerations? Much of Brian's workforce is in San Francisco; much of Bill's is in Chicago; and Sally has lots of employees in the St. Paul suburbs. When the cost of living is factored in, all salaries are on par. Since there are many factors that can impact the meaningfulness of the data, it's important to be aware of what makes the data relevant and meaningful.

Numbers have to mean something. Unambiguously. Keep in mind that numbers by themselves mean little. They are gathered and interpreted by humans—*and there's the rub*. What counts is how the numbers are gathered and how they are explained. But an even bigger compromise to clarity and credibility is how numbers are displayed graphically. Always be suspicious of graphs and charts.

Scene #2

Over dinner in a suburban neighborhood restaurant, the Stewarts and the Joneses begin talking about their children's schools. Mr. Stewart remarks on his concern about declining test scores: "Did you read this morning that in the Palo Alto schools—of all places, where Stanford University is located—half the kids are performing below average! Now that's startling."

Mr. Stewart might refresh his knowledge about the word *average.* In this example, it means the statistical mean: the result of adding the number of students from all the grades and dividing by the total number of grades. In any school—in any environment—half the people are below average on the item being analyzed and half are above. It's simple mathematics.

Now, if the main point is that the mean has dropped steadily over the last four years, we'd want to know what's going on. We would start by generating some hypotheses. How, if at all, has the test changed? Have there been any environmental changes, such as a global pandemic or any other socioeconomic phenomenon? How have the teachers or curriculum changed? The answers to these questions will provide meaning and direction to the data.

Scene #3

Some numbers beg the question "So what?" It's your twenty-year college reunion. Let's say you survey the salaries of those attending. Only 60 alumni out of 258 show up. Among them are five multimillionaires earning big salaries. The others include government workers and nonprofit professionals. Your survey published the average salary and reports it at the reunion dinner. But of what use is that number? Not everyone showed up for the reunion. The millionaires bombed the average widely. Not everyone chose to answer such a personal question. And some may have lied. The reported number also doesn't say anything significant about your college's prowess. Surveys must mean something.

Important Notes on Terminology

If you want to be credible, don't misuse numerical terminology. Statistical terms can be confusing, and thus, misinterpreted. Let's outline some simple definitions to help your clarity with numbers and your credibility.

The pitfall of randomness. In a nutshell, things happen by pure chance far more often than we're all willing to admit. We may have our beliefs about randomness and trust our intuition, but these things are typically in conflict most of the time. You toss a coin eight times and it comes up heads each time. Many coin tossers would say it is likely, even overdue, for tails to win on the next toss. Not so. Random. Same with a professional athletic team on a losing streak, prompting the firing of their coach. Which leads us to . . .

Correlation and causation. Someone in the next town says, "Wow, lots of people on this side of the river have cancer. Must be the water or something." Using some of our earlier principles, it is acceptable to generate hypotheses such as these, but not acceptable to draw any conclusions. Another hypothesis may show that most of those residents work in a coal mine or are smokers.

A teacher friend said their school did a survey study of kids who are avid book readers. The study indicated those students also chewed their fingernails. Does being a loner book fan prompt nail biting, to the exclusion of other traits?

Coincidence is random. The commonality of cancer in each area does not necessarily equate to a single cause to the exclusion of other factors. This is a common error of math, as well as lack of common sense, clarity, and credibility. Don't be the first in your organization to make a rush judgment that similar incidents of something must be the cause of some development. Stuff happens, but often for no reason. Economist and social theorist Thomas Sowell added it up with a warning, stating "One of the first things taught in introductory statistics textbooks is that correlation is not causation. It is also one of the first things forgotten."

Average. The average rancher in Montana has a horse stable. Average rancher? No mathematical calculation there. But if you said the *typical* rancher in Montana has a horse stable, you would likely get no argument. *Average* does not equal *typical.* We overuse the word *average* when we mean common, ordinary, normal, or the term "most people."

Here's a simple rule of thumb and a coaching tip to preserve your clarity and your credibility: Use the word "average" *only for a mathematical meaning*. In math, the most common or frequent value in an array of values (numbers), regardless of its location in that array, is called the *mode*. To remember that, think "popular mode." The number in the exact middle of all the numbers is the *median*. Think "middle median." But the result of *adding* all the values and *dividing* by the number of values is the *mean*—that old mean average. Three types of averages. To a knowledgeable colleague, confusing the three can become a distraction from your influence.

Regression to the mean. "Regression to the mean" is observed when variables that are much higher or much lower than average on the first measurement move closer to the average (mean) on the second measurement. In other words, one value in a set of numbers is unusual, either very high or very low, but the next measurement is more like the mathematical average—the mean. Simply put, things sometimes go up and then go down, but they tend to return to the average.

An example is the stock market. You notice the highs and lows of a stock you follow. But then you notice that the value comes back to the average sooner or later.

It's the same with your proud golf score during the last five to ten games. Eventually, you will fail to meet your par and drop to near average. Golf may be a game of skill, but it's also a game of chance with lots of numbers.

COACHING TIP: It is common with large datasets to remove extreme high or low anomaly data points so as not to bias the data. If you take this approach, you must footnote that.

This last coaching tip raises the question of data manipulation. It's important to understand the dataset in question. Instead of approaching this as manipulation, your objective should be to show the most realistic portrayal of events so that you and your organization can act appropriately. You should always clearly state how you have obtained and/or modified the data. Think back to the college reunion salary data. If we acknowledge removing the few millionaires' data, as well as those who are unemployed at the time of data collection, the average salary may be a more interesting and accurate reflection, assuming the group was honest when submitting their salary figures.

In Pitfall #6, on facts, we cited author Thomas Kida's list of six packs of problems. The first he describes as our tendency to prefer stories over statistics. We stash stories away and regularly call them up. But always resorting to our favorite anecdotes, without reevaluating and refreshing the issue, can compromise your reasoning, and thus your credibility.

Baseline blunders. In short, don't change the baseline when comparing events with numbers. Let's say your company's sales dropped from 1,000 units by 20 percent, meaning a loss of 200 units and sales of only 800 units. But the next week, unit sales increased by 20 percent. Phew . . . close one, right? Same percentage! Wrong. That's an increase of only 160 units (20 percent of 800), not the 200-unit decrease from last week. You made the mistake of using two baselines, 800 and 1,000, when only 1,000 should be used. Maybe you will get back to 1,000 units next week.

Another issue associated with the baseline example above goes back to context. You know your organization best. Should you simply be monitoring changes over a longer time horizon? Or is that 20 percent something you and the executive team should be aware of and act on? If so, do you just need basic awareness, or is this a crucial indicator? It's up to you to determine whether something should be ignored or celebrated, or whether the red warning flag needs to be raised.

This is about your judgment. Your credibility depends on getting this right. The good news is that you don't need to go about this alone. If you catch something in the data that looks interesting or out of place, seek a second opinion.

COACHING TIP: Seek a second opinion to validate data assertions.

Silly Sampling . . . and Influence Lost

A *sample* is a collection of people or things to be analyzed. The sample is not all those people or things, so the sample must represent them accurately. That is where bias comes into play. A sample could be gathered with an unconscious bias that throws off all validity. A sample could be gathered with an intentional bias that is kept secret. Example: political claims. Either sample is inaccurate.

Here's a workplace example of sampling bias. The head of HR reports that over 83 percent of associates are "very satisfied" or "extremely satisfied" with the company. It turns out that the survey was distributed to people who were only in their current role for six months or less. In other words, they were recently hired or promoted.

Scene #4

You are new to a nice Chicago suburb and must register your dog and take her to the vet. While waiting, you observe nine cats in line for shots.

Eight are all black with white markings. You conclude that about 85 percent of cats in this new city must be black with white markings, and pride yourself on such perceptive analysis. Guess what? Nine is not a reasonable sample number of cats in any town, even a small one.

Public opinion polling has gone through generations of sampling bias. In the 1930s, voters were telephoned regarding presidential preference. But that was the Great Depression, and the population of voters who could afford telephones was biased toward people of means who were likely Republican. Recent public opinion surveys have had to deal with the tendency of smartphone users to avoid answering phone numbers they do not recognize. Another issue is people who don't want to admit for whom they voted and choose to just lie, for whatever reason.

A good question to ask regarding any sampling survey: What possible biases, accidental or intentional, could have gone into this survey? The key to good sampling is making certain everyone in the sample is representative of the larger population you are surveying. Makes sense, doesn't it?

Another problem is terminology used in surveys. Suppose the question deals with formal education. What is that? Only a four-year degree? What about professional two-year degrees in such wide fields as allied health, which yield lifetime certifications? Do those with four-year degrees from small liberal arts colleges in nonurban locales think differently from those who graduated from state universities in large cities? How about the term *laborer*? We used to define that as unskilled folks in a factory who work with their hands. So do others who don't work on an assembly line. In a survey about poverty, what definition of poverty is used? Always ask, "Define what you mean by the specific subject in question."

Another issue is the difference between something purchased and the long-term happiness of the purchaser's decision. It's one thing to cite how many people use X (formerly known as Twitter), but even that statement does not define "use" regarding frequency (e.g., once per day, once per week). It's another thing to uncover how many people respect X and how many do not.

Same with books sold. A book that hits a bestseller list does not indicate how many buyers read the book to completion or gave the books away as gifts.

We are not trying to encourage you to call into question every single aspect of data. We want you to leverage data with positive intention and be good consumers of data. Keep in mind that the examples above are public opinion and political in nature, so there is an inherent value in the story being told one way versus another. Showing a certain belief or support can help drive additional momentum. Workplaces are no different. People have agendas—often associated with self-promotion or self-preservation—that may influence which data are focused on and how it is presented.

Be suspicious of ambiguous words and phrases as well as ambiguous numbers and statistics. It's your credibility at stake. One of our sources below, *Making Numbers Count*, is all about using simple examples to make big numbers clear and meaningful. Here's one example that makes the authors' point meaningful: A million seconds is twelve days, but a billion seconds is thirty-two years. Easy to understand those numbers, right?

Probability. Simply defined, *probability* is the likelihood that one or more results will occur among a menu of results. Unfortunately, most of us draw from personal data and images to guess what is probable in a situation. In short, we guess by recalling what we know from past incidents. For example, in eight of the last ten years, when the sales team achieved their midyear forecast, they went on to meet or exceed their year-end sales targets. What if they achieve their midyear sales goals this year? Recent history suggests that 80 percent of the time, they go on to achieve year-end goals. You may say there is a high probability they will achieve their year-end goals. But what if they missed their midyear goals? That's only happened two times, or 20 percent, in the last ten years. Would you say there is a high probability they will miss their year-end goals?

And we must go back to context yet again. What if you found out that in all eight of the ten years where they achieved both midyear and year-end goals, the finance team made a considerable investment in the marketing and advertising of their product. However, this year, they did not make such an investment. Would that change how you viewed the notion of high probability?

The words you use to describe data will impact your credibility—especially when you are trying to be predictive in nature.

COACHING TIP: When forecasting or using data to predict future outcomes, consider contextual factors and speak objectively of the data.

Unreasonable assumptions. With the advent of professional journalism standards many decades ago, metropolitan daily newspapers and daily news broadcasts have been regarded as providing unbiased, careful reporting of developments and facts, with strict rules for corroboration and flags for retractions. Then came cable channels with obvious biases, and now, even worse, social media sites with no professional journalism standards. A big difference exists between a story reported on CBS News and the same story reported on a social media site. As we have said elsewhere in this book, anyone these days with cash and a cause can be a publisher. It's the same with numbers, statistics, and surveys. As Mark Twain once joked, "Facts are stubborn, but statistics are more pliable."

The smell test. Some studies and their reported numbers may be stretching the bounds of credibility. Be observant of certain phrases found in conclusions because they may indicate hedging. Examples:

- may be as high as
- could reach
- might include
- could potentially influence

The "So What?" of Data

For all we've presented here about data, we would be remiss if we didn't talk about one of the key ingredients for utilizing data effectively. That ingredient is analysis. Or, as we like to informally call it, the "So what?" of the data. It's one thing to look at our company performance numbers over a five-year period. But, not to be flip, so what? Is five years a long-enough time period to see trends in your organization's performance data? What was going on in the environment? Did your company make any investments or other changes that could positively or negatively impact performance?

You need to be able to answer these questions, and we encourage you to do so with the input and perspectives of others. This will allow for a more balanced interpretation of the data. Your ability to do so—to view the right data, ask the right questions, appropriately engage others, appropriately raise issues requiring action, and to generate and pursue hypotheses effectively—will all contribute to your data fluency and credibility.

COACHING TIP: When it comes to data, know what is essential in your company and learn how to ask good questions—not to be confrontational, but to understand the various data relationships, meaning, and requisite actions.

As you've seen throughout this chapter, data by itself does not tell a full or accurate story. Your experience and perspective is necessary in order to be able to convey the contextual nuances and meaning of the data. What stands out? How can—or should—this data be explained? What action, if any, is needed?

One senior executive we worked with noted that for every failed project, he had a spreadsheet with data that showed it would be successful. Your job is to recognize the right data to look for and how to use that information to make decisions—not just at the outset of a project, but also throughout its life cycle. In other words, it's up to you to understand as full a picture as possible and to carefully interpret the data. If you see something off course, it's up to you to have the courage to raise potential issues and change the course of action accordingly.

This raises another challenge with analysis. Too often in organizations, data is reported up the chain without any additional context. By the time reports get to the senior-most levels, some key insights might be missed. Perhaps the more junior associate does not want to overstep their bounds, or perhaps they assume the executives already have certain insights into the matter at hand. Senior executives tend to have a keen eye for key data points, but too often, valuable insights may get lost.

COACHING TIP: Get input from the employees closest to the data to help provide analytical value and insights. Have them report both the data and what stands out to them.

Summary of Coaching Tips

- Embrace the role and power of data to drive decisions. Make it a priority to become fluent in the data and metrics that are important to your organization. Use the hypothesis-driven approach to solve business challenges and problems quickly and effectively.
- Use the word *average* only for a mathematical meaning.
- Be sure to footnote if/when you remove any extreme data anomalies that are skewing the data.
- Seek a second opinion to validate data assertions.
- When forecasting or using data to predict future outcomes, consider contextual factors and speak objectively of the data.
- When it comes to data, know what is essential in your company and learn how to ask good questions—not to be confrontational, but to understand the various data relationships, meaning, and requisite actions.
- Get input from the employees closest to the data to help provide analytical value and insights. Have them report both the data and what stands out to them.

Summary of Pitfall #8

Statistics are not pristine. They are gathered by humans who are fallible. Also, statistics almost always need interpretation to make them clear and credible. (You might check out some of the Additional Resources below for further guidance.) We wanted to spotlight the big pitfalls nearly everyone makes. Don't be one of them. And make no mistake: If you fear, ignore, or misuse data, you will lose credibility. And clout.

Moving you along. We covered the pitfalls of varying dialects, domestic and foreign. There's another human foible that exists in all of us, whether we're standing or seated, whether it's in person or on video calls. Nonverbal behavior and "tells," as poker players call them. Know when you are exhibiting body botches. On to Pitfall #9.

Additional Resources

- The classic in the field for decades: *How to Lie with Statistics* by Darrell Huff (New York: W. W. Norton & Company, 1993 [1953]).
- *The Drunkard's Walk: How Randomness Rules Our Lives* by Leonard Mlodinow (New York: Pantheon Books, 2008).
- *The Numbers Game: The Commonsense Guide to Understanding Numbers in the News, in Politics, and in Life* by Michael Blastland and Andrew Dilnot (New York: Gotham Books, 2009).
- *Making Numbers Count: The Art and Science of Communicating Numbers* by Chip Heath and Karla Starr (New York: Avid Reader Press, 2022).
- *Rationality: What It Is, Why It Seems Scarce, Why It Matters* by Steven Pinker (New York: Viking, 2021).

Pitfall #9: Body Botches

Distractions of the Nonverbal and the Near-Verbal

You can lie in any language on earth,
and body language is no exception.

—NOVELIST NENIA CAMPBELL

So far, this book has covered how words, phrases, dialectal differences, and cultural differences can be conspicuous. But our bodies often speak a different language, distracting others to our detriment, leading to a loss of our credibility. Managing nonverbal behavior—*the silent language*—is an essential element of how we get to influence. Clout.

You communicate even when you're not speaking. Your body language speaks volumes. Are you interested and engaged? Are you distracted, closed, confident, or angry? Does your body language match what you are saying? Some of your body language may be subtle and some is overt. But make no mistake: Your body language is sending a message. The real questions are, Is that the message you intend to send? And is it situationally appropriate?

We make it silently clear to people when we are uncomfortable with them, without saying a word. What's worse, we don't usually know if we are exhibiting discomfort, or why. Job interviews, meetings, presentations at a lectern, handling a microphone—a host of interactions. Eyes, hands, legs—*and how we dress*—can all become distractions that compromise your influence.

The Gist

It's simple. You want to be remembered for your critical thinking, your clarity, and your credible influence. You don't want to be remembered for your physical distractions. To be influential, you want colleagues to be attentive to what you write or say. You don't want to create distractions that kill attention. Distractions can be verbal, but they can also be nonverbal. They can be the result of cultural naiveté. All distractions to your colleagues' attention span can compromise your credibility, regardless of type.

COACHING TIP: Since self-improvement starts with awareness, ask a friend or colleague with whom you interact regularly to identify any of your nonverbal communication habits that you may not be aware of. Ask for specifics: What was one of your nonverbal cues? What message did it send?

Scene #1

Zak gets to his interview in plenty of time and nervously awaits his likely boss. First, he goes to the men's room to make sure everything is in its place. Back to the reception room. Deep breaths . . . more deep breaths. He wonders if he's fully prepared.

"Zak? Hi. I'm Jean Bowers. Come on back."

Zak is grateful for the relaxing walk to her office.

Throughout the interview, Zak sits with arms across his chest when he's not rubbing the tops of his knuckles back and forth with the opposite hand. He continuously rubs his nose and pulls on his ear.

"Tell me what your duties were at your last job?" asks Bowers.

Zak's eyes wander all about the room. More rubbing of knuckles, crossing of legs back and forth.

Finally, sensing Zak's unease, Bowers asks, "Well, what would you like to know about our firm and what your duties would be?"

Zak clears his throat. "Well, ahh, I looked up your, ya know, your website, but it's the same kind of jobs I've had, if you will, so I am eager to find out, ya know, more about your company."

Bowers notices everything and makes quick notes in her file before tossing it aside.

A blur of blinks, taps, jiggles, pivots, and shifts . . . the body language of a man wishing urgently to be elsewhere.

—TELEVISION JOURNALIST EDWARD R. MURROW

What were some of the nonverbal messages Zak sent during the interview? What impression did Zak leave with Bowers? What advice would you give Zak as he prepares for future interviews?

COACHING TIP: Spend time preparing for your most critical meetings. Focus on what your key messages are and how you will deliver them. To rehearse, consider practicing in front of a mirror or asking a friend or colleague to be your role-play audience.

You must ensure that your words match your actions. If you say that you are interested and engaged with what someone is saying, but then are looking off into the distance while they speak, your credibility will be negatively impacted.

Nonverbal communication includes a great deal. It's also how we react to others' customs and manners. This book would not be complete without spotlighting big distractions your colleagues may not point out, like your mannerisms or your physical presentation. It's all about how you show up, and, yes—how you dress matters. It matters in some situations and organizations more than others, but make no mistake: It matters. How well do you integrate with the culture or situation you are a part of? In some organizations, this is referred to as "fit" or "executive presence."

Ten Bodily Signs of Suspicious Credibility

Experts in nonverbal communication call it *kinesics*. Your "giveaways." It's all what you do with:

- your eyes
- your head
- your facial expressions
- your hands and arms
- your legs and feet
- your posture
- your tone of voice

Although we will review each of these nonverbal aspects one at a time, it is important to consider the message you might be sending when combining some of them, such as folded arms, crossed legs, and eyes focused on the people in the next meeting room.

Training your eyes. It should not be a surprise that eye contact is essential to a good conversation, especially in job interviews and meetings with staff. But it counts in any interaction. Darting eyes raise suspicions. Rolling your eyes is a sign of disagreement. Closing your eyes implies disapproval. Not blinking your eyes in a conversation is just downright distracting. Looking off into the distance or focusing your eyes elsewhere demonstrates distraction and disinterest.

Your eyes will contradict your words if your words contradict your thoughts and feelings.

—LIFE COACH / PSYCHOLOGIST SAM OWEN

COACHING TIP: Be present in the moment, and practice *tuning out distractions*.

Training your head. Being levelheaded sounds like a no-brainer for someone seeking to gain credibility and clout. But it is also a physical regimen *to be practiced*, as Cara Hale Alter points out in her book (cited below). Aside from good posture, keep a level head, both literally and physically. Speaking with your chin dipped can be perceived as being shy or uncertain. Holding your chin too high can appear condescending to some. However, speaking with your head positioned squarely on your shoulders is a universal sign of confidence.

We make so many gestures with our heads, and many of us don't realize what such gestures convey. For example, a timely head nod to someone who is speaking conveys active listening, interest, understanding, and engagement.

Scene #2

Co-author Roger once chaired a panel discussion of ten participants, half of whom hated the other half. The tenseness drew several hundred people, most of whom expected finger-pointing and fireworks. The panel chair was a tad nervous. Watching the videotape later, it was a revelation to Roger to see how he nervously looked left and right—for an hour—to check panelists' moods and reactions instead of listening closely to their comments. (Don't skip the section below on videotaping yourself.)

About those facial expressions. These are dead giveaways anywhere. Clenching your lips tight can be perceived as disapproving or even hostile.

It is possible that facial expressions can be misinterpreted. Co-author Tim recalls several times when he was speaking at a professional conference, as he scanned the audience, he would notice one of his professors in the audience with crossed arms, squinting her eyes, tilting her head, and generally wearing a puzzled expression. After several of these experiences, the speaker asked the professor if he was saying the wrong things, because her facial expressions and body language sent a message that she was confused, disappointed, or in disagreement. Her reply was that this was how she focused on what was being said. Interestingly, however, that feedback helped the professor to manage her expressions and mannerisms during his future presentations.

Training your hands and arms. In any conversation or group meeting or presentation, you want people looking at you—your face—or following the overhead slides. We have worked with several leaders who are very demonstrative and animated with their hand gestures. In fact, someone once asked one of those leaders whether they would be able to talk if they were unable to move their arms. While we are not encouraging you to be a statue when you speak, you need to find the proper balance when it comes to how and when you use subtle hand gestures to reinforce points rather than using them in an exaggerated way, the latter, of course, being highly distracting.

Scene #3

What follows was truly unfortunate. It was a night to hear from candidates for the school board. The first six candidates presented themselves in ways that ranged from formal to folksy.

Then came candidate seven. He was a good-hearted person who ran a shelter for runaway teens. But he finished nearly every statement by nervously tucking his shirt into his pants. Seven times his hands disappeared. Deep into his pants. Front and back. Side to side. *For ten minutes straight.* It wasn't intentional; he was not conscious of doing it. To say this was a distraction to his candidacy is an understatement. People were turning away in embarrassment.

Come election night, when the votes were tallied, candidate seven came in seventh. The lesson: Tighten your belt and hold on to the microphone or your notes instead. And don't let go.

What we do with our hands is telling. When you are talking with someone and they begin fidgeting with their pen, what's happening?

Nervousness? Folding our arms in a tough conversation can be perceived as protecting ourselves.

Americans love hand and finger gestures. But before your next international trip, train yourself to leave all hand gestures at home. That includes the good luck gestures, the okay sign, the thumbs-up signal, and the peace sign. You might get a very terse response.

The big mistake is using your left hand for anything just about anywhere outside the United States, especially when eating. Never touch your face or anyone else with your left hand. To put it delicately, the left hand in much of the world is associated with toilet hygiene (if you catch our drift). Likewise, never point with your left hand; rather, point with your whole hand and make it your right one. Big distraction. *Distractions delay credibility.*

COACHING TIP: As noted in Pitfall #3 on dialect downers and cultural clashes, it's important to familiarize yourself with local customs associated with nonverbal communications prior to international travel and/or business meetings.

When exchanging gifts in Asia, a common business custom, use both hands to receive a gift, and always with your palms up. Use both hands palms-up when handing money to a cashier. As we said earlier, never use your left hand.

Business card exchange is almost a ritual in Asia. Don't be an ugly American and stuff it into your pocket. That is a sign of disrespect. Use both hands to receive your guest's card, and then study it carefully and respectfully. That card's owner views their card as part of their person, not just contact information. Impatient hands can offend in many ways.

Training your legs and feet. Crossing and uncrossing your legs is perceived by many as nervousness, a lack of ease with others. Constantly jittering your leg is also distracting. It sends a message that you are nervous, not confident, or perhaps you need to use the restroom. Outside of the United States, in the Middle East and much of Asia, exposing the bottoms of your shoes is offensive. Remember the incident in the Middle East when a man in the audience hurled both his shoes at President George W. Bush? The ultimate offense.

Dialogue is not just quotation. It is grimaces, pauses, adjustments of blouse buttons, doodles on a napkin, and crossings of legs.

—AUTHOR JEROME STERN

Training your posture. Posture includes your legs and feet, and your back. Slouching sends a message of a lack in confidence. Further, Asian custom is never to turn your back to an elder. Many cultures have posture taboos.

COACHING TIP: Practice good posture when speaking or listening.

We cite in our Additional Resources below the work of executive coach Cara Hale Alter and her informative book, which includes the following true story about a client company.

Scene #4

The stakes were high in the search for the new chief executive officer of an architectural firm. Headhunters had reviewed and forwarded the résumés of several candidates to oversee the two-hundred-person company. Five highly qualified candidates had been selected for interviews.

After the first round of phone interviews, one candidate stood out. He sounded confident over the phone. Good track record. Excellent experience. The management search committee sensed he was the one and flew him out for an interview.

The interview went smoothly; the candidate seemed to fit the bill. Yet, after the candidate left, each member of the search committee voted against hiring him. When they discussed the reasons, they all realized it came down to one moment: At one point during the interview, the candidate stood up and walked to the counter to refill his coffee. His slumped posture and weak spine made him look tired and worn-out, and, in that moment, each member of the search committee concluded he was not the energized, engaged CEO they wanted to lead their company.

"You would never think something as superficial as bad posture could cost you a job, yet I heard this story directly from the search committee [as I was training their new CEO]," explained Alter.

Posture is a leadership language.

—ACTRESS JANNA CACHOLA

It's so easy to lie to colleagues. We could try to cover all the subtle signals that might be perceived as lying, but there are many. In poker, these are called "tells." When bluffing—or lying—one tends to repeat certain nonverbal cues, all subconsciously.

Check out the various tests and warnings by using the phrase "how to detect a lie" or similar wording in an online search. Your credibility can be the victim of your head movements, your eyes, your hands, arms, and fingers, your legs, your coughs, your lips, your mouth, and your voice.

COACHING TIP: Watch for "tells" in yourself and others. A videotape will help.

Multitasking in Meetings and during Lunchtime

We are glued to our smartphones, but texting while at lunch with colleagues is not a great display of common courtesy or respect. Likewise, darting your eyes about at a luncheon implies that your mind is elsewhere.

There is a reason that multitasking is a myth. Multiple studies have shown that it is physically impossible to provide focused attention on more than one task at a time. Our brains simply are not hardwired to do so. Once you shift your attention from one activity to another, you are in essence not focused on the second activity. This is not to say that people don't try to multitask; they may say or even believe that they do. In such an instance, your mind is jumping from one task to the next, which provides neither activity your full focus.

Has this ever happened to you? You're in a group meeting and one of your colleagues is presenting. Your phone buzzes. You quickly shift your focus to who sent you a message and perhaps a quick check on what was said. You quickly refocus on your colleague only to realize that you've missed one of her key messages. Or perhaps you are trying to get a project or emails done during a virtual training session. Can you imagine taking a phone call at lunch instead of blocking calls or telling the caller you will get back to them? But if you do not stay focused on the task at hand, what does that say about your credibility and clout?

Scene #5

Sharon was providing a year-end update and strategic planning for the year ahead to her seven direct reports. There was a lot to cover, and the meeting was scheduled to run for half the day. Each of the direct reports were to provide a brief update throughout the meeting regarding their respective areas.

During the meeting, Julie would glance to her phone. On more than one occasion she quickly responded to an email. She thought she was being quick and subtle, but all of her colleagues noticed. Several gave her side glances and head shakes. Julie never noticed. But as they were about to take their first mid-morning break, Sharon asked the group to wrap up any business during the break, so they could come back fully focused on this meeting. Everyone—including Julie—knew that Sharon's message was directed toward Julie.

What message did Julie's attempt at multitasking send? What do you think Julie's actions did to her credibility among her peers and her boss? If you were Sharon, how would you follow up with Julie?

COACHING TIP: Avoid multitasking. This may require turning your phone off or setting it on "silent" during meetings. Additionally, avoid a host of other multitasking situations altogether by focusing on one main activity at a time.

The Distraction of Physical Proximity Across Cultures

In some cultures, it is ordinary to stand quite close to each other when talking. Italy and France are examples. No distraction for them. Other cultures keep more distance. Such is the case in the United States, Germany, and Japan. In America, standing within a foot of someone can be perceived as being rude or even rather aggressive. Such a perception by others builds no influence on them. It may be why people on subways and elevators rarely strike up a conversation about last night's game. Try it and see how folks react.

Now, about your other distractions. Experts in nonverbal communication call them "artifacts." This includes clothing, jewelry, grooming, and makeup. If you want to be perceived as influential, you will get there faster by managing unnecessary distractions. Garish clothing, tattoos, facial studs . . . all distractions. Be aware that many people, here and abroad, think it rude to wear hats inside a building, especially in someone's home.

Scene #6

Dave recalls an interview he conducted decades ago for a large city planning department:

> *We had three job openings for what might be considered these days as a community organizer to work with neighborhood organizations. Because of civil service rules, current city employees had preference over outsiders. We had three openings to fill and scheduled the morning for interviews with the top five, the minimum we had to interview for three openings. All had city jobs already.*
>
> *One fellow walked in and sat down. He had never met me or my boss, who was the city planning director and ultimate decider. One chance to make a first impression, right?*
>
> *So how does he dress for a job interview? A Mickey Mouse T-shirt and jeans. Do you think it distracted from what he was saying? What was his message about us, or the job? I remember nothing of what he said, just the T-shirt.*
>
> *Of course, we had to hire him due to his civil service status, since he was in the top five, and we had no cause under the rules to send him away. He turned out to be an okay employee, but to this day, [I still wonder], What was he thinking? I would never have hired him in a million years but for civil service rules. Was I biased by his dress, or did his dress show he had no common sense or maturity?*

COACHING TIP: Don't let what you wear "speak" louder than what you say. It becomes a distraction. Wear attire that fits the situation and the culture (both organizational culture and broader societal culture).

What you wear has surely become more nuanced in recent years. Previously, when in business meetings, men wore a suit and tie, and women wore a well-pressed and tailored skirt or pantsuit. Practices have become more varied in today's business environment, with multiple views of business, casual, and business-casual. Don't assume that business-casual practices apply across all cultures. Make no mistake, though: What you wear can distract from your leadership presence.

Scene #7

Josh was early in his career as a consultant. Although he worked for a top global consultancy that was known as a conservative company, Josh's fashion style favored the trendy.

One day, Josh's boss pulled him aside and suggested he might want to tone down some of his more extreme outfits. Josh was quick to point out that there were no HR guidelines directing what he could or couldn't wear, and added that his ideas should matter more than the clothes he wore. All true points.

While this was all true, Josh never quite fit in with the organization's culture. Ironically, Josh's fashion made more of a statement than his other contributions. His clothing had become a distraction within and outside the organization. He was a good contributor, but after six years with the company, never advancing beyond consultant, he decided to move on.

We should point out that Josh's choice of attire was not the sole reason he was passed over for promotion. However, it was one of the nonverbal ways that showed he didn't quite fit with this organization.

COACHING TIP: Find an organization that fits your style. When you are deciding on your fashion choices within your organization, always look one to two levels up from yours for indications of what is appropriate.

I speak two languages, Body and English.

—ACTRESS MAE WEST

Training your voice. You may wonder what your voice has to do with nonverbal, but aspects of voice touch on more than words. Loudness, inflection, formal versus informal—it all matters in some situations. We have all encountered people who:

- speak too loudly in small quarters, like the guy in this morning's meeting or the lady at the restaurant table next to you (has anyone told you your voice is too loud?);
- load up sentences with filler words (e.g., ahh, ya know, well, like), as Zak did;
- talk so softly—and without confidence—that you get impatient, having to ask them to speak up.

Down with uptalk! Do you end sentences that are not questions with a habitual questioning intonation? It's commonly called "uptalk." Unfortunately, it can convey uncertainty or even subliminal, unintended deference to the other person. Either way, not good for credibility and influence. Here's an example:

Scene # 8

What a journalist should not do:

"Ms. Phillips? This is Frank Foster, from the *Daily Post*? I am doing a story on your latest product . . . okay? And I'm wondering if I can ask a couple questions, okay? Do you have some time right now . . . or later?"

Well, Frank, are you new to reporting and don't yet feel you're in the groove, or do you always go on like this and not stop to give Ms. Phillips a chance to say anything?

If someone mentions such behaviors in you, you are well advised.

Words mean more than what is set down on paper.
It takes the human voice to infuse them with deep meaning.

—POET MAYA ANGELOU

Doing the video test . . . on yourself. Here's a question for you: Have you ever seen a video of yourself talking or presenting? Get one done early in your career. Promise yourself.

Here's what Cara Hale Alter has to say:

> *The bottom line is that nearly all of us are unaware of our own bad habits and how they might undermine our image. The proof point that I offer my clients is this: It's a relatively universal truth that people hate to see themselves on video—whether that's giving a formal presentation or simply doing a speaking exercise in class. So why do we hate seeing ourselves on camera? Because we are surprised at what we see. The person on the video doesn't match our own internal image of how we think we represent ourselves. And usually not in a positive way.*

COACHING TIP: Have a colleague take a video of you while you speak. Do this in multiple professional settings to help identify your nonverbal communication patterns. Identify your positive and negative mannerisms and habits. Once you've identified the two or three areas of nonverbal communication you want to work on, identify an internal coach to provide you with feedback on those specific areas as part of planning for and feedback after future presentations.

Summary of Coaching Tips

- Ask a friend or colleague with whom you regularly interact to identify any of your nonverbal communication habits that you may not be aware of. Ask for specifics: What was your nonverbal cue? And what message did it send?

- Spend time preparing for the most critical meetings. Focus on what your key messages are and how you will deliver them. To rehearse, consider practicing in a mirror or asking a friend or colleague to be your role-play audience.
- Be present in the moment, and practice tuning out distractions.
- Familiarize yourself with local customs associated with nonverbal communications prior to international travel and/or business meetings.
- Practice good posture.
- Watch for "tells" in yourself and others.
- Avoid multitasking. This may require turning your phone off or putting it on "silent" during meetings. Better yet, avoid a host of other multitasking situations altogether by focusing on one main activity at a time.
- Don't let what you wear "speak" louder than what you say. It becomes a distraction. Wear attire that fits the situation and the culture (both organizational culture and broader societal culture).
- Find an organization that fits your style. When you are deciding on your fashion choices within your organization, always look one to two levels up from yours for indications of what is appropriate.
- Have a colleague take a video of you while you speak. Do this in multiple professional settings to help identify your nonverbal communication patterns. Identify your positive and negative mannerisms and habits. Once you've identified the two or three areas of nonverbal communication you want to work on, identify an internal coach to provide you with feedback on those specific areas as part of planning for and feedback after future presentations.

Summary of Pitfall #9

Sometimes what you do rather than say speaks louder than your words. It isn't just dialectal differences in English and other languages. It's the impressions we make nonverbally as well as verbally. Your nonverbal mannerisms, habits, and idiosyncrasies say a lot. Are they sending the message you intend to send? That you are confident? Focused? Honest? Are they reinforcing your credibility or detracting from it?

Filler words can make you sound uncertain about what you are saying. Uncertainty does not build credibility. Our cultural assumptions can be bad assumptions. Assuming what we do and say in America is a form of ethnocentrism—the incorrect belief that what we do is surely what everyone else does.

Moving you along. Trust is so important, but it can become an invisible pitfall if you are too trusting—not just of others, but of yourself. We are talking about intuition, reaching consensus, asking questions, and more. You could be making mistakes in all of these areas. On to Pitfall #10.

Additional Resources

- Executive coach Cara Hale Alter is president of Speech Skills (www.speechskills.com), a San Francisco–based communications training company specializing in verbal and nonverbal communication skills, and their credibility assets. Her seminars are well worth the time and cost. She also wrote *The Credibility Code: How to Project Confidence & Competence When It Matters Most* (San Francisco: Meritus Books, 2012). A must-have for all of you readers.
- *Going Dutch in Beijing: How to Behave Properly When Far Away from Home* by Mark McCrum (New York: Henry Holt & Co., 2007). A must-have before you get off the plane in any foreign country. It covers manners, gestures, gifting, food, formalities, and more.
- *The Definitive Book of Body Language: The Hidden Meaning Behind People's Gestures and Expressions* by Barbara Pease and Allan Pease (New York: Bantam, 2006).

Pitfall #10: Troubling Trusts

Common Assumptions to Avoid on Your Path to More Clout

Critical thinking, clarity, credibility . . . and clout. We call them the Four Cs of personal influence. In this chapter, we help you to avoid tripping on issues of trust by shining the spotlight on some critical missteps regarding trust. As author Joseph Campbell warned, "If the path before you is clear, you're probably on somebody else's path."

In this book, we have urged you to avoid the distractions outlined in the previous pitfalls. A leader—with or without a managerial title—avoids distractions and has a clear focus ahead. That's a leader who does not blindly trust everything that comes their way but stops to evaluate the credibility of the information or points of view encountered. That leader serves colleagues by being a thoughtful, introspective person who doesn't have to comment on everything. Rather, it's a prescient leader who raises the one pointed and naked question that brings colleagues to that silent recognition—even admission—that they have missed something.

Readers, that question or comment is your clear path to more influence. Both of us have seen colleagues' influence put on a pedestal with just one such comment or question, never to be forgotten. Do that only once and earn a big credibility token.

Shortcuts. Shortcuts are necessary for speed and efficiency in business. Taking a shortcut relies on trust, whether it be trusting in someone else's guidance or our own experience. We trust it will all work out.

However, much like distractions can detract from your credibility, so too can shortcuts. Whether we realize it or not, we often take shortcuts when it comes to judgments and business decisions. They require self-awareness and must be monitored so they do not hinder your credibility. When left unquestioned, they provide a lazy approach to your critical thinking. The interpretation of such an approach is "I'm too busy or lazy to think critically, so I will rely on my previous experiences, whether they are right or not."

Shortcuts with judgments take the form of biases. Rather than getting to know a person for who they are, we rely on our previous experiences with people who look or sound similar. Or perhaps they come from a certain area, background, or education. Shortcuts make it easy, but they can be faulty.

Taking a shortcut with a business decision is referred to as intuition. Although *intuition* has a more positive connotation than *bias*, it can be equally risky if it's faulty. Imagine the time and resources spent toward pursuing an intuition, or gut feeling. Great job if you are correct, but it can be costly if not. We recommend using intuition as a starting point for ideas, but we also recommend following up with probes and questions to validate intuition.

Both biases and intuition are rooted in trust—trust in self, trust in others, and trust in institutions. We are advocates of the "Trust but verify" approach. This allows you to consider your experience but encourages you to question it to avoid losing credibility. The best ways to verify include via data or others' input.

COACHING TIP: When it comes to making decisions based upon data, judgment, or intuition, *trust but verify* any assumptions.

Even so, you need to keep your focus and avoid stumbling. Think of stumbles as the little details that can trip you up on your communication and credibility. These details can take the form of distractions, shortcuts, or missteps, and they can be nuanced and situational.

The missteps on the path to influence are great:

- Your precious intuition is not always so trustworthy.
- Your infatuation with gaining a fast consensus can steer you wrong.
- Your problem-solving skills can miss the problem.
- Falling back on those old, trusted questions you always ask can trip you up.

In this chapter we spotlight more stumbles that we all make on our journey to influence. We typically learn about them the hard way, but you won't have to if you continue reading. Together, these issues of trust constitute another pitfall.

The Gist

We are deep in an era of complexity; simple answers are rare. All issues are gray; black-and-white answers to problems are naive. Who do you trust? What information do you trust?

As we highlight in this chapter, having strong intuition places a high degree of trust in oneself. The opposite of trust is doubt, and we are certainly not encouraging you to doubt yourself. We are encouraging you to be critical, independent thinkers. Yes, take your past into account, but do not rely exclusively on it without question.

Bring that same approach when trusting others' input or opinions. In fact, your ability to question others critically and constructively will help you to determine whether someone is sharing a fact, or an opinion. And let's not forget our proclivity to trust institutions—whether it's blindly trusting a point of view based upon where someone was educated, or based on their work experience. Don't assume that everyone who worked at XYZ company is brilliant (or knows nothing), just as you can't assume that everyone who went to a top Ivy League school is always wise.

This requires clear, critical thinking; but do we ask the right questions? If not, how can you trust any consensus on any important action? What are the risks of your gut hunches, those long-trusted intuitions that require little thought and never get challenged? What are the real causes and what are their effects? Identifying the wrong cause is a path to nowhere. When is a short-term solution better than a long-term fix—or is it the other way around?

The Challenge of Trusting Your Intuition and Insights Too Much; or How Well Do You *Really* Know Your Gut?

We all love to say "I rely heavily on my intuition," or "Hey, my gut feeling about this is *X*." From time to time we've all proudly touted our "feel" for things. Our perceptions are anchors of truth to us.

The anchors of intuition are typically based on our own experience. We apply this experiential lens to current issues. That makes a lot of sense. Otherwise, what's the point of our experience if we can't learn from it and apply it to similar situations?

But what if those judgments are wrong, outdated, or not applicable?

COACHING TIP: Since no two situations are exactly alike, when applying your previous experience (or intuition) to a situation, ask yourself what is unique and what is the same? And how do the answers to those questions inform your current approach?

Has it ever occurred to you that you may be locked into a prison of aged, trusted perceptions, and that such intuitions—*your gut feelings*—may be a tad limiting at the very least, or, at worst, highly inaccurate? We can be fenced in by our perceptions, and that makes it harder to be seen as credible.

We need to be able to quickly pivot—to be open to new information and perspectives that may challenge our old mental models. Think of this as a continuous-improvement mind-set, where you are constantly looking to learn and build upon experiences, adapting them to the nuances of each situation. Now that sounds like someone on their way to establishing strong credibility!

How we see things, our perceptions, are often based on just a few occurrences that get stuck in our heads and remain there. That becomes all we see. Social psychologists call that *confirmation bias.* Head noise. Biases or attitudes about things that get triggered and remind us of a past situation. It affects how we think about a host of issues: politics, religion, attire, consumer purchases, hiring decisions, management decisions, planning, and more. And we don't even realize it. Many gut feelings are first impressions based on limited experiences and biases, such as past relationships, hurts and rejections, criticisms and admonitions—or just the way you were raised.

Where's the logic? Polio vaccine scientist Jonas Salk pointed the way, saying "Intuition will tell the thinking mind where to look next."

Have you ever had a colleague, upon hearing your gut feeling about something, quiz you in depth? The colleague doesn't share the same biases and perceptions and may have a different conclusion about the matter at hand. Who's correct? Suddenly, you realize your gut feeling falls flat.

In the workplace, this can manifest itself in one of two ways: innovation or conflict. When two people are open to different perspectives, it can lead to creativity and to thinking differently about a situation, problem, or challenge. It is the realization of that old saying that two heads are better than one. On the other hand, when one or both individuals dig in their heels and remain closed to other perspectives, it can lead to conflict.

Daniel Kahneman is a respected psychologist whose book *Thinking, Fast and Slow* is cited below in our Additional Resources. Writing about intuition in his book, he said, "As we navigate our lives, we normally allow ourselves to be guided by impressions and feelings, and the confidence we have in our intuitive beliefs and preferences is usually justified. But not always. We are often confident even when we are wrong, and an objective observer is more likely to detect our errors than we are." His book is a valuable addition to your influence library.

Let's explore those gut feelings from the past. We encourage you to review Pitfall #5, Inner Isms, which spotlights the problems of our biases. We are not suggesting that you *never* listen to your gut. On the contrary, we are suggesting taking a critical approach when listening to your gut. Challenge yourself and be open to alternative perspectives. Our point: Understanding our gut feelings about colleagues is a way to manage those feelings. Otherwise, your credibility could be compromised.

Things to consider as you reflect on intuition:

- Was an intuition about something someone said limited solely to your upbringing?
- Did you ever have a gut reaction to something a former colleague did or said?
- Ever have a brain flash prompted by a prior workplace comment or incident?
- Have you ever reacted negatively to someone based on where they live? Or where they attended college?

Some questions to ask yourself:

- During a job interview, can you recall a gut feeling you got about the prospective boss?
- While interviewing someone for a job, did something they said spark a judgment about them?
- Have you ever made an investment decision based on intuition?
- In a workplace meeting, did something someone said forever label them a certain way in your mind?

It is human nature to rationalize our previous experience, whether it was a favorable outcome or a bad decision. So how does this affect your communication and credibility? Simple. You may find yourself advocating for a point you're absolutely convinced is correct based on intuition, only to find it to be faulty—and yes, hopefully you're the one who discovers it so you can save face and do damage control. As others discover faulty intuitions, your credibility can quickly fade.

Can you now see that trust is something you must manage? Albert Einstein practiced this. "I believe in intuitions and inspirations . . . I sometimes *feel* that I am right. I do not *know* that I am."

Scene #1

Jill is a director for a national cybersecurity consulting firm that provides strategic and operational advisory services and products. Her team needs to be good at planning and writing detailed, orderly proposals. As she sets out to build her team, she reviews the résumés of seven people, all of whom have relevant experience. One person, Phil, got his undergraduate degree in philosophy from a small liberal arts college in the rural Midwest. She concludes that Phil should not be called for an interview. "Why would anyone get a degree in philosophy and attend such an insular school?" she commented to her assistant.

Well, Jill, one of the attributes of being a philosophy major is building good arguments. Logic is their strength. Her gut feeling on Phil was based on a flippant attitude and perhaps her own personal bias, not an in-depth interview. This casual decision could turn out to cost Jill in the long run if Phil genuinely had the essential skills to be an effective proposal writer and consultant.

The Challenge of Trusting Consensus to a Fault as a Block to Problem-Solving

A well-accepted maxim is that once a decision is made, everyone in the organization works accordingly. It's hard to have a functioning organization if its members are working at cross purposes with different agendas and strategies. As a budding leader, raise your issue in the meeting in your role as a devil's advocate, but know when you might be seen as a distraction to the discussion. Understand there is a time, place, and way to raise issues. Your job is to find out which approach fits with both your personal style and the organization's culture.

COACHING TIP: Contribute critical questions and alternative viewpoints in a way that is consistent with your organization's culture. For example, it may or may not be well received to contradict a leader or colleague during a meeting. Some organizations encourage that type of approach in advance of a meeting. It's a delicate balance between being a contributor versus a disruptor. That balance is driven largely by an organization's culture, so we cannot be overly prescriptive here other than to say, Be aware of what is welcome in your organization.

The issue is getting to consensus but avoiding a process that's too rushed and lacking adequate study. The impulse to look ever so businesslike and to make bold, hasty decisions to feed the ego can result in big mistakes. As journalist Walter Lippmann said so pithily, "Where all think alike, no one thinks very much."

When no one in a group setting is critically thinking or questioning, there is a risk of groupthink. Groupthink occurs when a group of well-intentioned people conform to a less than optimal decision despite knowing it is not ideal. Groupthink reduces individual responsibility or accountability.

COACHING TIP: Avoid groupthink by actively seeking and welcoming diverse perspectives and making time for independent evaluation.

Individual decisions are nothing compared to getting consensus with colleagues in the conference room. But here is the first rule of consensus building:

Forget about getting 100 percent completeness! Seeking 100 percent completeness and perfection only frustrates your colleagues. If you and your colleagues reach 85 percent completeness, you will likely have the essentials nailed down.

Where are the trade-offs, and how do you arrive at those? Trust and credibility are again at the core of this stumble. Finding common ground is one way to achieve this. In business, common ground is often found in business outcomes, i.e., what is best for the business. However, beware of hidden agendas—*yours and others*—as they can confuse business interests with personal ones.

Scene #2

One leader we worked with, Gillian, had a useful approach to understanding the appropriate completeness for communicating and implementing initiatives. Gillian was new to her organization, and she simply asked other leaders: Is this the type of organization that requires something to be 100 percent complete and agreed-upon in order to move forward? Or were they okay with, say, 75 percent? What she learned was that "It depends." And no, that is not just a cop-out response. For Gillian's organization, the leaders supported partial solutions in most instances, but for anything that was high client-facing, the expectation was that it would be closer to 100 percent complete and agreed-upon. For her organization, alignment among leaders was very important. It presented a united front and strengthened messages.

COACHING TIP: As a leader or emerging leader, always critique and review ideas in advance of meetings if you anticipate alternate viewpoints.

In our Additional Resources, we cite a book by Nick Montoya, *The Magic Megaphone,* which outlines a simple tool for arriving at a workable consensus. Co-author Roger watched Montoya use his consensus tool to great success with assertive engineers and IT professionals. Where? Intel Corporation, a company known for driven, no-nonsense employees. As problems were discussed in meetings of five to fifteen people, Montoya would outline a solution and ask participants, "Okay, so is this 85 percent fix to the issue good enough?" His colleagues would look back and forth at each other and reply, yes, that covers it sufficiently. Montoya could do it in a thirty- to sixty-minute meeting. Everyone was on board. Meeting over.

Previously we mentioned shortcuts and how they can be a detriment to your credibility. But let's face reality: In a business setting, time matters. However, you cannot cut corners in the interest of time. Otherwise, most people would just individually decide and skip the consensus altogether. That would be fast, but you need to balance being expeditious with gaining acceptance.

This is the age-old debate about what's more important, process or outcomes? Involving others provides an opportunity to gain agreement. It allows for discussion, idea generation, and refinement. It allows others to have a voice and avoids them feeling bullied or overlooked.

Scene #3

Jake was an IT manager at a global organization. He had devoted over a year to developing a proprietary project management tool that would be extremely beneficial to multiple departments across his company. Throughout the project, he included multiple team members from those departments. He got their input and provided regular updates. Unfortunately, Jake's project got shut down just as it was nearing completion. The reason: He had overlooked one department with a particularly territorial leader. The leader of the other department argued that they didn't see the value or relevance of this new tool and that it wasn't worth all the effort. And just like that, a year's worth of effort was lost. Although this was a case of ego and power over common sense, it may have been avoided by including them.

COACHING TIP: Devote more time than you think you need on the process of seeking input and buy-in or risk longer-term outcomes—and your credibility.

When striving for group acceptance, and/or you sense your colleagues are about to get bold and become a gang in the conference room, consider the following:

1. In an intense group discussion, do you sense a hidden "elephant in the room" question that everyone is avoiding, either intentionally or naively? Seize the moment! Give that elephant room at the table and watch the mouths drop. You have just acquired a credibility token. Use it wisely.
2. Why, you ask, are your colleagues ignoring that elephant bumping into the conference table? Simple. Everyone has a domain to protect, either their professional view or the fleshy one twitching on their chair. You don't need to expose either to embarrassment, but others will get the picture.
3. What are the long-term benefits of the group's consensus brainstorm? More importantly, what are the long-term negatives?
4. The big question to ask: Can you ever have a consensus that everyone at the conference table agrees to? Even if consensus is royally declared, will everyone pull with the same enthusiasm? Imagine the meeting is over and someone, maybe you, says, "Hey, let's go to lunch." Will seven people all suddenly agree? No. Sometimes it takes the one person whose credibility and influence are solid: You. You say, "Come on, guys. Charlie's Deli has something for everyone, including vegans. Let's go." You earn an influence token.

COACHING TIP: In meetings, do not feel compelled to comment on everything. You don't have a quota on comments. Choose your shots. Take in all responses first. After all, that person in your group who comments on everything is giving you the gut feeling—the intuition—they can be ignored. (Note: Reread Scene #1.)

Meeting Discipline

What follows are some tips for assembling a meeting for a big issue, and why your clout is enhanced by proposing the following guidelines:

- If it's a serious issue, one that can derail the organization, meet in person. If it is a critical issue, online videoconferencing loses some nuance.
- What is the worst thing that could happen if no decision or consensus is met?
- Make sure all the stakeholders are recruited.
- Plan ahead on the time needed. This is not a "let's do it and get it over with" meeting.
- Connect with key stakeholders elsewhere as needed, and then return to the main group.
- Outline the short-term fix and the long-term fix.
    - Benefits and downside of the short-term fix
    - Benefits and downside of the long-term fix
- Does either fix require rethinking the organization's entire strategy?
- Carefully and honestly outline who in the organization will be affected, positively or negatively. Where possible, ensure that they are included in the discussion in advance of the broader meeting environment. This will help to identify potential roadblocks during the meeting.
- Structure the agenda so there is a break for any factions to discuss their position.
- Does the level of disagreement call for a professional, neutral meeting facilitator?

COACHING TIP: Always use business *outcomes and goals* as the unifying framework to establish common ground. If the conversation goes sideways and/or there are multiple competing perspectives, it's helpful to refer to the agreed-upon objectives.

But first, is it time for a brain retreat? Aside from the foregoing list, you need some quiet time to think through it all. Getaway time. Sitting at your desk in an office wing with lots of disruptions does not provide time to think it all out. For years, cognitive psychologists have written about how the best brainstorming takes place when you go someplace for quiet thought. At home in the backyard or by the fireplace, quiet music playing, yellow pad in hand . . . yes, get away from a keyboard. New settings work wonders. Don't believe it? Just try it.

COACHING TIP: Find the time and place where you do your best creative work. Seek that out when creativity and big thinking are required.

When discussing controversial decisions with colleagues, it takes someone who is the Master of Questions. Being a master of questions also requires being a master of listening.

The Challenge of Trusting Past Questions—*the Wrong Ones*

Often company leaders look at annual budgets and urge the strategy of zero-based budgeting. It's simple. Start with the original rationale for the project and rationalize why the project is still needed. It's a strategy that can reveal changes lost to everyone's memory.

Here, let's call it zero-based questioning. What is the base question that needs to be asked here? Author Isaac Asimov pointed the way: "A good question is, of course, the key by which infinite answers can be deduced."

We cite in Additional Resources a book all aspiring leaders need on their shelves: Andrew Finlayson's *Questions That Work: How to Ask Questions That Will Help You Succeed in Any Business Situation*. In his introduction, Finlayson spells out the issue for aspiring leaders: "Individuals and institutions must ask and encourage others to ask more questions. If you doubt the value of questions, let me argue that when careers collapse, it is often the result of a lack of insightful questioning. When corporations falter, it frequently is a lack of questioning that has brought about the crisis."

Remember this: As co-author Tim states in his book *Peak Leadership Fitness*, asking good, thoughtful questions is a sign of wisdom, not a sign of weakness.

Scene #4

Harold is customer service manager for a firm that builds, sells, and rents trade-show displays for companies with yearlong exhibition needs. He emailed the following question to all the client trade-show exhibit managers: "Are you satisfied with our customer service?" He received few replies, he told the marketing chief one day at lunch.

The marketing manager said the question should include a rating system: "on a scale from 0 to 10, 0 being not at all satisfied, and 10 being fully satisfied." He also urged Harold to ask for feedback on display quality, construction time, and delivery time.

Harold went back to the clients a few weeks later with the marketing manager's suggestions. This time he received replies from 82 percent of the clients, and the answers pointed to some issues.

Harold's first survey question was too rigid, too absolute. It pays to ask the questions *that make recipients think.*

The Challenge of Trusting Old Problem-Solving Ways

Organizational problems cannot be ignored. How you attack them can mean the difference between success and failure. You must be the one with the essential problem-solving algorithm and sequence. Author Edward Hodnett summarized the essence of a sequence of questions. "A good problem statement often includes a) what is known, b) what is unknown, and c) what is sought."

Define—no, *dissect*—the problem you are tackling in some detail. What is the downside? What are the long-term gains or losses? Can the problem correct itself with some new venture? The last thing you want is for a colleague to point out something you missed. The respected Swiss-French architect Charles Le Corbusier once said, "A problem properly stated finds its own solution."

It's not often that someone in an organization stops and asks, "Why do we do things this way?" Processes easily become embedded habits—good or bad, for better or for worse. As the environment changes (and it usually changes rapidly and often), we need to resist blindly accepting faulty old approaches. We need to challenge our old habits by constructively and critically questioning them. Those who do this are well on their way to high degrees of credibility and clout.

Problem definition. If a problem exists in an organization, a simple, quick definition and solution is unlikely. Albert Einstein had a rigorous approach to it all: "When I have one week to solve a seemingly impossible problem, I spend six days defining the problem. Then, the solution becomes obvious." The better defined the problem, the more it will help to facilitate buy-in, and, more importantly, clarity of direction and results.

Let's work through the basic steps:

- Who thinks it's a problem, and who does not?
- Who has a vested interest in fixing the problem? A hidden agenda?
- What is the stated cause of the problem and what is the stated effect?
- Is the problem within one department, and does that department recognize the issue?
- How is the problem affecting your organization, and who within it?
- What facts have been expressed?
- Have the facts been substantiated compared to mere opinions?
- What type of issue is it (e.g., HR, marketing, customer service, sales, finance)?
- Is the issue one of training or staffing?
- Is there a quick fix that can work?
- If not, what is the long-term fix, and what additional resources are needed for the latter?

The Four Cs

We have frequently cited the Four Cs. This pitfall alerts you to some common mistakes of trust that can negatively affect all Four Cs. In short: No trust, no influence, no clout.

- **C#1**—*Clear, critical thinking.* Do your homework. Listen. Probe. Make sure you understand what your colleague(s) value, what their experience is, and what is important to them. Unless you understand what makes them tick on the issue, how can you pitch your position with any assurance of success? This requires complete, clear, critical thinking.
- **C#2**—*Clear, unambiguous communications.* Be it formal or one-on-one, make sure you are devoid of any distractions, verbal, nonverbal, or artifacts—the kind we covered in Pitfall #9. The late Barbara Walters said it well after her early days as an aspiring television news anchor: "There are few times in your life when it isn't too melodramatic to say your destiny hangs on the impression you make."
- **C#3**—*Credibility that results from Cs 1 and 2.* In short, believability. Always keep in mind this question: Is it always right to be right?

Occasionally admitting you are not right isn't going to damage your credibility or influence.

- **C#4**—*Clout . . . the resulting influence . . .* earned. Call it clout closure. Do colleagues label the decision a success? Ask, "Do you agree with how this has developed? Any reservations?" In other words, close the deal!

Summary of Coaching Tips

- When it comes to making decisions based upon data, judgment, or intuition, trust but verify any assumptions.
- Since no two situations are exactly alike, when applying your previous experience (or intuitions) to a situation, ask yourself, What is unique and what is the same? And how do the answers to those questions inform your current approach?
- Contribute critical questions and alternative viewpoints in a way that is consistent with your organization's culture.
- Avoid groupthink by actively seeking and welcoming diverse perspectives and making time for independent evaluation.
- As a leader, or emerging leader, always share ideas in advance of meetings if you anticipate alternate viewpoints.
- Devote more time than you think you need on the process of seeking input and buy-in or risk longer-term outcomes—and your credibility.
- In meetings, do not feel compelled to comment on everything. You don't have a quota on comments. Choose your shots. Take in all responses first.
- Always use business outcomes and goals as the unifying framework to establish common ground. If the conversation goes sideways and/or there are multiple competing perspectives, it is helpful to refer to the agreed-upon objectives.
- Find the time and place that you do your best creative work. Seek that out when creativity and big thinking are required.

Summary of Pitfall #10

Our main point here is not to cast in cement how you gain consensus. Don't rely on the same old questions when trying to solve problems or you could miss something. And your gut feeling about things may be based on biases or past experiences that do not always apply to new situations. Think new. Clean slate. Tabula rasa. Zero-based thinking.

Moving you along. We have covered ten pitfalls that you need to avoid on the path to more credibility and clout . . . influence. That's part I. But you're not done yet. Now we are on to part II, the pathways of influence. In other words, further help in "closing the deal."

It is better to be looked over than overlooked.

—ACTRESS MAE WEST

Additional Resources

- *Thinking, Fast and Slow* by Daniel Kahneman (New York: Farrar, Straus and Giroux, 2011).
- *The Magic Megaphone: How to Get Your Projects Unstuck and Back on Track in Under 60 Minutes* by Nick Montoya, with Roger S. Peterson (Granite Bay, CA: Megaphone Publishing Co., 2006).
- *Questions That Work: How to Ask Questions That Will Help You Succeed in Any Business Situation* by Andrew Finlayson (New York: AMACOM / American Management Association, 2001).
- To read up on the research on influence, search for everything that social psychologist Robert Cialdini has written, because he is the master. This includes his book *Influence: The Psychology of Persuasion* (New York: Harper Business, 2021).
- *How We Decide* by Jonah Lehrer (Boston / New York: Mariner Books, 2009).
- *Problem Solving 101: A Simple Book for Smart People* by Ken Watanabe (New York: Portfolio/Penguin Group, 2009).
- *In Defense of Troublemakers: The Power of Dissent in Life and Business* by Charlan Nemeth, PhD (New York: Basic Books, 2018).
- *Peak Leadership Fitness: Elevating Your Leadership Game* by Timothy J. Tobin (Alexandria, VA: ATD Press, an imprint of the Association for Talent Development, 2019).
- *Originals: How Non-Conformists Move the World* by Adam Grant (New York: Viking, 2016).

Transition

From Those Pitfalls to Your Pathways

Moving from pitfalls to pathways requires that you hone your learning mind-set. This means you must become self-aware in order to recognize what you know and don't know about your organization; to know what your strengths and areas for improvement are; and to be open to learning and improving. You need to be inquisitive. Our attention shifts from avoiding the various distractions associated with pitfalls to proactive processes you can follow to pursue promising pathways.

Each pathway is meant to move you further along in your personal development. Your starting point and goals are unique to you. Expect your focus to shift over time as well. As you read about the various processes, vignettes, coaching tips, and core skills, and as you reflect upon and apply these insights to your unique situation, the pathways will provide you with an opportunity to make step-function progress in your communication skills.

Your personal pathway is paved with skills. An added feature to the next part of the book is that each pathway lists the skills that will help you move forward.

Once you've gained self-awareness and have your starting point, remember that practice makes perfect—especially when it is coupled with feedback. Observe and learn from those around you and roll up your sleeves to test out some of our recommended practices.

Take special note of the skills we list in each pathway and consider how you are doing with each one. Practically speaking, you can approach this part of the book by focusing on two or three of the core skills from a single pathway, or you may choose to select from skills from across multiple pathways. It's a question of depth versus breadth, and because this is unique to you, there really is no wrong answer. In this brief transition, we want to reiterate three areas that will further help you on your pathway to more clout: 1) purpose, 2) plan, and 3) skills.

We want you to begin with **purpose**—specifically, *your* purpose as it pertains to improving your critical thinking, clarity, and credibility. When you set out on a pathway, know where you're going, or you could find yourself wandering aimlessly. Be clear and decisive about your intentions. Plans emerge from structure.

If you haven't already done so, now is the time to establish or recommit to your 4-C personal improvement plan. Speaking of improvement, you should be open to *continuous* improvement. When it comes to establishing pathways, no one is perfect, so approaching this as a journey of improvement will allow you to experience progress along the way and learn from both your and others' successes and mistakes.

COACHING TIP: Take some time to think specifically about what you want to improve in terms of your a) critical thinking, b) clarity, and/or c) credibility. What does success in these areas look like for you? How will you get there—i.e., what specific actions will you take? *Write this down and keep it in a visible location*, as it will become your plan. It will be a great source of accountability to yourself as well as a way to monitor your progress.

In fact, what personal improvements come to mind *right now*? Jot them down here:

1. ______________________________
2. ______________________________
3. ______________________________
4. ______________________________

Metaphorically speaking, should your pathway be sturdy and made of flagstones, or flexible and made of gravel? In our experience, we have found that you need to combine a strong foundation with flexibility to adapt and grow.

When you set out to build a pathway, it's important to first lay the groundwork. This requires you to be proactive. Your communication pathways will not simply emerge without some thought and planning on your part.

But where should you start? This next section will help you do that.

With your purpose identified and plan well documented, you need the skills to execute your plan. You will hear words like *anticipate*, *navigate*, and *strengthen*. These are intentionally proactive words, because you need to be proactive on your journey of continuous improvement.

The following pathways will provide you with a structure, and yes, we will highlight specific skills you will need along your journey. However, it's important to also be flexible—to adapt and pivot as new information becomes available.

As you have learned through the first part of the book, three of the Four Cs are within your control: critical thinking, clarity, and credibility. As you work on being at your best with those, the fourth C—clout—will come.

In this next part of the book, we reinforce practice and reflection. You will continue to see practical vignettes and tips, and you are encouraged to reflect on how this applies to you and your unique situation. What communication skills do you have? Which ones do you need?

Don't simply breeze through the pathways. Reflect and consider what you can learn from these tips and examples throughout each pathway. How have you handled, or would you handle, a similar situation? And most importantly, how can you continue to improve?

We've done our best to provide you with coaching tips throughout this book, and as you continue to hone your skills, we strongly encourage you to share your experiences and coach others. If you've achieved a level of mastery, how can you help others improve?

As part of this intermission, we want to provide you with a vignette from our experience. Not only can you reflect on this, but it also provides you with an opportunity to put your coaching hat on.

Scene #1

Steve was an individual contributor at a large global professional services firm. He had ten years of professional experience, but less than a year at the firm. It was typical for associates at the firm to work on multiple projects simultaneously and therefore work with different project leads throughout the year. Steve took initiative, and this was initially recognized and appreciated by his project leaders.

However, Steve's approach had a fatal communication flaw: He had a habit of always saying "I got it" no matter what task or project came his way. As it turned out, this was less about initiative and more about follow-through. Project leaders would give Steve a task only to discover several weeks—or, in one instance, months—later that Steve did not "have it," which resulted in multiple project delays and setbacks. Steve volunteered for much but accomplished little.

Throughout the year, project leaders would meet to discuss project updates, including staffing information. At one of the meetings, it became clear that Steve's "I got it" and the similar lack of follow-through permeated across all of his projects.

What impact do you think this had on Steve's credibility? What advice would you give to Steve?

We encourage you to take this similar reflective, yet practical and advisory, approach as you proceed through the five pathways. Don't simply read through them; rather, put yourself in the position of the various people in the vignettes. In the story above, consider what it's like to be Steve; one of his project leaders; his boss; or his colleagues.

At every opportunity, consider what aspects you can incorporate into your personal communication practices, as well as what tips and advice you would give to the various characters in the story. Look around your own organization and recognize the multiple opportunities to learn from others and to showcase your newly developed skills.

Ready? On to part II!

Part II

Stepping Around the Pitfalls . . . for More Enduring Influence

Pathway #1

Anticipate the speed bumps of contemporary business

Whatever course you decide upon, there is always someone to tell you that you are wrong. There are always difficulties arising which tempt you to believe that your critics are right. To map out a course of action and follow it to an end requires courage.
—RALPH WALDO EMERSON

Speed bumps are obstacles put in place to slow you down. In the workplace, they are all around you. They can be immovable or flexible, small or large, perceived or real, and self- or organizationally imposed, and they may or may not be visible. To anticipate and navigate speed bumps requires knowledge, skills, and yes, as Mr. Emerson's quote suggests, courage. You must also be self-aware and know your business.

Your first impression may be that all speed bumps are bad. They get in your way and slow you down. After all, being slow in business can be detrimental. This is true, but keep in mind as you read this chapter: Not all speed bumps are bad.

Some speed bumps may be in place for your safety or the safety of the business. They may be in place to ensure that you get *better* business outcomes, or that you take a more *thoughtful* approach. They can allow for some often-overlooked critical thinking, and they can give you an opportunity to connect with others, or perhaps to reflect on a potential decision.

Although there are countless possible business outcomes, we argue that the majority come down to increased quality, quantity, or speed of decisions. Other more specific and tangible outcomes flow from there.

But wait. You may be thinking that all the tangible outcomes and metrics associated with productivity, revenue, and the like are the *real* business outcomes. This may be what you are ultimately pursuing, but they all stem from earlier decisions about what to prioritize, where to invest (or not), and how to communicate, reinforce, and recognize progress along the way. Every step along that pathway requires a decision.

So, when we emphasize words like *better* and *thoughtful*, we're talking about your ability to make the best possible decisions and to do so in a timely manner. In business, there will never be unlimited time or resources, so you've got to know when to move quickly and when to pause. For example:

- Did we communicate expectations clearly?
- Did we provide feedback to help calibrate an associate's performance?
- Did we coach along the way?

To accomplish this, it's important to recognize that some speed bumps are beneficial and allow for critical thinking and reflection.

Familiarity can be both beneficial and at times a barrier. If you are taking a common pathway for a certain recurring business activity—one that you experience with regularity—you may already know about all the speed bumps along the way. That can be good for anticipating them. For example, you will know the importance of involving certain stakeholders as part of the process.

However, it can be beneficial for both processes and outcomes to periodically and constructively question some of the elements designed to slow you down; for example, a new law regarding hiring, or the post-COVID-19 trend of working partly from home. This is not specifically or exclusively about the stakeholder example; rather, it applies to any recurring speed bumps. Do they still provide a benefit to the business?

Let's face it: We're talking about business, which brings with it an inherent and at times high degree of uncertainty. As you will see throughout this chapter, some processes and structures are intentionally put in place to help establish some level of certainty or a system of checks and balances. Recognize them and leverage them for their intended purpose.

At times, speed bumps may overwhelm us. But with awareness and the right approach, you can avoid them, or find ways to work with them—hopefully to the advantage of your organization, your colleagues, and you.

Awareness of both existing and potential speed bumps comes from experience. You may experience them firsthand, or you may base your knowledge on others' experience. And, yes, you can even gain awareness from reading a book, which is where we come in. We're here to provide you with awareness of the common speed bumps in contemporary business, as well as how to recognize and navigate them.

The opportunity for you to make a difference comes from seeing the speed bump with as much advance notice as possible, so that you can navigate it accordingly and ultimately get on with the business at hand. Remember that business is about results *and* how you get them. What you are known for—your brand, which we covered in Pitfall #5—is built upon both.

What exactly are the speed bumps of contemporary business? Broadly speaking, speed bumps stem from people, processes, structures, and culture. We will cover each throughout this chapter. We should also point out that each of the potential speed bumps is a critical component of an organization's strategy and operations. The idea that they also present as speed bumps can be situational, meaning they can occur intentionally or unintentionally, as previously noted.

COACHING TIP: Take a few minutes (or longer, as needed) and identify the speed bumps in your workplace. Revisit this list as you learn more throughout this chapter.

Beneficial speed bumps:	**Blocking speed bumps:**
1. ______________________	1. ______________________
2. ______________________	2. ______________________
3. ______________________	3. ______________________
4. ______________________	4. ______________________
5. ______________________	5. ______________________

The Gist

Pathway #1 is about identifying the various types of obstacles you are likely to encounter in the workplace. We want to help you anticipate them so that you can better navigate them.

We cover each of the broad categories of obstacles—people, process, structure, and culture. So that you can work on your personal development plan and how to improve, we also highlight the key skills you'll need in order to navigate the common speed bumps to contemporary business. Throughout this chapter, we assume that you are either in a leadership position or actively working toward achieving a level of leading others.

What do speed bumps have to do with clarity of communication? For starters, speed bumps are a form of nonverbal communication. Your job is to determine whether slowing down is good for intended outcomes or not, what to do with the briefly slower pace, and how to move toward a better business outcome.

You have seen throughout our book our emphasis on critical thinking. When you encounter an obstacle, this is an opportunity to practice your critical thinking skills. You may also recall that in Pitfall #1, we suggest you practice "benign neglect." This is an intentional brief pause that allows you to reflect on your words, the actions you are considering, and potential outcomes.

Secondly, how are you communicating potential speed bumps to others? If you are aware of them, do you help others anticipate them? Do you help remove them? Do you ask others to figure them out for themselves? Or are you there to answer questions and provide navigational guidance?

COACHING TIP: Whether you have a leadership title or not, your job is to help others succeed by seeing speed bumps, understanding why they are in place, and helping others navigate around them.

People-Centered Speed Bumps

People-centered speed bumps fall into two broad categories: talent and relationships.

Talent is a pathway that involves your ability to identify talent, as well as to coach and develop people. This starts with communicating expectations. Are you able to identify the skills and characteristics required to accomplish a task? And can you properly select or develop people who either have these skills or can learn them?

This may take the form of a job description, or it may be connected to how you set out to form a project team. If you're correct in your assessment, the project—and the person—are much more likely to succeed. If you are wrong, you put the project and the associate's reputation at risk.

But what about times when you inherit a team? Since you won't have the ability to identify or select the talent, it will be crucial for you to develop the requisite skills among your associates. You *will* have control over how you identify and communicate priorities—which skills are needed—as well as how you continuously develop the people you are working with to accomplish objectives.

You cannot have a "set it and forget it" approach to leadership. If you do, neither you nor your associates will succeed. You must be committed to clear and frequent communication.

Scene #1

Eli was a mid-level manager at a manufacturing company with a team of nine associates. He described himself as a hands-off manager and one that provided his associates with a lot of autonomy. Since Eli rarely provided his associates with any feedback, they each assumed they were on track and meeting expectations. During the company's annual review period, several of them received a different message. For four of his associates in particular, Eli outlined the various ways they had fallen short of performance expectations throughout the year. The problem, the associates argued, was that there were never any expectations established. Eli's response was that they had been around the organization long enough to know what was expected. Those associates were dejected, and that feeling eventually worked its way into the morale of the rest of the team.

What advice would you give Eli? What advice would you give his associates? How could this situation have been avoided or handled differently from the outset?

COACHING TIP: Don't assume associates will intuitively know what is expected of them. Be clear. To be successful, you must establish clear performance expectations and provide frequent feedback to your associates.

If you're a leader, or an emerging one, your job is to help people succeed. You lead for them. This involves two critical tasks. We just covered the first, setting clear expectations. This ensures alignment and allows you to hold yourself and others accountable. The second requires removing barriers. This ensures efficiencies and will likely result in some lessons learned along the way.

Think of your reputation as your brand. When it comes to talent, there are implications for your long-term reputation. Are you known as the leader who identifies and develops associates? As you evolve your career as a leader, your credibility will relate to your ability to honestly and accurately do so.

Associate performance can become a speed bump. Sometimes, even when you set clear expectations and provide clear and timely feedback, not all associates are able to achieve the skills required to do the job effectively. In those instances, and once you've exhausted all feedback and development options, you may be called upon to decide how to proceed in the best interests of the associate and the organization.

- Can you find a different, more suitable role on the team or within the organization for the associate?
- Is their level of performance acceptable enough for the team, or would the associate and organization be better off parting ways?

These decisions are never easy, and they are highly personal and organization-specific. How you assess and develop talent will become part of your own reputation.

The second area of potential people-centered speed bumps is *relationships*. You will likely encounter many differing viewpoints throughout your career journey. On one hand, some are simple, honest, different mind-sets or opinions. For example, if you are in a finance role, your point of view will likely be different than the way someone in a marketing or human resources department sees the world.

On the other hand, other people-related differences may be more driven by competing agendas or priorities. For example, you may encounter someone who is looking to advance their career at all costs. We are not against people advancing their career; on the contrary. But we are not supportive of the "at all costs" aspect of career growth.

Two pieces of advice on this topic. One, don't be this person. There is plenty of opportunity to grow your career *and* develop strong, supportive relationships across your company. If not, you may not be at the right organization. The second piece of advice is that if you come across as someone with this "advancement at all costs" mind-set, you'd better watch your back. We have seen more than one professional take credit for another person's work or make one employee look bad so they look good.

Scene #2

Becky was very aspirational in her career, and she would do anything to climb the corporate ladder. She joined her organization as an individual contributor, and she actively sought out projects. She especially liked being on projects with access to senior leadership. Whenever a project went well, she was very visible and quick to take credit. When projects didn't go as planned, she would point blame along the way, mostly behind the scenes. She was quite savvy with her approach—always positive in front of the team, but working behind the scenes to discredit her peers and colleagues. The good news for Becky is that she eventually got the promotion she desired. However, eventually, word got around about the things she said and did, and as a result, no one wanted to work with her. She was not someone that could be trusted, and therefore had zero credibility.

What feedback and guidance would you have given Becky when she started at the company? How would the feedback and guidance have changed if you learned that she was taking credit and placing blame? Lastly, if your first opportunity to provide Becky with feedback came after her promotion and after her negative reputation had been cemented, what advice would you give her?

Getting back to the cross-functional relationships, in all relational aspects, your role is to find a common language that allows you to work across teams and viewpoints. We have found the best common language is centered on business results. Keep in mind that a business result to someone from the finance department might look different than a business result from someone in the marketing department; nonetheless, it provides an excellent starting and ending point for discussion. Your responsibility is to facilitate common ground.

You may even find that some business outcomes benefit from having multiple points of view represented. If that speed bump can be navigated well, you stand to experience potential innovative solutions or a multiplier effect, whereby the sum of the collective is greater than its individual parts.

Scene #3

Brenda led a cross-functional team at a large financial services company that developed a product that achieved significant results. Todd was the CEO of the company. He championed innovation, and wanted to understand what they did to achieve such results so that it could be replicated throughout the company. Todd hired an outside consultant to review the team's processes and outcomes.

The prominent finding that differentiated Brenda's team from any others in the organization was that they were a virtual and cross-functional team comprised of functional subject-matter experts from across the company. Brenda had handpicked experts from the departments she believed were integral to the development of the product and had gotten them engaged at just the right time. The virtual aspect meant that those subject-matter experts came together as an intact team only a small number of times, first, to ensure that the objectives and roles were clearly understood, and then for periodic status updates. Those team members got involved only as their specific expertise was required. For example, the marketing expert was more heavily involved in the mid- to late stages of the project. Although it was Brenda's leadership and innovation that made the biggest difference, the unprecedented results came from a collaborative effort.

The vignette above is an example of overcoming potential obstacles, and how Brenda used a multiple of them to her advantage. Resource constraints drove the need to make the team virtual. To ensure that talent did not become an obstacle, Brenda had the foresight to hand-select subject-matter experts whom she knew could contribute to the objectives. And the processes Brenda utilized were effective, as she leveraged expertise from across the organization. She also had a strong appreciation for the team members' time. Since nothing like this had been attempted before at her company, Brenda's approach required courage. In this case, insight plus courage led to innovation and extremely positive results.

COACHING TIP: Be aware of how your professional viewpoint shapes your perspective and be open to others' viewpoints. When approaching business challenges or projects, seek common ground in business outcomes.

Process-Focused Speed Bumps

Process-focused speed bumps include two areas: stakeholder alignment and managing expectations.

Stakeholder alignment could easily find its way into the section on people- or culture-related speed bumps, but we want to include it here so you know it's a step in the process that must be intentionally built into your projects. Your personal success as well as any associated organizational success often involves obtaining acceptance as part of project management—especially when projects pertain to others' work areas.

COACHING TIP: Involve stakeholders early and often for idea generation, alignment, and acceptance. Approach cross-functional projects in a collaborative, partnership fashion. This will enhance your credibility, the influence of your personal brand, and business outcomes.

At a minimum, key stakeholders need to be aware of any discussions affecting their respective areas. No one likes surprises, and it gives you a chance to gauge support, clarify topics, address resistance, generate ideas, and identify issues ahead of time.

This involvement can take a wide variety of forms, including identifying key stakeholders as part of the planning process and inviting them or a representative to all meetings. Or it may involve periodic email or phone updates or one-on-one check-ins with the stakeholder prior to any final decisions being made. In this way, timing of involvement is more important than simply "check-the-box" involvement.

COACHING TIP: When it comes to stakeholder involvement, when in doubt, it is best to ask each stakeholder at the beginning of any project what level of involvement they would like to have.

It is also highly likely those stakeholders will want to be involved in shaping any recommendations, so be open to their involvement. Without their involvement in a timely, clear, and thorough way, your efforts will likely meet some resistance later. Further, while this speed bump may seemingly slow a project down, neglecting it will have future and potentially long-term implications for your credibility and clout. It may also result in a larger slowdown later in the project.

Managing expectations is an important part of any project. These often involve deadlines and related demands. Whether you work for a large organization or are an individual consultant, you face a variety of pressures and expectations every day. Setting aside any of these demands we put on ourselves, they otherwise come from the people we interact with. At the root of these demands is communication.

COACHING TIP: Under-promise and over-deliver. Stretch where possible, but be realistic. And never intentionally misrepresent potential or intent (i.e., "sandbag") to gain an advantage.

Yes, deadlines exist, and they are real. However, they likely stem from commitments we impose. For example, if your boss asks you whether a project can be accomplished in thirty days and you say yes to appease your boss, knowing full well this project cannot be done in that time frame, you risk losing credibility. Specifically, this will be a direct reflection on you and your ability to manage a project.

It is imperative that you are clear and as accurate as possible about timelines and resources from the outset of a project. Of course, change occurs. You can encounter a wide variety of speed bumps we've discussed here. And when that happens, it is your job to clearly communicate the changes and the impact as soon as possible. Ignoring the speed bumps rarely makes them go away. There is a saying in business that good leaders want good news fast and bad news even faster.

Fear not. You are in control of setting expectations and managing them along the way. You need to build it into your processes. In project management lingo, these are called *timelines* and *contingencies*. This is a skill that requires insight and expertise. How do you know how long something will take? Typically, the way to determine this is from experience with similar projects. When that is not an option, seek others who have such experience.

COACHING TIP: Always build in contingency in your projects for the unexpected speed bumps that arise.

Structural Speed Bumps

Structural speed bumps also fall into two categories: hierarchy and resources. Each presents unique challenges that must be understood to be navigated.

Hierarchy refers to your organization's structure:

- How are people organized to make decisions and get work done?
- Who has decision-making authority?
- Are there many layers of approval, or can decisions be made quickly?

The specific translation of these questions to our overall theme is: Who do you need to communicate with to get decisions made and work done? And subsequently, how, and when, do those messages need to occur?

An associate from one organization we are familiar with used to say "Every associate has the power to say no, but no one has the power to say yes." As you can imagine, this was not the most effective or efficient approach, and the business results and levels of associate engagement often reflected that.

Make sure you have a solid understanding of the various approval processes and "chain of command," or you may find yourself running up against speed bumps that you created by neglecting these structural hierarchy considerations.

You may be tempted to take structural shortcuts. Depending on your organization and the leaders involved, that will have varying degrees of negative impact. In the same organization mentioned above, there were numerous stories from associates who tried to work around the structures in the interest of expeditious progress and positive business outcomes. In some instances, they were able to make short-term steps forward only to take multiple steps back later on. Other associates were not so lucky, and did not last in that organization.

COACHING TIP: Respect your organization's chain of command. Do not try to take shortcuts or circumvent it.

When it comes to *resources*, the focus is on whether there are realistic time expectations and the tools and resources required to do one's job. Time is not infinite—especially in business. There are several considerations associated with time, including time management, deadlines, and readiness to launch various initiatives.

How do associates manage their time? And how do you help others to manage their time? Are deadlines realistic? Do associates routinely work nights and weekends to meet deadlines? Is it better to launch an initiative quickly or completely?

When it comes to time management and deadlines, all companies are different, and it's fair to expect to occasionally have to work some nights or weekends, depending on your role, of course. However, if you or your associates find yourselves regularly working nights and weekends out of necessity, your organization may have a resource challenge.

Speed matters, but so, too, does accuracy. You need to understand and clearly communicate when it is acceptable to implement a product, service, or message that is incomplete—say 60 to 70 percent ready—versus when the launch must be close to 100 percent.

We cannot tell you whether it's important for you and your team to be quick versus accurate, but you will need to understand this within the context of your organization, and perhaps even with each specific project.

The answer is, "It depends." Regardless of the answer, you must clearly articulate this information to your team to avoid unnecessary setbacks.

COACHING TIP: Don't rush to failure.

A popular employee engagement question asks whether the associate has the tools and resources to do their job. It's a basic question that you should use when you check in with your associates. If they answer "No," you need to be prepared to advocate for the resources they need to do their jobs, or to clearly communicate why they won't get what they deem as the necessary resources.

In our experience, it is common for leaders to want to grow their team, but any such requests should be driven by business needs and how well the new resources could contribute to organizational objectives versus creating more busywork. We like to refer to this as "building more stuff" versus making a difference. As a leader, you need to discern when to pursue such requests and how to do so versus when to coach your associates to work within their current resources.

COACHING TIP: If you find yourself needing to advocate for or request more resources, always focus on how those resources will contribute to the various business strategies or related critical results.

Scene #4

Terri was a new, first-time manager. She managed a team of three associates, and she was eager to grow her team. Within two months in her role, she approached her boss asking for permission to hire three more associates.

If you were Terri's boss, what questions would you ask Terri to determine whether this is something you could advocate for? How would you advise her? If you were Terri, how would you have approached your new role and such a request?

The primary skills you will need in order to navigate the structural hierarchy speed bumps are organizational/political savvy, time management, and project management. Developing these skills will help you understand not only who to communicate with but the navigational aspects of how and when to do so. You will also need to learn how to anticipate and communicate project timelines and resource requirements. As with the other speed bumps, your ability to do so accurately will directly impact your credibility.

Culture-Related Speed Bumps

Culture can be one of the most challenging and potentially most crucial of speed bumps. Culture embodies the *ways work gets done* and *how associates interact* within a company. Those practices and norms consist of the values, beliefs and behaviors that drive the interactions.

COACHING TIP: Know and respect your company's culture. Never ignore or override the culture in favor of expediency. What appears to be a near-term shortcut could come back to become a much bigger roadblock later.

What makes culture so challenging is that many characteristics of an organization's culture can be tacit or implicit, including the *ways work gets done*. When discussing culture, the metaphor of an iceberg is often used to depict what is visible on the surface compared to the vast amount that exists below the surface.

Scene #5

Hailey was new to her organization. She joined the company as a director overseeing a department of seventeen associates. She was one of thirty directors in the company. Wanting to make a good first impression, Hailey was very focused on results. She never understood why she had to involve her peers in various business aspects that she believed only slowed her progress. In her first several months, she made several missteps because she circumvented some essential processes associated with keeping her fellow directors informed of her projects.

She was becoming known among her peers as a renegade. A recent example brought the issue to a boiling point. She invited associates from across multiple teams to a daylong ideation session without consulting any of the other directors. The issue was not so much that she included the associates, but that she did not coordinate or even inform any of her peers. For some of her peers, that posed a problem due to impending deadlines. Moreover, it presented a problem because it was contrary to the collaborative culture of the company—*how associates interact* with each other.

What advice would you give Hailey as far as this specific situation goes? What recommendations would you give her going forward?

If you are new to an organization, trying to guess about its culture may not be the most effective approach. While people tend to exhibit more patience for new people, the trial-and-error approach may have longer-term implications for your credibility.

COACHING TIP: Ensure that you have a strong and supportive relationship with someone within your organization who knows the company's culture well. This is likely someone who has a longer tenure. When you have questions about your company's culture, seek their input. When in doubt, seek their input.

Failure as a Speed Bump

No one likes the word *failure*. From a very young age, we are taught that failure is bad. It is usually associated with either lack of effort or lack of competence.

The same interpretation can be applied in the workplace. No one wants to be known for their failures. In fact, in our professional experience, there are countless stories of associates who failed big once, or multiple times, and thus did not last at their respective company.

> *You may not control all the events that happen to you,*
> *but you can decide not to be reduced by them.*
>
> —MAYA ANGELOU

While we are not encouraging you to go out there and fail, we do advocate for recognizing that there are setbacks (i.e., failures) that can help us get better. How many have heard the story about Edison trying to invent the lightbulb? His research assistant asked him whether he was getting frustrated failing more than seven hundred times to invent the lightbulb. Edison replied that he had succeeded at finding over seven hundred ways that didn't work. It's all in your perspective.

There probably aren't a lot of bosses or organizations who are going to be patient enough for an Edison-like track record, unless perhaps they are part of an R&D or innovation department. Our point is much more about your frame of mind than anything else.

This really ties into having a learning and growth mind-set. We all encounter setbacks and speed bumps throughout our professional journey. When a project does not go your way, or the organization's way, don't simply give up. Learn from it. Help others learn from it. You will be better as a result. Furthermore, your resilience and persistence will send a strong positive message about you.

Essential Skills for Anticipating and Navigating Speed Bumps

Throughout this chapter, we have introduced many potential speed bumps that could hinder or help your communication. How well are you prepared to develop your capabilities to anticipate and navigate these speed bumps?

We are including the top, core skills and characteristics required to excel with this pathway. No one is perfect in all areas, so as you review the list, consider which ones you stand to make the greatest gains with, along with your communication and brand, and include those as top priorities in your personal development plan.

- Critical thinking is the impartial and unbiased analysis and evaluation of a topic to form a judgment. Analytical skills are essential. See appendix B for an extensive review and description of critical thinking.
- Communication is the ability to convey ideas in a clear, concise, and effective manner without misinterpretation or misleading others. This includes active listening, along with written, oral, nonverbal, and contextual communication.
- A learning mind-set is the personal belief that one's attributes and capabilities can be developed.
- Relationship skills involve forming and maintaining healthy connections with others. It involves strong communication, cooperation, and conflict management skills.
- Knowledge of your business involves a strong understanding of the core business functions, operations, and strategies of your business. It also involves an understanding of who the competitors are and the essential differentiators.
- Knowledge of your corporate culture includes knowing the values, beliefs, and behaviors which can be tacit or implicit that determine how the company's associates and management interact.
- Organizational/political savvy requires demonstrating integrity, character, and authenticity to achieve a combination of career success, team achievement, and organizational results.

- Coaching skills involve constructive questioning and active listening to support the growth and development of associates for the purposes of improved performance.
- Project management requires the application of processes of knowledge, skills, tools, and techniques to deliver a valuable outcome upon established objectives. The approaches used are time- and resource-bound.
- Time management is the ability to use one's time effectively and productively. Consideration must be given to time and resources.

Summary of Coaching Tips

- Take the necessary time to identify the speed bumps in your workplace.
- Whether you have a leadership title or not, your job is to help others succeed by seeing speed bumps, understanding why they are in place, and helping others to navigate around them.
- Don't assume associates will intuitively know what is expected of them. Be clear. To be successful, you must establish clear performance expectations and provide frequent feedback to your associates.
- Be aware of how your professional viewpoint shapes your perspective and be open to others' viewpoints. When approaching business challenges or projects, seek common ground in business outcomes.
- Involve stakeholders early and often for their idea generation, alignment, and acceptance. Approach cross-functional projects in a collaborative, partnership fashion. This will enhance both your credibility and business outcomes.
- When it comes to stakeholder involvement, when in doubt, it is best to ask each stakeholder at the beginning of any project what level of involvement they would like to have.
- Under-promise and over-deliver. Stretch where possible, but be realistic. And never intentionally misrepresent potential or intent (i.e., "sandbag") to gain an advantage.
- Always build in contingency in your projects for the unexpected speed bumps that arise.
- Respect your organization's chain of command. Do not try to take shortcuts or circumvent it.
- Don't rush to failure.
- If you find yourself needing to advocate for or request more resources, always focus on how those resources will contribute to the various business strategies or related critical results.

- Know and respect your company's culture. Never ignore or override the culture in favor of expediency. What appears to be a near-term shortcut could come back to become a much bigger roadblock later.
- Ensure that you have a strong and supportive relationship with someone within your organization who knows the company's culture well. This is likely someone who has a longer tenure. When you have questions about your company's culture, seek their input. When in doubt, seek their input.

Summary of Pathway #1

Speed bumps in the workplace abound, but not all are considered negative. When presented with a speed bump, you will need to navigate the obstacle in an effective manner. Broadly speaking, speed bumps fall into the four areas covered throughout this chapter: people-centered, process-focused, structural, and cultural-focused. Those that can be anticipated provide you with the opportunity to plan effectively.

Unfortunately, even with great planning, some unexpected speed bumps will still arise. In all instances—anticipated or unanticipated—it is essential that you maintain clear and effective communication to your associates, stakeholders, and leaders. For your credibility, it is equally important that you are proactive in your communication, as it's all about your ability to anticipate them.

To support your development, we identified the core skills that will help you anticipate and navigate the speed bumps you encounter. Prioritize two or three from the list that can make the greatest difference in your development and include them in your personal development plan. We encourage you to revisit the list and your progress often and modify accordingly.

Moving you along. Pathway #1 requires that you be proactive in identifying and navigating speed bumps you know about or may encounter along your pathway to success. We ask that you keep that momentum going for Pathway #2, where you will learn about what it takes to be proactive and engaged with your communication.

It is about more than just word selection. Yes, words matter, but so too do your actions. For greatest clarity, you need to take a proactive versus passive role in what you communicate, to whom, how, when, and why. As you will see in the next chapter, *proactive* does not mean quantity of participation. It requires that you be deliberate and thoughtful with your messages. Whether you take the proactive or the passive pathway, you will find commensurate implications for your credibility and clout.

Additional Resources

- *Peak Leadership Fitness: Elevating Your Leadership Game* by Timothy J. Tobin (Alexandria, VA: ATD Press, an imprint of the Association for Talent Development, 2019).
- *Crunch Time: How to Be Your Best When It Matters Most* by Rick Peterson and Judd Hoekstra (Oakland, CA: Berrett-Koehler Publishers, 2017).
- *Quiet Influence: The Introvert's Guide to Making a Difference* by Jennifer B. Kahnweiler, PhD (Oakland, CA: Berrett-Koehler Publishers, 2013).
- Cited in Pitfall #10, a good project management guide is *The Magic Megaphone: How to Get your Projects Unstuck and Back on Track in Under 60 Minutes* by Nick Montoya, with Roger S. Peterson (Granite Bay, CA: Megaphone Communications, 2006).

Pathway #2

Be proactive and engaged with your communication

Choices are the hinges of destiny.

—PYTHAGORAS

Being proactive and engaged with your communication is a choice. You can choose to sit back and wait for people and information to come to you, or you can choose to be motivated, bold, and take charge of the flow of information. This is not about micromanaging or spinning messages. It is about establishing trust, making connections, and building strong interpersonal and professional relationships.

As a leader or emerging leader, you must communicate proactively if you want to have credibility. Proactive communication allows you to connect with your leaders, peers, colleagues, and associates. And you cannot do that from a closed office or behind your desk.

Whether you are presenting to a single individual, a small team, or a large group, you need to know when and how to deliver your message. You must know what is important to your audience. What do they want or need to know? Although strong presentation skills and executive presence skills help, our focus here is on the processes associated with delivering your message.

What does it mean to be proactive and engaged with your communication? Being *proactive* means that you are highly anticipatory and preemptive. Being *engaged* means connecting with those you are communicating with. Let's take a moment for a quick review of each, and then we'll dive into how, why, and when to be proactive and engaged.

You are proactive when you identify needs for information, potential problems, and other related interests before they become issues. It is about anticipating versus reacting or responding. Implicit in being proactive is the importance of being honest in your communication.

Being engaged requires consistent effort. Get to know your associates and others you work with on both a personal and professional level. Those connections are priceless when it comes to making strong connections. It is through those connections that you build trust and establish awareness of what matters to your various audiences. It also allows you to establish communication priorities and to speak their language.

COACHING TIP: Get to know your associates and colleagues on both a work and a personal level. This will help you build trust, make connections, understand issues and priorities, and speak the same language.

Think about proactive and engaged communication as a management tool that will increase productivity and avoid any potential speed bumps. This requires you taking a lead role in determining the message, as well as when and how it will be delivered. This is a skill that requires both art and science.

The Gist

This chapter is about the *how* and *when* of your message. You must establish a connection to those you are communicating with, and this pathway helps you to do so. We will describe how and why to be proactive and engaged.

Sometimes opportunities present themselves situationally, while others require a concerted effort on your part. Additionally, as you will see, the timing of your message may impact how it's received.

In this chapter, we introduce you to concepts like making strong connections, being true to yourself (i.e., authenticity), and finding the right cultural fit. Not every culture fits with every communication style, and that's okay. What's important is that you find the best fit that allows you to be authentic. We'll share vignettes and coaching tips and provide you with the essential skills required to help you enhance this pathway.

How to Be Proactive

Be inquisitive. Be a seeker of information. Be open to feedback. And have a learning mind-set.

To be proactive means that you need to be observant and learn from experiences, your own and others'. You should learn from both successes and mistakes. Continue to refine your learning mind-set over time so that you can learn more quickly with each passing experience. This skill allows you to pivot, modify, and eventually, to anticipate.

The more you can learn about your organization and your associates, the more informed you will be about what is important. Being proactive will potentially allow you to learn about issues before they become issues. You may also identify ways to make processes more efficient and products more effective.

Begin by knowing your audience. We have previously discussed the importance of asking the right questions. When you are being proactive in your communication, there is a fine balance between being inquisitive and curious versus being overbearing. Here, as you are getting to know your audience, we reinforce that it's not just what you ask, but *how*. Don't be antagonistic and confrontational in your approach. Be genuinely curious. For example, you may simply say "Help me understand" whatever the topic is. And then your job is to actively listen.

Sometimes you have the luxury of tailoring all aspects of a message, and other times you may need to simply deliver a message. Either approach takes time, thought, and planning. Being engaged with your communication is an excellent opportunity to develop your ability to ask questions. Here are some sample questions to consider asking about your audience:

- Who are they?
- What do they want or need to know?
- What are their communication preferences?

Scene #1

Eileen was a long-tenured associate who recently got promoted into her first leadership role. She had two direct reports, each of whom had two direct reports of their own. She wanted to establish good communication processes from the start, so she added a one-on-one weekly meeting with each of her direct reports. She set up the same weekly cadence of meeting with her boss as well. This ensured she had clear direction and support from her boss, and it allowed her to learn about any roadblocks her team leaders may encounter.

About a month into her new role, she had an idea to add a monthly all-team meeting and quarterly skip-level meetings. A skip-level meeting is one in which a manager meets separately with the associates of her direct reports. To ensure there were no surprises, Eileen let her direct reports know she would be meeting with their associates, and these meetings allowed her to meet one-on-one with her entire team. Her proactive approach proved to be a success. She had some of the highest associate satisfaction scores in the organization, and she routinely anticipated issues before they became issues.

COACHING TIP: Schedule a regular cadence of status update meetings with key stakeholders.

When you are being proactive with your communication, timing matters. *When* is just as important as what and how. Your message should not be about an information dump as soon as your associates walk into the office. Nor is it about checking the box that indicates you shared the information. Being proactive requires thought, planning, and timing.

Proactive and *spontaneous* do not mean the same thing. Even the savviest communicators plan their message in advance. They may look as though their message is natural or spontaneous, but in almost every instance we're familiar with, those messages were planned. There is an art to crafting and delivering a message. That art strongly considers the recipients.

COACHING TIP: When it comes to conveying a message, especially an important one, don't wing it.

In many instances, you may not have 100 percent of the information required to convey a message. Do you have *enough* information to address the audience's needs and questions? Are you prepared to give the message? And, not to be overlooked—is the audience ready to receive it?

Learn how to read the room. Is the person/people you're talking to ready to hear the message? Or are you running down a checklist of topics you need to check off your list and overwhelming the recipient? You will probably feel great at the end of the conversation because you just unloaded a lot of topics, or one important one. Unfortunately, your message may be lost due to timing. There is a simple way to mitigate this as you are running down your list of topics. Check your audience's reaction: Are they receiving it, or do they have blank expressions, their eyes glazed over?

Here are some other ways to read the room and see whether your message is being received. Look for nonverbal cues as to whether your messages are being received by the audience. Head nods are good indicators. Side conversations, looking at their phones, staring out the window, or wrinkled brows are signs that your message may not be getting through.

When you are communicating to a larger group, there may not be the opportunity for immediate back-and-forth dialogue. Your delivery of the message may be one-way, from you to them. Even in those instances, though, we would encourage you to read the room and be aware of the signals the audience is giving off.

Being proactive sometimes means shifting your direction. If it appears that people are shutting down, perhaps you've gone on too long or your message is simply not resonating. It's not okay to keep going if your message is not getting through. It is okay to pause and come back to the group using a different strategy to ensure your message is received. This may require a different time, format, or even a different person to deliver the message.

COACHING TIP: Do not ignore nonverbal signals from any audience you are delivering a message to. They may not be saying anything, but they are giving you valuable feedback all the same.

How to Be Engaged

There are two primary opportunities for you to be engaged with your communication: first, in the moment; and second, by getting to know the people you work with.

Situational and in-the-moment opportunities to be engaged means listening, being present, focusing, and eliminating distractions. This applies to both verbal and nonverbal communication. Have you ever been part of a conversation where the other person is constantly glancing down at their phone? How does that make you feel? It's safe to say that the person glancing often at their phone is not focused or engaged in the conversation.

Scene #2

At a weekly team business meeting, Teddy checks his phone often, about every one to two minutes. Sometimes he looks to see if a new message has come in, while other times he quickly responds to a message. It's clear that Teddy is not listening to anything being said in the meeting, and what's more, his behavior has become a distraction to the others in the meeting. At the end of the session, Teddy is the first to get up and leave, all the while staring at his phone.

What impact do you think Teddy's behavior has on his credibility? What messages do you think Teddy's behavior sends to those present? Whether as Teddy's boss or a peer, what advice would you give him?

The other way to engage with your communication is to get to know the people you work with. Management by walking around. Get to know your associates and colleagues. Ask questions. Listen. Engage. You don't even have to have a specific topic to discuss.

COACHING TIP: We highly recommend "management by walking around" as an approach to improve proactive communication. However, don't be a leader that only walks around at 4:00 p.m. on a Friday afternoon. This presents a "gotcha" approach rather than a genuine interest in your associates.

It's amazing what you can learn by asking someone how everything is going or how their weekend was. The personal conversations help to establish the trust and credibility necessary to pave the way for work-related conversations and requests—especially when those requests are challenging.

COACHING TIP: When giving feedback, first ask "Are you open to some feedback?" It puts people in a ready state.

Why Be Proactive and Engaged?

Being proactive and engaged with your communication is a very powerful leadership tool to have at your disposal. And the great news is that you are in control of it. You get to choose the level of proactivity and engagement you exhibit.

On an individual level, being proactive and engaged helps to build strong relationships. Questioning shows genuine interest. Listening builds trust and credibility. Together, they demonstrate empathy, authenticity, and transparency.

From a process standpoint, it is an efficient form of communication that allows you to control and prioritize what is communicated, when, how, and to whom. It allows you to control the message.

This is particularly important during times of uncertainty because, in the absence of communication and information from leadership, associates tend to get bits and pieces of information from which they create their own story. Or they may share their opinions as facts. In either case, it is highly likely that the information conveyed is not accurate, nor is it the information you would want communicated.

That's how rumors get started and inaccurate information gets spread. In these instances, your role shifts from offense to defense. You must explain away all the inaccurate information before you can even get to the accurate messages. Not only can this cause delays, but associates can become overwhelmed trying to make sense of the various mixed messages. You risk your message being lost or not believed. It can also be lost if there is any history whatsoever with inaccuracies in the past. The seed of doubt will have been planted, and once again, you risk your message being lost.

Implications of Your Communication

Words are powerful. They drive action. And some of these actions may have unanticipated consequences of shifting resources away from other priorities. The next two vignettes will show you how a leader can unintentionally shift strategies and resources with just a few words.

Scene #3

Deborah was the newly appointed director of a highly regarded international association. The association had over six hundred associates and several successful global initiatives under way. Outside of work, Deborah loved hiking. In some of her earliest speeches as the new director, she would often reference some of her hiking experiences. She would even use hiking as a metaphor for the rewarding work that lay ahead for her association. The associates connected with her message.

However, it wasn't long before everything around the office took on a hiking theme. Associates at all levels and departments looked for ways to shift some of their strategy to fit a more hiking-centric focus, even at the risk of some of the currently prioritized successful global initiatives. It was simply a case of misreading her messages. Deborah had never intended this shift in some strategies and resource allocations, so she quickly pulled her leadership team together and requested that the association return to its original focus that had been established around the global initiatives.

Scene #4

Alberto was the executive vice president of his division. He spent a significant portion of his week reviewing reports and providing updates to his peers. Alberto relied heavily on data and analytics. He would occasionally wonder aloud about various business topics. At a recent monthly meeting with his team leaders, he casually said, "I wonder how many months over the last ten years productivity scores were above 80 percent." Although it was simply an offhand remark, his leaders took it as a request from him. Alberto did not intend for them to set out on a new project to find the answer to this, but because of the power of words and who they came from—in this case, from a senior executive—that's exactly what happened.

The problem with Alberto's comment was that their organization had only started tracking productivity scores three months ago. His leaders did not want to disappoint him, so after the meeting they got together and identified three team members to get the answer to Alberto's question. Each associate stopped what they were doing to focus exclusively on that task. Because it was a manual task covering ten years and required that information be pulled from multiple sources in order to validate it, Alberto's casual comment became a task that soon turned into a project.

After almost two weeks, the three associates provided a report. Alberto was both surprised and pleased, even though he'd long since forgotten that he had wondered aloud about it. He added it to a stack of reports, and the associates' findings got a brief mention at the next executive meeting. Had Alberto known the level of effort required to obtain this data, he never would have supported the work. He never thought to ask, and no one ever thought to seek clarity. Unfortunately, this was one of many instances where Alberto's wondering aloud became a project for someone else.

Both vignettes show how powerful words can be. Implications stem not only from what is said, but who says it. In both instances, being proactive without seeking clarity of expectations proved detrimental. As you can see, words have both intended and unintended consequences. They can be quite costly in terms of time and resources. The message here is not to start ignoring your leaders. That would be bad. The message is to seek clarity, manage expectations, and have candid conversations about intentions and level of effort.

Words can also have an emotional impact as well. Have you ever said something that you wish you hadn't? What happens when you say something and come to regret it? Being proactive sometimes means making amends when necessary.

You may have to troubleshoot following a previous communication, whether it was an honest mistake of inaccurate information, or information changed, or perhaps you said something angrily. This is not about placing blame; it's about getting the message right.

In the services industry, there are studies that suggest if a customer experiences something negative and that problem gets resolved, the person will rate that experience higher than if they had experienced no problems, or if they had a problem that wasn't resolved. In some instances, this may apply to communication as well. If you recognize and take responsibility for a misstep, associates may be more likely to respect you and view you as credible than if you ignore or try to spin it.

Ignoring messages that you wish you hadn't communicated does not make them go away. It often compounds the issue. Depending on the issue, of course, you may have the opportunity to strengthen your credibility based upon how you handle it.

We have previously stated that communication is irreversible, and unfortunately that is true. So, whether you say something, write something, or do something that you regret, make no mistake—it's out there. This is why we have advised previously to avoid knee-jerk communications and to take some extra time to consider the implications of your message.

This sounds good on paper, but occasionally communication missteps do happen. We get it. When that happens, there is a different type of being proactive. In those instances, you must own it. You may have to apologize for it. And you will likely have to reposition around it.

Depending on how many people you've isolated with a particular message, you should seek input on how the original message landed with the audience and the impact it had. As you work on any follow-up communication, you should run the message by someone you know well and trust, ideally someone who was part of your original message and understands the situation. That feedback will be invaluable as you are proactive in your cleanup.

COACHING TIP: If you write, say, or do something that you regret, own up to it quickly and apologize to those impacted.

This is like your own personal crisis communication, which is a whole other perspective on being proactive; although we hope you don't encounter it often, if you do, your job is to do damage control. And we do not recommend making excuses, shifting blame, or spinning it. Those approaches may appear at times to work on the surface, but people are not fools. More often than not, they see through the spin and excuses. The longer you pursue that strategy, the more damage to your credibility and clout. In fact, we have seen multiple occasions where taking that type of approach only serves to exacerbate the problem and worsen the overall impact.

On the other hand, we have seen the more successful approach, and more positive outcomes, when the messenger takes responsibility for their message. Further, being proactive also demonstrates a higher level of customer service.

COACHING TIP: If you do not know something, it is better to say "I don't know" or "Let me get back to you" than to make something up on the spot.

Proactive Communication, Culture, Authenticity, and Fit

Whether you are supportive of proactive communication or not, as a leader, you are building a culture. It becomes a question of whether you are building the culture you want.

When you encourage proactive communication among your associates, you encourage them to raise issues and opportunities. Their input will help you to become more proactive. It becomes a virtuous cycle.

Associates working day to day with various aspects tend to know what is working well and what isn't, as well as where potential issues and opportunities exist. When you actively seek out their input, you are building a culture of proactive communication. You may not be able to pursue every single issue or opportunity raised, but you will gain greater insight into the business.

It's the fine line between authenticity and corporate culture. Yes, we always encourage you to be yourself. Being authentic still requires you to be situationally appropriate. After all, you are part of a professional organization. There is a time and place to share your non-work-related views. Also, keep in mind that being your unfiltered, authentic self may have ramifications.

Just as you may determine you don't align with the views of others within the organization, the organization can decide you don't fit. It is difficult for us to coach or guide you on subjective, judgment, and often situation-specific events. However, our simple guidance is to be culturally aware of your organization's beliefs, values, and practices. You should not feel pressure to conform to them, just as you should not expect their values to conform to yours. For that reason, find the organization that best fits with your values and beliefs and allows you to be your authentic self.

Essential Skills for Being Proactive and Engaged with Your Communication

The following skills and traits lend themselves to proactive and engaged communication:

- *Project management*, which is also mentioned in Pathway #1, requires the application of processes of knowledge, skills, tools, and techniques to deliver a valuable outcome upon established objectives. The approaches used are time- and resource-bound.
- *Active listening* involves being fully aware of what is being said by listening and responding to a person, either verbally or nonverbally. It improves and helps clarify mutual understanding of a topic or issue.
- *Empathy* refers to one's ability to recognize and share the feelings of another as a way of acknowledging, understanding, and appreciating what they are experiencing.
- *Emotional intelligence* is the ability to perceive, interpret, and manage emotions to communicate with and relate to others constructively. It is referred to as EQ (versus IQ) and serves to foster relationships.
- *Authenticity* refers to being confident in who you are, including your values, personality, beliefs, and principles. You do not compromise your point of view for the comfort of others.
- *Presentation skills* include the ability to deliver compelling, engaging, and informative presentations in a clear, concise, and effective manner so that your key messages are understood and acted upon appropriately.
- *Executive presence* is based upon your ability to inspire confidence among your associates, peers, and more senior leaders. It is based upon capability, reliability, and results. This often stems from experience, knowledge, reputation, and ultimately trustworthiness.
- *Giving feedback* requires providing helpful input and responses to someone's work. Feedback can be positive, negative, or neutral, but should always be constructive, and as objective and specific as possible.
- *Focus* is a thinking skill that allows us to pay attention in order to complete a task. It involves a simple decision on where you place your attention, and it can be learned through deliberate practice.

- *Conflict management* is the process of identifying and managing interpersonal issues fairly and effectively. The issues in question often stem from differing opinions, interpretations, needs, objectives, or agendas. Approaches include collaborating, competing, avoiding, accommodating, or compromising.

Summary of Coaching Tips

- Get to know your associates and colleagues on both a work and a personal level. This will help you to build trust, make connections, understand issues and priorities, and speak the same language.
- Schedule a regular cadence of status-update meetings with key stakeholders.
- When it comes to conveying a message, especially an important one, don't wing it.
- Do not ignore nonverbal signals from any audience to whom you are delivering a message. They may not be saying anything, but they are giving you valuable feedback all the same.
- We highly recommend "management by walking around" as an approach to proactive communication. However, don't be a leader that walks around only at 4:00 p.m. on a Friday afternoon. That presents a "gotcha" approach rather than a genuine interest in your associates.
- When giving feedback, ask "Are you open to some feedback?" It puts people in a ready state.
- If you write, say, or do something that you regret, own up to it quickly and apologize to those impacted.
- If you do not know something, it is better to say "I don't know" or "Let me get back to you" than to make something up on the spot.

Summary of Pathway #2

This pathway is about you taking initiative and anticipating your audiences' needs for information. It requires that you use a proactive approach to your communication as a management tool to achieve business efficiencies. Doing so allows you to make stronger connections with your peers, colleagues, associates, boss, and other senior leaders.

Proactive communication allows you to manage the message. However, you must know what message your audience wants, needs, or expects. Honesty and authenticity are paramount.

Walk around the office. Have an open door, but don't wait for associates to come to you. Check in with your associates. Engage with them. Get to know them on a personal and professional level. This level of engagement will allow you to build strong connections with them. It builds trust and rapport. Getting to know your associates will help you understand what's important to them, so that when you are formulating messages, you can speak their language.

We have provided you with the ten essential skills to help you become more proactive and engaged. Which are the select few that resonate with you as an opportunity for you? How can you incorporate them into your development plan and day-to-day routines?

Moving you along. Excellent work. Since you have gotten this far, we assume that you have kept the momentum going along the pathways. We hope that you've been able to refine your personal improvement plan along the way and perhaps even put some of the coaching tips into practice.

The next chapter provides guidance around driving business results and understanding what matters to your various audiences. Results are important, but only provide a partial picture of credibility. There's a natural connection between business results and how you tell the story of those results.

We place great emphasis on developing your ability to tell the story of results in a language that people care about and understand. As you will see, sometimes that story may be your own, your team's, or your organization's.

Additional Resources

- *Everyone Communicates, Few Connect: What the Most Effective People Do Differently* by John C. Maxwell (Nashville, TN: Thomas Nelson Publishing, 2010).
- *Am I Asking the Right Questions?: How to Focus on What Matters Most* by Michael McGaulley, JD (independently published, December 17, 2020).
- *Invisible Solutions: 25 Lenses That Reframe and Help Solve Difficult Business Problems* by Stephen M. Shapiro (Herndon, VA: Amplify Publishing, 2020).
- *Start with Why: How Great Leaders Inspire Everyone to Take Action* by Simon Sinek (Westminster, London: Portfolio, reprint edition, 2011).
- *The Power of Listening: How to Improve Relationships by Becoming an Active Listener* by Damian Blair (independently published, May 13, 2021).

Pathway #3

Drive meaningful business results—and how to tell the story

Strive not to be a success, but rather to be of value.
—ALBERT EINSTEIN

Being of value means matching and applying your capabilities and passions with the needs of the business. Where can you be of greatest value for your company? Your team? Take a few minutes to think about that and jot down your answer below:

____

____

Being of value in a business environment means you are contributing to results that matter. In fact, this is so important that driving business results is a core competency in many organizations. To be effective requires priority setting, perseverance, communication, adaptability, negotiation, and maybe even conflict management, to name a few specific skills.

Results speak volumes. What was the significance of the results? How did you or others achieve them? What was your role?

We would argue that results are the language of business. Individually, they say a lot about you as an associate, how connected you are to the business, and your ability to apply those essential skills—leveraging resources, working with others, overcoming obstacles, and helping your company.

Those who deliver results well and do it repeatedly develop a positive reputation. They strengthen their credibility which can in turn fuel future results. You may hear things like, "There goes Tom. He sure did some amazing work on that last project." Or "Stephanie is amazing to work with . . . and she always exceeds her targets."

Depending on the results, how you get them, and how you tell the story of those results, it can become a virtuous or vicious cycle. Never overlook the *how*. Business results are great, but it is important to know which results matter most and how to get them. Therein lies the value associated with your contribution. What are your contributions and results saying about you? In short, what is your story?

Expectations for results may be explicitly stated or more implicitly understood. Therefore, you must ensure clarity when it comes to what constitutes an important result. That's right—just ask.

COACHING TIP: Find out today from your boss what the three most meaningful results you could deliver are. Ensure that you are managing your calendar and work activities around those priorities.

Make no mistake: Results matter. They are a way to communicate contribution, value, and progress—progress from the past, from established goals, or progress relative to competitors. Results help to answer the question "Are we on the right track?"

Achieving results is not a solo endeavor. It may feel like it under some circumstances, but it's a team effort that requires strong connections and mutual understanding. The best leaders know how to motivate and inspire others. They communicate a compelling vision, connect with people, align them on essential priorities and initiatives, remove obstacles, hold them accountable to expectations, give credit, and celebrate their collective successes. For the sake of your credibility, it is important that results are attributed fairly and accurately.

Scene #1

Jordan was an established leader who had big career aspirations. She was one of nine mid-level leaders on a ninety-person professional services team. An important focus for the team was business development, and associates were recognized for generating revenue. Associates that generated significant revenue or developed it consistently over time were promoted.

Jordan and her peer Phil were nearing the end of a project. While at a closing meeting with the client, they proposed some significant follow-on work. The work would entail six consultants working full-time for nearly a year to develop additional process improvements and ensure successful implementation. The project was proposed at $1.5 million, and the client accepted. This was a big deal. Jordan finalized the contractual paperwork.

At the next professional services team meeting, it became apparent during the update that Jordan had put her name down as the sole winner of the contract. Phil's name was not included on the win. Everyone on the team knew that Jordan and Phil had both worked on that project, so there were many side whispers when the report was projected on the screen.

What do you think happened to Jordan's credibility following that meeting? What advice would you have for Jordan? For Phil?

COACHING TIP: Always give credit for business results where credit is due. When it comes to giving credit, always tell the whole story.

Once results are achieved, why should you have to review the story? Results speak for themselves, right? Don't count on it. As you will see, results can be misinterpreted. To avoid this, you must own the narrative associated with any results you are connected to. We'll show you why that's important and how to do so in this chapter.

The Gist

Whether you are an emerging or current leader, it should be clear by now that you must achieve business results. Without clear, demonstrable results that are agreed upon with your boss, you can't be successful at your company. It's also likely that your company won't be very successful either if they employ people who don't deliver results.

But which results? How do you know where to focus your efforts for the most meaningful results?

The value of MBLs. This chapter will help to provide you with the fluency required to speak multiple business languages. Note that we did not say *multiple languages.* Fluency in *multiple business languages* requires you to know your stakeholders, what's important to them, and how to best connect with them.

This pathway focuses on where you should start. We highlight the importance of knowing your business as a foundation for business results, how to determine what constitutes meaningful results, and the actions you can take to drive results.

As we noted in the introduction to this chapter, results alone are not enough. How you go about achieving them also matters. Do you work with integrity, fairness, and collaboration? Or are you a lone wolf?

You will also need to tell the whole story of the results. Doing this well requires that you know the business and what information your various stakeholders (i.e., audiences) want and how they want to receive it. There can be a fine balance between being humble and deferential and being misguided and overbearing.

If you are someone who believes the results should speak for themselves, fair warning here that you are leaving the message open to misinterpretation. If you are involved in achieving results, you are also responsible for communicating about them.

Know your business. The more you know, the better informed you will be. Leverage that knowledge along with the many communication techniques we've discussed in our book to refine your clarity and gain credibility. Here's where you should start to really know your business:

- Know your company's strategy.
- Ensure you understand who your stakeholders are. Who are the people who have the greatest interest in the results? And what is it they care most about?
- Identify who your company's competitors are and how they are similar and different from your company.
- Know your company's history, strategy, goals, and key performance indicators.
- Have a clear understanding of the products and services your company provides.
- Know how and where to obtain essential data and reports.
- Understand what differentiates your company from others.
- Know how your company is funded or makes money.

Armed with this knowledge, you will have a strong foundation to better understand what constitutes meaningful results at your company. Additionally, knowing these areas facilitates the discussion about how you're doing as a company, as well as what, if anything, needs to change.

COACHING TIP: Get a PhD in your company (and once you do, teach others).

Since businesses are dynamic, knowing your business is not a one-time activity. You need to constantly listen and learn what is important. Your operating environment shifts. New information becomes available. And if you rely on what you knew about your business two years ago (or even one), you may miss the mark.

Knowing your business also requires that you know what external environmental forces can affect it, both positively and negatively. For example, is there a new regulation, technology, or political change that impacts your business? No one can predict the future, but the more you know and understand your business and the surrounding environment, the more you will be able to anticipate changes.

You will become a more strategic thinker. This knowledge will help contribute to the discussion surrounding the direction of your company in more meaningful ways. Building this skill can positively influence your ability to think critically and strengthen your credibility.

What Constitutes Meaningful Business Results

There are two main points in this section. First, meaningful business results vary by organization, department, functional area, and even stage in your career. Second, context matters.

Each program, project, stakeholder, and department may have more refined definitions of what constitutes *meaningful results*. For example, you may find that the head of the sales department views a certain result as meaningful whereas the head of human resources has a different view. Neither is necessarily wrong. It is up to you to understand the variations so you can better connect with the various stakeholders. We're confident that over time you will develop fluency in the language of meaningful results for your department, but this cross-department knowledge will help you speak *their* language.

Early on in a career, the focus on results is typically very narrow. For example, junior-level associates may be responsible for a specific program, or even more narrowly, some aspect of an existing program.

COACHING TIP: As an individual contributing employee or manager, it is important that you seek clarity to determine what constitutes meaningful results. If you are a leader, it is your job to provide that clarity.

As you take on more leadership responsibilities, expectations will grow as well. Results may include broad aspects, such as program execution and maintenance, process improvements, participation, satisfaction, or budgetary achievements. Additionally, a more-senior-level associate may have multiple aspects of the program they need to deliver on, or even multiple processes or programs.

As the scope of your responsibilities changes, so too do the expectations for delivering results. You will also need to coach and develop those you lead, and as a result, you will have some level of responsibility for their results. To achieve this optimally, you will need to maintain some level of engagement and retention among your team.

There are several ways that, as a leader, you can help drive engagement and ultimately results. Some ways are directly related to communication, while others are more indirect. On the direct side, providing clear expectations and timely, specific feedback are at the top of the list. On the indirect side, delegation and task significance both help to drive engagement. Clarity is critical to both engagement drivers.

Delegation is when you assign one of your associates a task, such as gathering data, writing a report, or any of a number of other assignments. Task significance is connected to helping associates find meaning and purpose in their work. As a leader, it is important that you help your associates understand where the work they do fits into the bigger picture.

There is an art associated with delegation—an art that relies significantly on communication. First, you should not simply delegate the unattractive, tedious tasks. When delegating, communicate expectations clearly.

When it comes to task significance, there is an additional benefit for you in providing clarity around the importance of the work they're doing. Helping associates understand how they are making a difference and adding value helps them to find purpose and meaning in their work. Remember that work you did at the beginning of this pathway around identifying your value and contribution? Now you are passing this along to those you lead.

Our second point around what constitutes meaningful results is the importance of *context*. Results by themselves seldom mean as much as when they are compared to something else, such as past performance or competitors' performance. Consider these questions: How is your company doing? Relative to what? Goals? Performance over the last year, last quarter, or some other time frame? Performance of your competitors? Something else?

Putting this section's knowledge all together, from careers and departments to context and relativism, your job as a leader is about connecting the dots. In other words, you must put the various pieces of information together and communicate how they fit together. You need to understand the business and what's important in order to help others do so.

COACHING TIP: As a leader, communicate how various pieces of information fit together and how they contribute to overall business results.

Up until this point, we have taken the position that business results are positive. After all, the section is focused on what constitutes meaningful results that are positive in nature. However, before we move on to the next section, we want to recognize that not all business results are meaningful or positive. In those instances, it's important that you raise any potentially problematic issues before they become bigger issues. Avoiding the issue because it is bad news or uncomfortable to talk about will not make it any easier over time. This falls under the category of being proactive.

How to Drive Business Results

Results come from taking action that leads to achieving or exceeding goals. This section highlights the key actions and attributes to consider. We also touch on the most common roadblocks to achieving results.

Three key actions help you drive results:

- establishing and aligning on expectations;
- providing status updates; and
- ensuring accountability.

All three rely heavily on you communicating with clarity.

First, discussions involving *establishing and aligning on expectations* should focus on project goals, objectives, resources, timelines, and any other expectations. In other words, how will the work be accomplished? When? And what will the results be? Keep in mind that there are often multiple stakeholders, so there may also be dialogue where multiple parties contribute to the expectations.

COACHING TIP: When setting personal or project goals, focus on the goals and supporting actions that lead to improvements in performance and processes.

"Stretch goals" are those that expand beyond your current skill set and can lead to the best results. But are the expectations realistic? Are the proper resources available?

There is no room to assume what the expectations are. Ask. Discuss. Clarify. Align. It is important that you are on the same page as those who are expecting results, such as your boss or other stakeholders, or else your project—and dare we say, your reputation—could be at risk. Getting the expectations wrong or misaligned can have significant implications for a wide range of outcomes, including allocation of resources, overall project success, and your personal reputation.

Second, *provide periodic progress updates*. As a leader, it is imperative that you are proactive not only in setting expectations but keeping the appropriate stakeholders informed on the progress.

Agree on a progress update schedule with your stakeholders in advance. What do *they* need to know? How often do *they* want updates? Do *they* prefer a written update or to meet in person? (Notice the emphasis on *they*.)

Some projects may require more frequent updates or meetings that include multiple stakeholders. Topics to consider at progress update meetings include progress relative to timeline, recent accomplishments, what's working well, resource- or budget-related updates, obstacles, risks, and risk mitigation ideas, to name a few.

COACHING TIP: Establish frequent opportunities to communicate progress updates. In the event progress is off expectations, this allows for course corrections in real time versus after the fact.

Third, *ensure accountability*. This extends to you, your team, and anyone else involved in pursuing results. If progress is not going as planned, speak up. By being proactive, you can more easily course-correct, which will save time, money, and potential frustration. If you continue to let progress go off course, the risk and impact becomes exponentially worse. It's a rare occasion when ignoring an issue allows it to resolve itself.

With clear expectations established and agreed upon, it is easier to have productive conversations if progress goes astray. Such conversations could go something like this: "A few months ago, we all agreed that expectations were *X*. We're falling short of those expectations. What are some of the reasons? What do you need to get us back on track? How can I help?" A discussion like this shows a true collaborative approach to business results. It takes a servant leadership approach with an emphasis on business results.

Accountability does not just mean coming down on people when expectations are off. By recognizing people when expectations are being exceeded, you will motivate, inspire, and ultimately build credibility.

Achieving incremental wins can be easily overlooked. Tracking progress allows you to manage stakeholder expectations as well as to showcase and celebrate wins. That is beneficial to stakeholders and can be a source of motivation and inspiration to the team.

Tracking progress requires intent and planning. You need to have a plan on what to keep track of and how to do so. You also need to differentiate between the mundane and the significant. Recognize the difference between a task and an outcome.

COACHING TIP: Keep track of your performance, both project-specific and major personal accomplishments throughout the year. The latter will provide a reminder for end-of-year and ongoing performance reviews.

Scene #2

Jill was a highly regarded project manager. She was known for delivering projects on time, on budget, and often exceeding performance expectations. Prior to every project, she met with all the key stakeholders individually and then as a full group. She was proactive, and she kept people informed.

She clarified expectations around roles, timelines, goals, and even their preferences for status updates, including frequency, what to include, and how to deliver the updates. Jill often relied on her extensive experience to further refine their expectations, so the stakeholders' expectations were exceeded. She celebrated the team wins with the team as well as with the broader audience of stakeholders, which kept her team engaged. On the occasions where a project encountered a roadblock or setback, she was quick to alert her stakeholders about what had happened and what she and the team were doing to get the project back on track.

What are the best practices that Jill utilized in her approach? Can you think of anything she could do differently, or better? Which are the practices from above that you utilize or could utilize in your approach?

As you read Jill's story, it may appear to come off as being so natural to her. Driving business results may come easier to some people than to others. The four attributes that lend themselves to driving results are determination, persistence, inclusiveness, and resourcefulness.

Determination is demonstrated by your commitment to meeting or exceeding goals. It involves having confidence in your decisions. *Persistence* is all about having the drive to overcome obstacles and not letting anything get in your—or your team's—way when working to achieve the established goals. *Inclusiveness* ensures that you work well with others. You get the right people involved at the right time. And *resourcefulness* ties it all together to ensure that you and your team find quick and novel ways to overcome obstacles, solve problems, and achieve results.

Telling the Story

You may have heard this philosophical pondering before: If a tree falls in the forest and no one is there, does it make a sound? Similarly in business, if results are achieved, and no one knows about them, do they matter?

Sometimes it may appear that business results speak for themselves. However, to ensure your credibility—and ultimately, your clout—do not count on that being the case. You've already learned in Pathway #1 about the importance of being proactive with your communication. It is up to you to manage the narrative associated with your business results. Otherwise, you risk stakeholders missing the essential elements of the story.

Why spend any energy on telling the story? Stories are memorable and they provide a deeper level of understanding than just a snapshot, chart, or graph. They provide a learning tool within your organization, and they help to reinforce the company culture. Stories allow you to recognize the team for their work, which can go a long way toward future contributions. They also help build or reinforce your trust and credibility.

Storytelling requires a framework. Here are some simple questions for you to consider that will provide a starting framework for how you can tell the story of business results.

- What was done?
- Who was involved?
- What obstacles were overcome?
- How are these results relative to our past? The past could include the last quarter, or it could consider the last year, or the last five or ten years. It's up to you to determine the appropriate contextual time frame.
- How are these results relative to our competitors' results?

There are several dos and don'ts associated with storytelling. We hope they mostly go without saying, but just in case, we're going to share them below for your quick reference:

- **Don't** let the story of business results that you are associated with speak for themselves. Provide context.
- **Don't** fictionalize the story. Never fabricate or exaggerate the story associated with business results.
- **Don't** alter any of the facts or data to reflect a story you wish were true. It is difficult for associates to recover from these types of missteps.
- **Don't** give or take credit inappropriately.
- **Do** convey the story of the results in a way that your audience will understand. There is no need to try to show off your analytical skills if your message is going to be lost.
- **Do** put yourself in the audience's shoes. This will allow you to be proactive in your storytelling.
- **Do** get to the bottom line up front.
- **Do** anticipate questions. You will need to know your story well, and where you don't know it well, don't try to fake it. Prepare ahead of time by listing the likely questions and the best answers.

A word of caution when telling the story of business results that you are connected with: Beware of success fatigue. We have worked with some very good storytellers, people who promoted themselves or their team quite well. But one of the unintended consequences of doing too much storytelling is that some peers may get fatigued by your stories. Unfortunately, we have seen this take a negative turn, where others may try to detract from the story or poke holes in some of the results. Similarly, we have seen some tensions rise when some teams excel at telling their stories while others do not.

Essential Skills to Drive Meaningful Results and Tell the Story

Driving meaningful business results means that you know how to use the tools and resources at your disposal to get work done. This applies to entry-level associates all the way up to the president of the company. At every level of your company, there are several essential skills that will help you to utilize results as a communication vehicle. Developing these skills will help you know the message you're sending, why it's important, and how to effectively communicate it.

- *Analytical skills* are those that allow you to gather, display, and integrate data. These skills allow you to see patterns, derive reasons, draw conclusions, and find solutions that enhance results.
- *Creativity* brings together critical thinking, problem-solving, and communication to be able to think about something in an original way.
- *Storytelling* allows you to capture your audience's attention, engage them, and convey essential information in a compelling and memorable way.
- *Public speaking skills* are those that allow you to sustain a positive presence, connect with your audience, and communicate clearly to deliver your ideas.
- *Motivational skills* are an interpersonal skill that draws on empathy, goal setting, communication, and feedback to allow you to obtain a desired behavior, outcome, or response from another.

Summary of Coaching Tips

- Find out today from your boss the three most meaningful results you could deliver. Ensure that you are managing your calendar and work activities around those priorities.
- Always give credit for business results where credit is due. When it comes to giving credit, always tell the whole story.
- Get a PhD in your company (and once you do, teach others).
- As an individual contributing employee or manager, it is important that you seek clarity to determine what constitutes meaningful results. If you are a leader, it is your job to provide that clarity.
- As a leader, communicate how various pieces of information fit together and how they contribute to business results.
- When setting personal or project goals, focus on the goals and supporting actions that lead to improvements in performance and processes.
- Establish frequent opportunities to communicate progress updates. In the event progress is off expectations, this allows course corrections in real time versus after the fact.
- Keep track of your performance, both project-specific and major personal accomplishments throughout the year. The latter will provide a reminder for end-of-year and ongoing performance reviews.

Summary of Pathway #3

Driving meaningful business results begins with knowing your company. Understand the business priorities. Know your department's and your company's key performance indicators (KPIs). Align on what success looks like. Goal clarity is essential. It is up to you to know what constitutes meaningful results in your company, for your boss, and for a particular project.

Often, business success is highly quantitative. For example, productivity was increased by *X* percent. Or we realized *X* in cost savings or ROI. However, do not discount qualitative achievements.

The most meaningful results consider relativism and making connections with various related data. Are the results strong *relative* to past performance, competitors, or established goals? When you relate the business results data to something important, you help answer the question of "So what?"

Business results on their own *may* be powerful. Or just as easily, they may not. You need to help people understand what is important, and why. You do this by telling the story associated with the results.

You will likely know the messages you want to convey, but you must also know what your audience wants to hear. Who are your stakeholders, and what is important to them? It is up to you to own the narrative associated with any business results you achieve.

There is a risk of not getting this right. If what you deem as meaningful is not viewed that way by others, your credibility suffers. You appear disconnected.

A more positive way to think about this is that your clout depends on your ability to consistently achieve meaningful business results. However, your credibility will be tied directly to how you go about achieving and communicating them. Transparency, integrity, and authenticity win out here and will set you up for the best success.

Moving you along. Our attention in the next chapter is on you and how you can strengthen your influence. We are confident that if you have been working to avoid the pitfalls and making progress along the previous pathways, strengthening your influence will come a bit easier. You will have laid the foundation, modified some of your communication practices, and let your actions speak for you in many instances.

We will warn you, however, that if you have not fully embraced our other lessons, this next pathway will not come easy. In fact, you will *not* have established a strong foundation. You will *not* have cemented your credibility. Your influence will be shaky at best. So please, do not take shortcuts and circumvent the pathways that came before. They are there to help set you up for long-term success.

As you will see in the next chapter, your influence is built upon who you are as an associate and ultimately a leader. It will be based upon your character, strength of your relationships, authenticity, and your experience.

Rest assured, though, that you are not alone in strengthening your influence. Like all aspects of communication, it is a two-way street. Your peers and colleagues play a role. In fact, as you will see with the next pathway, sometimes they play a more critical role than you can even imagine. And if you can understand this important role and how to leverage it, you can further strengthen your influence.

Have we piqued your curiosity? You'll want to read on.

Additional Resources

- *Start with Why: How Great Leaders Inspire Everyone to Take Action* by Simon Sinek (Westminster, London: Portfolio, reprint edition, 2011).
- *How to Develop Self-Confidence and Influence People by Public Speaking* by Dale Carnegie (New York: Gallery Books, reissue edition, 2017).
- *The Power of Storytelling: The Art of Influential Communication* by Ty Bennett (Lehi, UT: Verbal Technology, Inc., 2013).
- *Creativity: Flow and the Psychology of Discovery and Invention* by Mihaly Csikszentmihalyi (New York: Harper Perennial, reprint edition, 2013).

Pathway #4

Strengthen Your Credibility and Influence

All leadership is influence.

—AMERICAN AUTHOR AND ORATOR JOHN C. MAXWELL

Let's connect the key concepts we've put forward throughout the book. You've put the foundation in place. You know how to avoid communication pitfalls. And you've begun to move along the pathways. But why? To what end?

Yes, clarity is one piece of the puzzle. We should all strive at a minimum to communicate clearly. Clarity—especially when coupled with critical thinking—leads to credibility. And yes, those with credibility are viewed as reliable and trustworthy. These are all good traits and characteristics to have, but there's more. And exactly what constitutes the "more" is what we've been setting you up for.

Displaying credibility over time leads to clout, and another word for clout is *influence*. It is your ability to transform and shape the opinions and behaviors of others. It means people may be inclined to follow you. The more credibility and influence you have, the more likely your point of view will be respected. This does not mean everyone will agree with you, but they will listen.

The Gist

In some cases, people are bestowed with the ability to influence with very little effort on their part. This may be associated with people who have charisma or other similar characteristics. However, for most people, gaining influence requires conscious effort. In our experience, credibility is the heartbeat of influence. So, the effort we refer to is around credibility.

We assert that anyone who wants to have influence can have it. However, wanting it and having it are two very different things. Influence must be earned. It starts with intent and requires thoughtful effort. Yet effort alone is not enough. The actions that contribute to strengthening your influence must be sustained over time. It must become part of who you are—your *professional* DNA.

The Virtue and Value of Voice

Influence is about having a voice. We know that technically everyone has a voice, but when you have influence, you have a voice that people will listen to and act on. While having a voice may sound appealing, you have an obligation to use that voice for good—for the betterment of others and for the organization.

COACHING TIP: Avoid promoting a personal (or team-specific) agenda over what's best for the organization.

In business, the ability to influence is a true differentiator. It is the essence of effective leadership. Remember, you are on a journey. We've pointed out the pitfalls and you now know where they are. You can start, stop, change direction, and generally go at your own pace. We want to ensure that you are supported throughout your journey.

COACHING TIP: Be open to your possibilities, potential, and subsequent responsibilities to have influence.

Regardless of what level of leadership you aspire to, we hope that you can think critically and communicate clearly. If you do this consistently, you will build your credibility. Because you will be viewed as trustworthy, people in your organization *will* look to you for your thoughts on various subjects. You will be viewed as a credible thought leader—someone with valuable insights; someone with a voice.

Here are five points for you to consider as you work to strengthen your influence:

1. You don't have to have a leadership title to be a trusted thought leader. This is referred to as "influence without authority."
2. Just because you have a leadership title does not mean you have influence. People may follow you because they have to, not because they think you're a clear, credible leader.

3. This is not about some kind of power trip. Those who believe it to be one often find their influence fleeting.
4. When influence is wielded properly, it's a way to set yourself apart and to make a meaningful difference—not only for your company, but in the lives of those you work with.
5. Achieving influence is not a solo endeavor.

For those who wish to proactively take that step toward having greater influence, we are going to help you focus your efforts. In this chapter, we'll cover the role of credibility in having sustainable influence, why one would want to have influence, the sources of it, how to put influence into practice, and the skills you should develop to strengthen your influence.

We cannot promise you a promotion, and we hope that alone is not your intention. However, for many people, following along this pathway can lead to greater leadership responsibilities. And it will likely allow you to have a voice in the direction of your team and company. You may be sought after for your insights. You may be asked to help solve problems, contribute to the strategy, or be a champion of change within your organization. If this sounds intriguing to you, this pathway may be particularly helpful.

People with influence are often viewed as leaders, and they can be informally or formally designated as such. You don't have to be a director or vice president at a company to have influence or be a leader. Similarly, just because you are a director or vice president or hold a similar leadership title does not mean you are a great leader or that you have credibility or influence.

Scene #1

Travis worked in his organization as an individual contributor for almost three years. Because he had worked on multiple projects during his tenure, he was well known across many teams. Although he was a self-described introvert, he connected with his colleagues. He exhibited genuine interest in learning more about their respective areas. He didn't dominate meetings, but he listened and thoughtfully contributed—either by asking questions or providing insights. As a result, Travis garnered the respect of his colleagues and supervisors.

One day, his senior vice president and his direct manager stopped by his office and invited him to be part of a team working on reviewing and modifying some of the existing critical business processes that cut across all teams at their organization. Since many people would be impacted by the new processes, the work was to be confidential until the new processes had been fully redefined and approved.

The work went on for several months, and, at one point during the process, Travis asked his manager why he had been selected for this team. His manager replied that Travis had established valuable insights that spanned the organization, and that this broad view would be helpful in defining new processes. His manager also stated that since he'd garnered respect and credibility from so many people across the company, they wanted him to be one of the primary people to lead the change-management efforts once the new processes were ready to be implemented. The senior leaders knew he could connect well with the rest of the company—that he could speak their language and help to influence the adoption of the new processes.

Credibility and Influence: Putting Ten Key Concepts into Practice

Influence must be built upon a foundation of credibility to have the greatest positive impact. Travis had credibility, and you should strive for the same. While this sounds good on paper, you might be wondering how to go about establishing and maintaining credibility. We've collected our top ten ways to do so. Consider these a collection of coaching tips for building your credibility. You'll see some familiar concepts we've gathered from throughout the book—all of which contribute to one's credibility.

1. Think clearly, be honest, and act fairly.
2. Align your words and actions. Be consistent and authentic.
3. Be thoughtful in your interactions—not only with what you say, but how you say it.
4. Prepare in advance. Here are two situational examples:
   - We all know leaders who make communicating look easy—like they just whipped up some information right there on the spot. That may happen on a rare occasion, but more than likely that leader has prepared in advance. They know the select few (two to four) points they want to make ahead of time.

- Furthermore, on a micro level, plan ahead for meetings you will attend by knowing the core topics and having a point of view on items requiring one. If you don't have a point of view, that's okay. Work to develop one throughout the meeting by listening to others' views.

5. Actively listen.
6. Welcome alternative points of view. You don't have to agree, but listen, learn, and respect them.
7. Establish and maintain connections. Don't simply seek out people when you need something from them; rather, look for ways to connect with them on a personal level as well.
8. As a leader, set a clear and compelling vision—one that is challenging yet attainable. Let people know where they fit within the vision; set realistic expectations; give feedback, coach and develop others; and hold yourself and others accountable.
9. Recognize and reward hard work and effort and be others' champion where earned.
10. Take a servant leadership approach. Ask "What can I do for you? How can I help you be successful?"

Why have influence? People may set out to have influence for a variety of reasons—some positive, and some more nefarious. On the positive side, there are opportunities to make a difference on both a micro and macro scale. People may want to motivate, inspire, and develop others. They may want to help contribute to the direction of the team or company. Some refer to this as having a "seat at the table."

COACHING TIP: Develop a personal plan that includes why you want to have influence. Consider where you want to have a positive impact. But be honest with yourself; don't allow the plan to come across as selfish. Consider the overall organization so peers can recognize your valuable voice.

The ability to influence others helps leaders to motivate people and make their teams more productive. In some instances, having influence will help you become a leader, while, in other instances, it's a skill you can learn as you gain more experience as a leader.

If your level of influence were strengthened, what are some areas where you would want to make a difference in your organization? Any considerations of impact broadly, beyond your organization? Grab a pen and your branding notebook, or feel free to jot down your ideas in the blank lines below.

____

____

____

On the negative end of the spectrum, people with a more sinister side may want influence so they can manipulate others, or for their ego. We won't delve into the psychological characteristics of people fitting this description, but they tend to be considered narcissists or megalomaniacs. Unfortunately, people like this continue to exist and even thrive in some instances, but we are firm supporters of using your influence for good.

The Core Four Sources of Influence

Influence comes from the following core four areas:

1. Knowledge, skills, values, and experience
2. Structure and authority
3. Situations
4. Relationships

Knowledge is power; so too are skills, values, and experience. These are all cornerstones to credibility and influence. Together, they allow you to expand your perspective and make more meaningful contributions to business decisions. But what do you need to know?

First and foremost, you need to know your organization or business. What is its business strategy? Who are your competitors? And how do you differentiate them from the products and services you offer? Along those lines, how do you and your team specifically contribute to the company's strategy and goals?

Second, you should have either a depth of technical knowledge, breadth of knowledge across multiple areas, or both. For example, if you have depth of knowledge in accounting, you can be viewed as a subject-matter expert. You would likely know a lot about accounting, and certainly much more than the average employee.

Depth of knowledge is typically developed through some combination of formal learning and experience. Through various institutions, you will learn the fundamentals of your subject matter, and experience will allow you to apply that knowledge.

Formal knowledge such as a degree earned at a highly prestigious university may provide you with initial opportunities. But if you are not able to put the knowledge into practice, your credibility will reach its limits early. In fact, if you are unable to put concepts and formal education into practice, that could very well negatively define you. The risk with being an expert, of course, is that you may be limited in your worldview. You may see the world only through the eyes of an accountant, a lawyer, or any other number of functional areas of expertise. Such tunnel vision can label you quickly.

Not everyone needs to be an expert, and there are some benefits to being a generalist. Generalists are those that know a fair amount across a broad range of functional areas. For example, you can know a fair amount about human resources, marketing, and accounting. Add some applied business knowledge specific to your company, and those insights can be extremely valuable.

Scene #2

Sean started out in the mailroom of his company. He was looking to make some money while he went to school. He did his job well and got to interact with people from across the company. After a couple years, he applied to a part-time job in facilities. As he was nearing his college graduation, a leader approached him and suggested he apply for an open position with the communication and events team. This role happened to be part of the human resources department. He got the job and worked on a variety of tasks over a six-year period. Along the way, he was promoted and took on a team of four, followed by another promotion to a team of nine. This pattern of expanding roles remained consistent for Sean. Every two or three years there were new opportunities to increase his experience—from leading bigger teams to working with other departments. Sean embraced each opportunity, and after eighteen years, he was promoted to chief operating officer (COO) of the company.

Up to this point, notice how we have not said that you must be a leader to have influence. When you are not a leader by title, yet you leverage your knowledge, skills, values, and experiences to optimize your influence, this is referred to as "influence without authority." These leaders are respected for what they know versus their title. The best organizations want to foster more input and contributions from whoever is in the know, regardless of title. If you have influence without authority, utilize the myriad of other communications skills to maintain your credibility.

For all the talk about knowledge, skills, values, and experience, credibility and influence are more than that. How you utilize your knowledge and experience can also factor in to your credibility. We have known people who believe they are the smartest person in the room, and they were the first to let others in the room know about it. They did so through their words, tone, body language, and actions. The lesson: Whether a subject-matter expert or experienced generalist, if you flaunt your knowledge and make others feel small, your credibility will suffer.

COACHING TIP: Use your knowledge to educate others and contribute to the broader organizational discussion rather than to put people down and make them feel inferior.

But I'm the boss! Some people believe that having a leadership title ensures that they have influence. There is some merit to this, but it is not guaranteed. Although some may have a degree of influence because of their title, they will not have the requisite credibility needed to sustain their influence. They certainly won't motivate and inspire others to act. This reliance on structure alone may meet some short-term needs, but rarely will it help to drive motivation or engagement, since those leaders may be feared more than respected.

Leaders that solely rely on their position as their source of influence tend to have a very "command and control" approach to leadership. They may expect you to take on tasks because they said so.

People with leadership titles do, in fact, have some level of influence by the mere fact of their title and position in the company's hierarchy. They can influence the strategy and goals of the company, as well as a wide variety of staffing and career development decisions.

Although titles can provide a source of influence, there is increasing risk for those who lead by fear or take a command-and-control approach to leadership. That type of influence without a foundation of credibility can be fleeting. That's right: Influence can disappear if not obtained or maintained correctly. For leaders relying too heavily on their title as a source of influence, their career longevity is at risk because of the negative impact they can have on a company's culture and team engagement.

Up to this point, you may think structural sources of influence are only negative. Not true. But we have devoted additional focus to this topic because of the risk associated with relying solely on your title as a source of influence. When structural influence is combined with a foundation of credibility, it can be quite a powerful combination. Employees are more likely to follow and be motivated and inspired by you. You will have stronger relationships with your associates, and they are more likely to be engaged with the company and in their work. Therefore, your goal as someone looking to strengthen their influence should be to ensure that it's built upon credibility.

COACHING TIP: Take a servant leadership approach; focus on helping others you work with, and lead with both your head *and* your heart.

Renowned business author and consultant Ken Blanchard nailed it when he said, "The key to successful leadership today is influence, not authority."

Situational influence. Think about influence as a dimmer switch rather than a simple light switch that is either on or off. Early in your career, you might find yourself in certain situations where you can contribute more than others. Perhaps it's a certain project, a task within the project, a brainstorming session, a meeting, or any of a number of other unique situations where you can contribute something meaningful. That something could be an idea, a recommendation, or a question. It's a way for you to showcase your level of engagement and understanding of the business or a particular issue. This is your opportunity to shine. Relish it. Learn from it, and build upon it.

COACHING TIP: Read the room. Learn to recognize when to contribute your thoughts, ideas, recommendations, and questions, and when not to—especially early in your career.

Relationships are a source of influence. People must have a reason to be influenced by you. You must say or do something that resonates with them. They must trust you.

Connections are built in a variety of ways, such as identifying a need that a person or group has, having something in common with them, or solving a problem they have. The more you can connect with people and understand what resonates with them, the more likely you will have influence, and the greater it will be.

Empathy and emotional intelligence are characteristics that facilitate connections. Those characteristics come more naturally to some than others. Depending on where they stand for you, those interpersonal skills will dictate the level of comfort you have—and the effort required—in making connections. Unfortunately, there are few if any shortcuts. If people don't trust you, they are not likely to follow you or be influenced by you.

The result of multiple connections is the basis for your professional network. You need a professional network for a variety of growth and development reasons. However, your network can also provide other benefits. Individuals in your network can be a sounding board for messages—especially if they pertain to them. You can also establish early buy-in and identify potential pitfalls prior to delivering your message to a broader audience. In short, people in your network can help you succeed.

COACHING TIP: Start a breakfast or lunch group of people in your position who work in different organizations and may well be facing the same issues.

Credibility substitutes. Strengthening your influence should not be a solo endeavor. In fact, we would argue that if you want to maximize your credibility and influence, it *cannot* be a solo endeavor. You need the help of others. You need people to vouch for you. Think of this as seeds of credibility being planted.

There's a name for people who speak highly of you in your absence—credibility substitutes. Since it would be awkward for you to scream from the proverbial mountaintops about how amazing you are, you need credibility substitutes to do it for you.

Credibility substitutes are people who voluntarily speak highly of you in your absence, almost by impulse. They are indirect yet powerful contributors toward strengthening your influence. Credibility substitutes may also provide professional opportunities and open doors. They can come from anywhere in your network, including peers, colleagues, direct reports, and supervisors. They should have already established their own credibility within your organization. People with influence (typically leaders) should know and respect them. They should be viewed as trustworthy, a good judge of talent, and have a seat at the leadership table. The best ones are established, trusted leaders from other parts of the organization. While your boss is an excellent source, a different leader vouching for you can be more powerful because that shows you have connected across the business.

You're probably asking yourself, "How do I get some of these substitutes?" Quite simply, credibility substitutes emerge because of your actions and overall performance. Never through requests.

Think about it this way: Why would someone want to vouch for you? Do you take the initiative? Do you accomplish tasks above expectations? Find comfort knowing there is not one single answer, because part of having credibility substitutes is about understanding what is important to them. For some, there are universal factors, such as initiative, consistent outcomes, or valuable insights. It often comes down to a simple question:

How are you helping a particular leader, colleague, or the organization look good?

If you must ask someone to speak highly of you, there is something missing from the equation. Besides putting someone on the spot, it removes some of the authenticity from the process. Furthermore, if your performance doesn't stand on its own, being asked to say something nice may frankly not be accurate. The power of credibility substitutes is that they self-identify and *want* to speak highly on your behalf.

You may consider who might provide this role for you based upon your work with them—who do you work with often, and who holds you in high regard? There's nothing wrong with wanting to do your best work and be recognized for it. However, you should never ask someone to be a credibility substitute for you.

Take a few minutes to consider the following questions: Who might be a credibility substitute for you? What are some ways (i.e., through current or upcoming projects) to help facilitate or reinforce this? Consider where you can exceed expectations and/or set yourself apart from others. Again, grab your branding notebook, or jot down your ideas in the blank lines below.

What do credibility substitutes say, and where and when do they say it? They may speak highly of you during a leadership meeting, when a project team is being identified, during a talent review, or even during a casual conversation between leaders. What they say varies depending on the context. During a leadership team meeting where they are providing project updates, it may be something as simple as "Julie has really stepped up on this project. She's someone we need to keep an eye on in terms of her future opportunities." Boom. Done. A credibility seed has been planted.

More often than not, other leaders will begin to see Julie's initiative, and it will likely extend to similar positive support. Julie may never even know these conversations are happening. That's okay. The primary point here is that Julie is doing a noticeably impressive job.

We have a word of caution if you are a leader who wants to be a credibility substitute for others. Choose who you advocate for very carefully. If you are reading this and suddenly want to advocate for your entire team, you will dilute the truly high performers. Similarly, if you advocate for someone who isn't that strong of a performer, it will reflect on you and negatively impact your future credibility.

Scene #3

Darcy was a mid-level manager. She was often the first to raise her hand for challenging assignments. Several leaders took notice of this and spoke highly about not only her initiative, but her ability to solve complex problems. Her boss knew about and shared with her an upcoming job posting from a different department that she would be well-suited for. She was one of nearly one hundred people to apply for the job.

Under normal circumstances, Darcy's résumé would have sat in the stack. The chances of her getting an interview, let alone the position, would have been slim. Given her bosses' and several other leaders' high praise about Darcy to the hiring manager, she was among the few selected to interview.

In a very real sense, Darcy had been "interviewing" for this role through her performance over the previous two years. She was ultimately selected for the role—not directly because of who she knew, but rather because people had experienced her initiative and problem-solving skills firsthand and knew she would excel in this role. Her credibility substitute helped Darcy to get her foot in the door, but being chosen for the position was based upon Darcy's earlier contributions, as well as the excellent job she did preparing for the interview.

COACHING TIP: Take initiative for complex projects where you think you can contribute.

Five Essential Skills and Characteristics for Strengthening Your Influence

To help you strengthen your influence capabilities, we've identified the five most helpful skills for you to develop. As you've seen throughout this chapter, it's not a single skill or characteristic that builds influence, but rather a combination of them.

Strengthening your influence can be complex. In addition to those listed below, continue to focus on developing the following skills covered in the previous pathways: motivational skills, empathy, emotional intelligence, critical thinking, communication, and active listening. Since strengthening your influence happens over time, this is about putting many of the skills together as part of your development plan, along with everyday practice.

1. *Consulting* relies on a combination of skills, including creative thinking, analyzing, problem-solving, communicating, time management, and collaborating.
2. *Negotiation skills* allow you and others to work through issues to reach an agreement acceptable to all sides.
3. *Political savvy* is a skill requiring diplomacy and tact while effectively relating to people across various levels and/or groups.
4. *Intuition* often exists based upon experience. It is the ability to understand a point, concept, or issue immediately and with little to no thought, reasoning, or further research.
5. *Persuasion* involves convincing someone to believe or do something that they may not have been inclined to do previously.

COACHING TIP: As part of your personal development plan to strengthen your influence, write down the specific actions you will take to develop and maintain your influence. Be specific, and consider incorporating elements from the Core Four sources of influence.

Summary of Coaching Tips

- Avoid promoting a personal (or team-specific) agenda over what's best for the organization.

- Be open to your possibilities, potential, and subsequent responsibilities to have influence.
- Develop a personal plan that includes why you want to have influence. Consider where you want to have a positive impact. But be honest with yourself; don't allow the plan to come across as selfish. Consider the overall organization so peers can recognize your valuable voice.
- Use your knowledge to educate others and contribute to the broader organizational discussion rather than to put people down and make them feel inferior.
- Take a servant leadership approach; focus on helping others you work with, and lead with both your head *and* your heart.
- Read the room. Learn to recognize when to contribute your thoughts, ideas, recommendations, and questions, and when not to—especially early in your career.
- Start a breakfast or lunch group of people in your position who work in different organizations and may well be facing the same issues.
- As part of your personal development plan to strengthen your influence, write down the specific actions you will take to develop and maintain your influence. Be specific, and consider incorporating elements from the Core Four sources of influence.

Summary of Pathway #4

Influence is about having a voice within your team or organization. With influence, you can help to set strategy, drive action, and motivate and inspire your team. You can make a difference and have a positive impact.

Credibility is the heartbeat of influence. When credibility and influence are connected properly, they create a circuitous relationship. Together, they can provide a strong foundation for effective leadership—whether formally by title or informally. When the two are not intertwined, influence can be unstable, fleeting, and tumultuous.

The Core Four. We see four essential sources of influence:

1) knowledge, skills, abilities, and values
2) structures
3) situations; and
4) relationships.

Furthermore, what adds to the power of influence is when you combine all of the Core Four sources. In other words, you are in a position of power which you have achieved and maintain through what you know, and you apply your knowledge and experience as dictated by specific situations. When that occurs, you are likely to realize the benefits ascribed to credibility substitutes. People will speak well on your behalf, which will in turn fuel your credibility and influence.

With credibility and influence, your point of view will be sought after. Regardless of the sources of your influence, you have responsibilities to take a constructive and developmental approach to those people and organizational issues requiring your input. There is a saying: With great power comes great responsibility. Influence fits this saying well.

You also have an obligation to listen to and respect others' points of view. Help facilitate the best solution or course of action—even if it's not yours. Don't consider influence as a zero-sum game where if you win, someone else loses, and vice versa. Winning is about what's best for the organization and its employees.

Moving you along. In the next chapter, our focus continues to be on you. We want you to maximize the impact you can have on yourself, your career, and others. You'll see words like brand and legacy. You'll be challenged to think about *your* brand and legacy. That sounds serious, and while it certainly can be, it's also something that should evolve and grow. You will see how you can turn your vision and goals into a reality through practice.

Pathway #5 is an opportunity for you to reflect on where you envision yourself from a career and capability standpoint, the mark you want to leave on your colleagues, team, and organization, and to further refine your plan based on your unique goals. We don't want you to simply reflect for the sake of reflecting. This is an opportunity for you to provide clarity for yourself. Our hope is that your new sense of clarity will drive purpose and action.

Additional Resources

- *The Power of Influence*, 2nd ed., by John C Maxwell (Colorado Springs: David C. Cook Publishers, 2001).

- *Impactful Influence for Modern Leaders: How to Use the Power of Influence to Lead Other People toward Success* by Paul A. Wyatt (London: Eagle Ridge Books, 2022).
- *Influence: The Psychology of Persuasion* by Robert B. Cialdini (New York: Harper Business, expanded edition, 2021).
- *Influence Without Authority*, 3rd ed., by Allan R. Cohen and David L. Bradford (New York: Wiley, 2017).

Pathway #5: The Power of YOU

Take control of your personal leadership brand

Your legacy is being written by yourself. Make the right decisions.

—AMERICAN BUSINESSMAN AND AUTHOR GARY VAYNERCHUK

Results are, of course, essential in business, but so too is how you go about achieving them. The entire communication life cycle—from setting expectations and connecting with others through providing feedback—will influence what you are known and remembered for.

- So, what do you want to be known for in the workplace?
- What can people expect from their interactions with you?
- Are you consistent?
- Are you someone that people generally want to be around? Do others seek you out for input and counsel?

If you've come this far, you realize that if you want any shot at credibility or influence, clear communication is the basic entry point. After all, if someone can't understand you, how can they support you or be influenced by you? We should all strive for and want to be known for communicating clearly. But do your words influence and motivate others? What difference do you want to make for your team or company? Do you want to be known as someone who contributes thoughtfully and meaningfully to organizational discussions? Being known as someone who thinks critically and has credibility becomes part of who you are and what you want to be known for.

We hope our book provides some considerations and provocative questions to ignite your thinking. Don't simply nod your head, say to yourself "Sounds good," and turn the page. Which of the questions above struck a chord with you? We encourage you to pause here and really reflect on the questions before you proceed.

When all is said and done, this goes to the core of who you are. It is really about your workplace identity. It's your reputation. Your brand. A personal brand exists where your personal values, beliefs, and convictions intersect with your actions. Think of it as a process to build your aspirational personal brand (APB).

You and Your Brand

You are in control of your brand. None of this happens on its own. It starts with self-awareness and requires deliberate action—both of which are covered throughout this chapter.

Stating your intentions regarding your personal brand is not enough. Your words and actions drive your brand. You must walk the talk. You must put your aspirational ideas about what you want to be known for into practice.

- Do your words and actions match?
- Do you take time to build connections?
- Do you ask thoughtful questions?
- Do you listen?
- Are your words and actions intentional?
- Are they always aligned?

Warning: If you never give your brand another thought, *you will still be known for something*. You will still have a brand, but will it be the one you intend? Here is your chance to take control of and shape your personal brand.

The Gist

As you can tell from our introduction to this chapter, this pathway encourages you to reflect on some potentially deep concepts. Reflection relies heavily on your inner voice. How does your inner voice impact your outward communication? Are you positive or negative? Optimistic or pessimistic?

This is your opportunity to look at yourself in the mirror. What do you see? No, not just physically, but the type of person you are. How do you interact with others at work? What is the energy that you bring? This energy we refer to can be quite contagious, and it says a lot about you. Are you the one who inspires others, or do you weigh them down?

One of the best ways to initiate reflection is through questions. You've gotten a taste of this already in our introduction above, and you will see many more questions throughout this chapter. Grab your branding notebook, or jot down your ideas in the space below. You may not have all the answers, and you may want to revise some of them by the chapter's end. That's okay. Remember—*this is all a work in progress.*

____

____

____

At the end of this chapter, we hope you will have clearer thinking around what you're known for in the workplace, what you want to be known for, and how to get there.

To help facilitate your reflection, this pathway facilitates self-awareness and alignment of your brand; provides you with a variety of questions designed to help encourage reflection; introduces a variety of factors that will help you to shape your brand; and provides vignettes and tips to help you further develop and refine your brand.

Applying Product Branding to Personal Branding

Product branding was put into practice long before the notion of personal branding emerged. There are four core concepts that we can glean from product branding that will help you think about your personal brand. The personal brand application is noted in each sub-bullet.

Here, imagine a conversation you could have had with an older acquaintance—someone who considers themselves more traditional and less tech-savvy.

1. *Awareness*: "Yeah, I've heard of Amazon for shopping versus my old brick-and-mortar retail stores. I have a friend who uses Amazon."
   - Are people aware of your strengths, capabilities, and interests? How can you further expand this awareness?

2. *Trial*: "Okay, I got some grass seed on Amazon to save gas and time running over to the garden shop. It's okay, and it was really easy. I can see the benefits."
   - How can you get involved in projects that allow you to showcase your talents?
3. *Preference*: "I'm now using Amazon for stuff that's too heavy for me to lift into the trunk, bulky stuff that's hard to carry to the house."
   - How can you establish credibility substitutes (see Pathway #4) and become top of mind for meetings, general insights, specific projects, and possibly expanded roles that allow you to apply and develop your best skills?
4. *Loyalty*: "I'm sold. I default to Amazon for a lot of things—especially when I lack the time to run to the store."
   - How can you become a frequently sought-after contributor on a wide range of business topics?

Scene #1

Sally is a new employee in the service department. After only a month, she sat in for her boss at a managers' meeting and asked some thoughtful questions that got lots of positive notice. She was credited with challenging the status quo because she asked sharp questions only a newbie would think of. Everyone noticed and commented in the hallways. That was a positive sign of awareness of Sally's brand. Thoughtful, challenges the status quo, and confident to speak up and contribute meaningfully.

Next went the brand trial stage for Sally, or, "Let's have Sally look at this . . . she's good at this." She was asked to head up a subcommittee on a growing issue. She did very well in the role, which further reinforced her brand.

A year later her manager left and Sally was promoted into that role after multiple recommendations *from others in the company*. Through these credibility substitutes (defined in Pathway #4), there was a clear preference for Sally (Sally's brand) heading an important department.

Other department heads now regularly seek Sally's input for problems they encounter, because her service department is so closely aligned with their departments. Brand loyalty for Sally.

COACHING TIP: Plan ahead before attending meetings. Know the topic, have a thoughtful point of view, and be prepared to contribute where appropriate. If you sense that the more tenured are not asking a key question, be prepared to offer it.

A word about meetings. You'll see we reference meetings quite a bit in this chapter. Although you likely have many types of interactions in your workplace, meetings are a Petri dish for personal brands. There are so many variables at play; they are a ripe venue for brands to flourish or perish. Are you (or others) prepared? Do you show up on time? Are you focused or distracted? Do you contribute or do you remain silent? And are your contributions thoughtful and relevant? Are you respectful of others' ideas? Do you bring positive energy? Do you make connections—with people and concepts? What do your tone, expressions, and body language say?

We could go on and on, but hopefully you get the picture. All the concepts we've covered throughout this book are on full display in meetings. Yes, people are watching. And yes, it is shaping how you are perceived.

It's "You" Time: An Activity

We are advocates of personal accountability. We believe that it's important for you to take ownership and control of becoming the person you want to become, and what you want to be known for. This requires a high level of clarity on your part.

We don't want you to be someone who simply checks the box and moves on. Remember, there are no shortcuts, so you're not off the hook by nodding at the terms *clarity*, *critical thinker*, *credibility*, and *influence*. Those words by themselves can be too subjective and abstract.

It's time to roll up your sleeves and get to work on you. We hope you've been doing that all along the way, but our focus here is on refining your personal brand. Before reading on, take some time to answer the two questions below.

1. What are you known for (three to five words that capture your brand as it is today)?

   ____

   ____

2. What do you *want* to be known for (three to five words that capture the personal brand you aspire to)?

____

____

For the rest of this chapter, we encourage you to revisit and refine your aspirational personal brand statement. We want you to not just *think* about how you can move toward your aspirational personal brand, but to *write* a plan for how you intend to get there. Be as specific as possible. Recall how in Scene #1, Sally's journey occurred over time. Perhaps the best description of Sally's APB is that she asks the best probing questions no one else seems to offer—or dares to offer.

For those of you who are already at your aspirational personal brand, your job is to document how you are going to maintain and reinforce it. Or, if you would like to take this activity to an even more advanced level, establish a plan for how you will help others achieve their aspirational personal brand.

As you reflect on where you stand now regarding your brand and where you want to go, consider your strengths, interests, and where you could improve. To help facilitate your thinking, we'll cover strengths and interests in more detail later in this chapter.

COACHING TIP: Never stop improving. Always have another trait or goal you want to add to your APB.

Consider specific examples of key aspirational concepts you strive to achieve. This may include personal examples from your experience or observing how others have modeled the ideal behaviors. Who do you know that exhibits these characteristics? How can you incorporate some of their skills and behaviors into your own activities? What are specific examples of when you exhibited—or struggled with—these behaviors? What can you learn from those experiences?

Ten Questions to Consider

As you've already seen by now, this chapter includes a lot of questions embedded within each section. They are all here to help you refine your brand and become known as you want to be known.

To help further inform your reflection, we've included below additional questions for you to consider. These are additional thought starters, and we encourage you to incorporate your own reflection questions as well.

As you consider your responses, also consider whether they help to contribute to your aspirational personal brand or whether they detract from it. For the detractors, jot down what you could do differently to turn your answers into actions that will support your aspirational brand.

1. How do you prepare in advance of meetings?
2. Are your contributions at meetings constructive, or do you prefer to play a contrarian role?
3. How do you continue to learn about your company, the industry, and your competitors?
4. Are you known as someone who has your colleagues' backs, or someone who talks behind their backs?
5. Do you tend to sit at your desk and focus on tasks with little social interaction at work? Or do you have a plan to connect with colleagues formally and informally throughout the day?
6. Are you a quiet, thoughtful leader? Or are you more energized and animated?
7. Do your words and actions match each other and the situation?
8. What aspect(s) of communication make you most uncomfortable (e.g., conflict, networking, public speaking, contributing at meetings, etc.)? What are you doing to overcome these and become more comfortable?
9. Who are your role models for personal brand? What can you learn from them?
10. How, when, and why do you provide feedback?

COACHING TIP: Consider your professional interactions like an emotional bank account. Make sure you are making more deposits than withdrawals.

Aspirational Personal Brand Is All about YOU

Think of the word *you* as an acronym that stands for:

Your
Optimal self
Unleashed

What does the best version of you look like? What do you need to be at your best in the workplace? There are some factors you can control. For those that you cannot directly control, you may be able to manage if you are aware of what they are and how they influence you and how you are perceived.

Attitude may be the best example of something you can control. Are you generally positive or negative? Are you going to be constructive and positive? Or are you going to be adversarial and look to derail ideas and progress?

We recognize that this is a delicate subject that requires a delicate balance. We are not advocating for groupthink and simply being robotically agreeable to everyone all the time.

You will see us also advocate for authenticity. Be yourself. We hope that being yourself does not mean being perpetually unhappy, negative, and adversarial. That would not be an enduring brand.

And we also recognize that mental health is a very real issue for people. We are not advocating for you to cover that up. In fact, quite the opposite, in all cases. Seek help where needed. Look for the positive in everyday encounters. And find ways to constructively disagree when necessary.

Sometimes we need to work harder at displaying the best version of ourselves. Even still, we all have bad days when it comes to how we interact with others. Just don't let the bad days define you. Focus on what you can control.

COACHING TIP: Do this gratefulness activity every day for two weeks, either first thing in the morning or last thing at night. Set aside one minute (timed) and write down everything in life you are grateful for.

Being Your Best Self

We all have triggers that cannot be ignored. Triggers are environmental factors that influence your behavior. Some of the common ones include sleep, food, space, and timing (i.e., beginning vs. end of the day).

COACHING TIP: Take the show on the road. Occasionally change the setting of meetings. For smaller or one-on-one meetings, consider having them at lunch or while going for a walk. This has the potential to change your energy and outlook during and after the meeting.

You may also be impacted by your surroundings—both the physical space and the organizational culture. An organization's culture is built upon values. These values drive action and interaction. When there is misalignment between the organization's values and its action or between the organization's values and yours, the impression can be profound. The impact of these can be subtle and occur over time—sometimes without you even recognizing how your outlook and personal brand have been impacted.

Scene #2

Noah was a rising star who worked for an industry-leading organization that maintained a strong reputation as being a great place to work. For many it was. A couple of their stated core values were collegiality and collaboration. However, this did not always translate to action. Leaders across the company were known to be disparaging of their colleagues behind their backs, despite being supportive in person. It was pervasive. In fact, some leaders spoke openly about it and noted that it was a survival skill within that organization.

Noah took note and witnessed the behavior on many occasions, across many leaders. At first, this didn't sit well with him. It didn't align with his own values, and it had really changed his outlook, making it more negative than he was used to. Over time, he either ignored the behavior or looked the other way. He had become numb to it. He even found himself contributing to the negative conversations. He was complicit, and had fallen into the trap of that behavior being a survival skill within that organization. He knew that was not who he was or wanted to be. He was disappointed in himself.

As unhealthy and egregious as it sounds, the organization and many of its people thrived. Those who couldn't embrace and navigate those behaviors and actions left the company. Noah was moving in the opposite direction of being his best self, and he became one of those individuals. The company had lost another rising star.

Other factors at play. Your best self today may very likely look different than your best self of ten years ago, just as it will look different ten years from now. People change, and your career stage will impact your personal brand. We hope that as you grow, your brand evolves right along with you. However, you cannot count on your brand to automatically change on its own without any effort on your part. It may change, but not likely into the brand you intend. And without effort on your part, it may not change at the pace you intend, either.

Scene #3

Early in her career, Charlotte was one to sit back in senior-level meetings. Even though she was asked by her boss to be an active participant, she wanted to observe, learn, and process the information during and after meetings. After all, the pace of the conversations tended to be very quick. She also wanted to be respectful and deferential to the more-senior-level leaders who were speaking. As a result, Charlotte never contributed anything in the meetings.

After attending several senior-level meetings, her boss pulled her aside and provided her with the feedback that she was starting to get a reputation as someone who didn't have anything to offer, and that there was a growing perception that the discussions were over her head and difficult to understand. Upon reflection, Charlotte realized that the discussions had been moving quite fast for her, and that she preferred to have additional time to process all that was being discussed. She also realized that if she didn't change her approach, her personal brand would be solidified by her actions (or inactions).

Charlotte began to review the agenda prior to each meeting so she knew which topics would be covered. Prior to the meeting, she also spent time establishing her own point of view on select topics where she had something to offer. Her contributions in these meetings started slowly—a question here, an idea there. Over time, she learned to refine her thinking and even to have counterpoints prepared. It wasn't long before she was a regular contributor at senior-level meetings.

The secrets for Charlotte's growth were no secret at all. It required advance preparation, strong listening skills, and the courage to contribute. An added benefit for Charlotte was that over time, she learned to refine her thinking in the moment and, although she still prepared in advance of the meetings, she was able to be spontaneous as well.

COACHING TIP: Take a proactive approach in establishing and reinforcing your personal brand. *Proactive* means knowing what you want your brand to be and identifying daily and weekly opportunities to showcase your capabilities.

Personality Characteristics and Finding Your Voice

Of course, quiet, shy, and introverted people can communicate effectively, be great leaders, have a strong personal brand, and make a great impact.

Similarly, not all extroverts are excellent communicators or leaders. You've got to be true to who you are. You've got to be authentic.

COACHING TIP: When it comes to defining your personal brand, be authentic and genuine, but also recognize that being the best version of yourself may require developing strategies to overcome any number of characteristics that may stand in the way of achieving your aspirational personal brand.

Just because you're quiet or shy doesn't mean you are excused from effective communication or having a brand. And shyness or being an introvert doesn't need to define you unless you want it to. You may simply have to work harder at it at times, and in certain situations.

To be fair, just because you're the loudest, most outgoing person in the room, you are hardly guaranteed any level of success with your message. You too may need to refine your approach. You may need to tone it down a bit.

In both cases, you may find yourself having to get comfortable being uncomfortable.

Build your brand around your strengths and interests. Your brand should be unique to you. What sets you apart from those you work with? Often, this comes down to strengths and interests. What are you great at? And what do you love to do? Additionally, consider what sets you apart, both negatively and positively.

Easier said than done, right? Most people have a difficult time talking positively about themselves. Understood. Humility is an admirable trait.

Therefore, for this next activity, you can answer the questions on your own or you can ask someone from work who knows you well for their perspective. Even if you choose to do this yourself, it's a good idea to check your answers against what someone else sees in you. You'd be surprised how often what you think you're known for—or want to be known for—is not how others see you.

What are your top three to four strengths in the workplace? And what are examples of you displaying them in action? Grab your notebook, or jot down your ideas in the space below:

____

____

____

People tend to get energized around the activities they love the most. That energy shines through as part of your personal brand. Keep in mind: Passion can come from specific tasks, outcomes, and the company mission.

What do you love to do? If you're in IT and love writing code, or you love managing projects, this is going to shine through. Similarly, if you find certain tasks and aspects of your role tedious, that will likely show through as well.

Below, write down the three to four aspects of work that give you the greatest energy. What gives you purpose and meaning?

____

____

____

Notice we didn't say to pull that from your current job. For some people, their current job may not provide them with work they truly love to do. It's an unfortunate reality, and we don't want you to feel like you are being forced to love your current job. One final word of caution: We're not looking for where you might have had a good or bad day. Think about this in terms of consistency. And rather than seeking out a boss or colleague for their input, consider running your thoughts by a close friend, family member, or spouse—someone who is more likely to be on the receiving end of some of that good energy as you talk about a certain day or project.

COACHING TIP: If you did not find characteristics of your current job that you love and that provide you with purpose and meaning, consider how you can modify your role or environment to find your true interests.

Scene #4

Ben was looking for his first job out of college. He knew he wanted to be in higher education, and he knew he wanted to help others, but he wasn't sure in what role. He had sent out many résumés but was not getting many interview requests. Finally, he received a call from a local community college about an admissions counselor role he'd applied for. Ben was thrilled. The idea of being a counselor appealed to his desire to help others find their path. This job aligned well with his passions.

During the interview, he learned more about the role. He was so excited about the possibilities—and frankly, he needed the work—that he overlooked the interviewer's discussion about meeting admissions targets.

Ben got the job, and it was explained to him that for his first ninety days, he would have a probationary status, meaning long-term employment was not guaranteed. This didn't bother him. It was common practice, and he knew he was committed to doing the best job possible.

He started out with enthusiasm, ready to make a difference and have a positive impact on the school, as well as on those applying for admission. After his first month on the job his boss called him into her office and reprimanded him for his performance. He was not closing deals, or making his daily or weekly quotas.

Ben was shocked. This job was not at all about helping others find their path. It was a sales job. His perspective had been completely turned upside down. He was never able to fully embrace the transactional nature of the role he had signed up for. On his eighty-ninth day, Ben and his boss met and mutually agreed to part ways. The vision of who he wanted to be and the type of work he wanted to do was too dissimilar from what the job called for.

COACHING TIP: Never compromise your values or your passions.

Ten Fundamental Tips for a Strong Personal Brand

Amid all the time, effort, and reflection you are putting in to find your unique brand, there are some fundamental aspects we believe are core. Everyone should strive to incorporate all of these characteristics into their brand.

All the work you've done throughout this chapter will help to establish the aspects of your brand that are unique to you. The following ten fundamental tips should become part of both who you are and what you do, related to your interactions. Is it possible? Yes. We think it's not only possible, but essential.

1. Communicate with empathy and emotional intelligence. Be a good colleague to your coworkers.
2. In all of your interactions, be positive, constructive, and respectful.
3. Help others and be a developer of others.
4. Maintain a business-first mind-set. Keep the focus on the business priorities and agenda, not a personal agenda.

5. Be known as the champion of your company and team. Be fair and honest in your assessment of talent.
6. Find a balance between patience and urgency.
7. Be an independent thinker (vs. being a yes-person or contrarian). Hone your ability to think quickly and decisively. Don't just show up; plan ahead and have a point of view. Be ready to contribute.
8. Know your limits. It's better to bring in an expert than pretend to be one.
9. When it comes to communication, be a role model. Be thoughtful, fair, and consistent. Match your words and actions!
10. Take initiative. Take on the most challenging tasks that no one else wants. Involve others. Get the right people (i.e., those impacted by the project) involved throughout and incorporate their input where possible.

Essential Skills and Characteristics for Developing Your Personal Brand

- *Self-awareness* reflects a deep understanding of one's values, strengths, weaknesses, and aspirations. It includes an understanding of where there is alignment. It allows for more accurate self-evaluation and adjustments that are the core of personal growth and development.
- *Self-confidence* relies on a strong yet accurate belief in one's abilities. It requires a high degree of self-awareness and knowing one's strengths and weaknesses. It is usually developed over time, and through feedback and practice.
- *Self-motivation* is inherent in those that clearly identify, prioritize, and accomplish tasks. They overcome obstacles and setbacks and demonstrate commitment to what they want to achieve.
- *Adaptability* ensures that people can adjust to changes in their environment. The changes themselves may be within or outside of one's control, but this skill represents one's ability to pivot and navigate in order to be effective within the new environment.
- *Positive energy* is a skill that involves consistently thinking, speaking, and acting with an optimistic outlook. There is often a strong solution orientation associated with this skill.
- *Networking* is a skill that supports the development and reinforcement of one's personal brand. It requires individuals to be proactive in establishing and maintaining strong interpersonal relationships.

- *Drive* for results represents a persistent and at times relentless focus on successfully completing tasks on time and on budget. This individual strives to exceed expectations and can effectively navigate obstacles.

Summary of Coaching Tips

- Plan ahead before attending meetings. Know the topic, have a thoughtful point of view, and be prepared to contribute where appropriate. If you sense the more tenured are not asking a key question, be prepared to offer it.
- Never stop improving. Always have another trait or goal you want to add to your APB.
- Consider your professional interactions like an emotional bank account. Make sure you are making more deposits than withdrawals.
- Do this gratefulness activity every day for two weeks, either first thing in the morning or last thing at night. Set aside one minute (timed) and write down everything in life you are grateful for.
- Take the show on the road. Occasionally change the setting of meetings. For smaller or one-on-one meetings, consider having them at lunch or while going for a walk. This has the potential to change your energy and outlook during and after the meeting.
- Take a proactive approach in establishing and reinforcing your personal brand. *Proactive* means knowing what you want your brand to be and identifying daily and weekly opportunities to showcase your capabilities.
- When it comes to defining your personal brand, be authentic and genuine, but also recognize that being the best version of yourself may require developing strategies to overcome any number of characteristics that may stand in the way of achieving your aspirational personal brand.
- Never compromise your values or your passions.
- If you do not find characteristics of your current job that you love and that provide you with purpose and meaning, consider how you can modify your role or environment to find your true interests.

Summary of Pathway #5

Throughout this final chapter, you have had various opportunities to reflect on and develop your personal brand. You've seen the multiple factors that can influence your brand, and we've provided several foundational characteristics that should be part of your brand. Incorporating them into your unique approach is not easy. It requires practice. And above all, once honed, it requires consistency.

We hope you've made the progress you want to see toward developing your brand. This should not be a static exercise. Your brand should continue to grow with you.

Moving you along. But wait, there's more. Before you close the book and put it back on the shelf, we want to leave you with some parting thoughts. As you will see, we don't like to think of what's next as the conclusion.

Additional Resources

- *Own the Room: Discover Your Signature Voice to Master Your Leadership Presence* by Amy Jen Su and Muriel Maignan Wilkins (Cambridge, MA: Harvard Business Review Press, 2013).
- *The Power of Story: Change Your Story, Change Your Destiny in Business and in Life* by Jim Loehr (New York: Free Press, 2008).
- *Your Leadership Story: Use Your Story to Energize, Inspire, and Motivate* by Timothy J. Tobin (Oakland, CA: Berrett-Koehler Publishers, 2015).
- *Unleash the Power of Storytelling: Win Hearts, Change Minds, Get Results* by Rob Biesenbach (La Vergne, TN: Ingram Publishers, 2018).

Conclusion

Your Journey Continues

Don't go where the path may lead.
Go instead where there is no path and leave a trail.
—RALPH WALDO EMERSON

Is this the end—or the beginning? That is entirely up to you. We hope you think of this book and what you've learned along the way more as a launching pad than a conclusion.

From the start, our book has been intended to meet you where you are on your journey and to help set you up for success with various communication pathways, all while avoiding pitfalls. The beauty of it (in our humble opinion) is that as you elevate your communication skills, grow in your career, and evolve your goals, there are aspects of our book that can continue to support you at any point throughout your journey.

Remember that any journey is taken one step at a time, and moving from clarity to clout is no different. You can take it as far as you'd like. Take detours as you wish. Move at *your* pace. It's up to you. You are in control of your journey.

We hope that as you've read our book you've been able to learn from our experiences and those of others whose stories we've shared. We hope you've been able to put the myriad of ideas and concepts into practice. And more importantly, we hope you have seen and continue to see the results you are seeking.

We have seen firsthand the power of our concepts when put into practice. The people we have worked with over the years that have had the greatest impact on others and their organizations are those that are self-aware, open to feedback, and have a "continuous improvement" mind-set.

To make the most of the possibilities, here are five reminders to carry along with you:

1. **Have a plan.** Write down your goals. These can be lofty career aspirations as well as more tangible, near-term improvements in any aspect of your communication. We highly encourage you to include both short- and long-term goals. Be as specific as possible with what you will do to achieve your goals.
2. **Practice** your new skills often.
3. **Get comfortable with being uncomfortable.** Be sure to challenge yourself to operate outside of your comfort zone. For example, if one of your goals is to be a better public speaker, you will need to put yourself in a variety of public speaking environments.
4. **Seek feedback** and incorporate it into your new practices. We can only improve through practice and feedback.
5. **Monitor** and adjust your plan as you make progress or your goals change.

You have been introduced to a lot in our book. After all, communication is complex. It involves so much more than the verbal aspects. To communicate clearly and effectively is a process that requires careful thought and planning. You need to know your audience, be aware of dialectal nuances, and watch your tone and body language. The words you use matter, and you need to match your words and actions. You need to ask questions and listen.

You know that effective communication has much to do with thinking critically and making connections. To do so requires removing distractions and appropriately leveraging shortcuts.

You know the benefits of clear, effective communication—to yourself, others, and your organization. Communicate clearly within your organization, and there is greater alignment and process efficiency. When you communicate clearly with others, stronger connections are made, and conflict is more likely to be handled respectfully. The personal benefits you receive with clear communication will directly impact your credibility and clout.

We hope that by using our tips and insights to help you navigate the various pitfalls and pathways on your journey, you will be able to find the promise of your potential fulfilled.

Think. Plan. Practice. Repeat.

Do this, and we believe the best is yet to come. And always remember to enjoy your journey!

—Tim and Roger

Appendix A

The Crystal Rule—Ten Guiding Principles for Trouble-Free Communication

I'm always interested in how people use language to not say what they mean.

—ACTRESS AND DIRECTOR GRETA GERWIG

Ahhhh, our good friend, communication. We all do it often—some might say, all day, every day. You might be thinking, "I don't talk to people all day." That may be true, but you are still very likely communicating, even if you are not speaking. Many people don't give their communication a second thought, and unfortunately, it shows. We're here to help improve the clarity of your communication, whatever the frequency or medium.

Do you work in an office setting? Perhaps you keep your door closed at times throughout the day, so you are not disturbed. Or perhaps you have an open-door policy. Guess what? You are sending a message about your availability and priorities. That is not necessarily good or bad, but it is reality.

Maybe you're among the growing number of people who work remotely. You're not off the hook in terms of communication. You are still communicating verbally and nonverbally. Does your virtual office show you as available? How quickly do you respond to people? Are you on phone calls or video meetings? In all of these scenarios, make no mistake—you are communicating.

But is your intended message heard? How do you know whether it is or not?

On the surface, communication might seem simple and straightforward. We say something to someone, they hear it, and they take the intended action. Simple enough. Unfortunately, that is not always the case. And the risk is high and implications costly. In short, it means people spend time doing the wrong activities or trying to decipher what you meant. In either case, it is valuable time and productivity wasted.

The Telephone Game

Have you ever heard about or played the telephone game? It's where you sit in a long line or circle (with at least ten people) and the facilitator whispers a message into the first person's ear. They are to whisper the exact same message to the next person, and so on, until the final person stands up and says the message out loud. As you can imagine, by the time the message gets to the last person, it has been altered—sometimes significantly, to the point where it's not even recognizable. Inherent in that game is the reality that relying on memory and interpretation can be risky.

Communication is complex. It includes verbal and nonverbal; there's body language and facial expressions to consider. It involves the sender of the message and recipient (or recipients). And, oh, how the number of recipients add to the complexity, because the way each recipient interprets a message can vary.

Communication is irreversible. Once your message is out there, it's out there. You may try and retract it, explain it, or, if it was an error of judgment, apologize for it. But make no mistake: It's out there.

Have we mentioned the various media available for communication? How we communicate continues to evolve. There's face-to-face and a wide variety of ways to communicate through technology. We won't cover them all here, but some common ones include email, text messages, and a growing number of social media apps. Some of these apps, such as Zoom, FaceTime, and Skype, even allow us to blend the virtual with the in-person. Of course, there is also the telephone. Remember when we used to use the telephone to call someone, to talk to them?! It almost feels awkward now.

Speaking of awkward, I was in the grocery store a couple weeks ago. I was in the produce section and there was a lady holding her basket in one hand and staring very intently at the tomatoes. Then suddenly, she began speaking to the tomatoes. "I can't pick you up," she says. "Sorry, but it's just not happening."

She moves over to the broccoli. "I understand your friends just got a pretty stern talking-to. How do you think they are feeling?" There is no response from the broccoli, and after several moments of silence, she turns away from the vegetables. She catches me trying not to stare, but my eyes are wide, part curiosity and part concern. Then I spot the tiniest of earpieces and realize she is talking to one of her children. The lesson: Context matters. (Also, it's not polite to stare. But that's another lesson for another day.)

The Crystal Rule

When it comes to communication, there are people who deliver the message, those that receive it, and occasionally casual observers. In all cases, perceptions are formed and applied, and there is room for misinterpreting any aspect of the message—from the intent to the message to any associated outcomes. In each aspect, clarity is paramount.

We're barely scratching the surface of the complexities of communication, but we wanted to set the stage for helping you make sense of these intricacies. The rest of the book goes a bit deeper into these nuances and how best to navigate them. In the meantime, there are two basic questions to consider as we start to unpack the complexities of communication.

- How can you ensure that your intended message is received? This question goes to the core of clarity.
- How well do your words and actions align? The answer to this goes to the heart of credibility.

It's easy to get overwhelmed and make occasional—and often costly—communication missteps. Fear not. We are here to help you navigate the many complexities of communication.

You've heard of the Golden Rule? To treat others how you want to be treated. For many, it is the cornerstone of their upbringing.

We developed the Crystal Rule (think: *crystal* clear). It is like the Golden Rule, but applied to how you communicate.

Our Crystal Rule is to communicate as clearly with others as you would want them to communicate with you.

Since that statement can be a bit ambiguous, we've identified ten guiding principles to better inform your communication in accordance with the Crystal Rule. These principles apply to all forms of communication. Follow them to be an empowered and responsible communicator, avoid common communication mistakes, and to improve your communication clarity.

Using the Crystal Rule and associated guiding principles helps you keep in mind how clarity affects your credibility and, eventually, your influence. Your adherence to these principles will directly impact how you are perceived by others. Each one is described below, along with why it's important and the implications of following the rule (or not).

Principle #1: Think before you talk (or hit "send").

This principle can be summed up in one word: *intention*. It is in place to ensure that you communicate the message you intend. It requires thoughtfulness and planning.

You've heard the expression, Look before you leap? In its literal translation, it is a matter of safety, so people don't run themselves off a cliff or otherwise hurt themselves or someone else. The same guidance applies to your communication.

With your communication, it's okay to pause before you respond. For electronic communication, one tip is to write the message you would like to reply with and set it aside. You may set it aside for a few minutes or even a day or two. If you find yourself pausing for a longer period, consider a quicker response to the sender that acknowledges you've received the message and you will respond shortly (or by *X* day, if that's the case).

We refer to this pause period as "benign neglect," where you intentionally set something aside and come back to it later. You'd be surprised how often you will reframe or edit your reply, finding—and correcting—mistakes. Perhaps you want to rethink the message or tone; maybe you need to review your message for grammar, punctuation, and sentence structure; or maybe you will choose to not send it at all.

There are many times where benign neglect is especially helpful. Specifically, if your emotions are heightened for any reason (e.g., you're angry, in a hurry, you've had some alcohol, or other similar reasons). In these instances, it is better to simply step away from your device. You may think you are being witty, funny, checking a box, clearing the air, or whatever, but consider the implications of how your message will be received and the immediate and lasting impact it will have on others—not to mention on your reputation, credibility, and ultimately your influence. Your brand. It's better to respond later than to respond prematurely.

Also keep in mind that when it comes to emails, texts, and other electronic communication, once you hit "send" and put a message out there, it's out there forever. There are countless examples of people regretting what they've sent, even if they thought it was a private conversation. Take the former Las Vegas Raiders football coach Jon Gruden, for example. Private—and very negative and inflammatory—emails he had sent an associate surfaced after many years. After his highly insensitive and crude emails became public and cost him his job, endorsements, and his reputation.

LESSON

Don't write anything you wouldn't want to appear on the evening news. This is about discoverability and accountability.

For in-person communication, benign neglect is a trickier balance between speed and thoughtfulness of response, but it can be equally important. The challenge comes when people may expect a response during a meeting or conversation. You can't always say that you'll get back to them.

As we discussed in Pathway #5: The Power of YOU, Charlotte received feedback that she was too quiet in meetings. When we pressed her on it, she agreed and acknowledged that the pace of conversations and decisions in some meetings moved too quickly to allow her to contribute meaningfully. She preferred time to reflect, formulate her opinion, and to provide more thoughtful input. What she didn't realize was that her approach was negatively affecting her leadership brand. Her peers and colleagues viewed her as aloof and disengaged. With that self-awareness and some minor modifications to how she planned for meetings in advance, she was able to be better prepared to contribute *in the moment*, which shifted the perception of her engagement and leadership brand to positive rather than negative.

LESSON

Whether you choose to wait to respond or plan better in advance of interactions, you will be more likely to have the response you intend.

FIND A WRITING BUDDY

Part of this principle has to do with how you plan before you set out to communicate. Are you having a one-on-one meeting with a direct report? Meeting with a colleague? Looking forward to a meeting, either as the meeting leader or a participant? Giving a presentation? In all cases, take the time to prepare:

- What is the purpose of your communication?
- What message do you want to give?
- Do you need any actions in return (e.g., decisions, recommendations, or feedback)?

Part of your preparation may include—and sometimes *should* include—having a writing buddy to review your work. One tip is to print off these ten guiding principles of the Crystal Rule (just the principles, not the details) and hand them to your writing buddy, along with a copy of your message. Ask them to review and provide feedback and recommendations.

The people who make it look easy have one thing in common: They prepare. You just may not see the work they put in to make their communication clear and seamless. Once Charlotte had begun to prepare better, she became more involved and added immediate value to the discussions. For guidance on how to plan, see Principle #5 (*Be wise—compartmentalize*) and Principle #10 (*Have an exit strategy*).

Principle #2: Be succinct.

Given this principle—Be succinct—our original thought was to leave it at that. However, we wanted to provide some additional context and rationale to make this principle more memorable. It mostly applies to emails, but it can just as easily be applied to face-to-face interactions and meetings.

When in a business setting, your audience typically does not have the time or attention span to read long emails. We've worked with some executives who receive up to one hundred emails a day. That translates to a significant percentage of their day spent reading and responding to emails, making it difficult to devote time to other, more strategic activities. This is your chance to be part of the solution and not the problem. What are the (no more than) four points you want to make? Think of this as the executive summary of your message.

Whether that's how many emails you receive each day or not, the purpose behind the principle is the same. Be thoughtful and considerate with how much you say or write. Imagine you must pay a dollar for every word you use. You might budget your message a little differently.

The reality, however, is that you do not have to pay a dollar for every word. It doesn't mean there aren't costly implications to lengthy messages. The other more subtle risks of sending lengthy emails including the potential to quickly lose your audience, key messages getting lost, and having your message deprioritized. You may feel great thinking you've sent a very detailed and comprehensive email. You've said everything on a topic that needs to be said. But how effective is the message if the recipient/s don't read it?

THE FOUR-FINGER RULE

Okay, so how long is too long? As we discussed in Pitfall #1: Speed Sprawls, a good rule of thumb for emails is known as the "four-finger rule." As you draft your email, place four fingers up to the computer screen. Yes, this includes the greeting and the closing. And, no, you cannot spread your fingers apart. Quite simply, never send an email longer than four fingers. If you find your message extending beyond those four fingers, consider an alternative delivery approach such as phone call or in person.

The good news is that attachments don't count. So, if you are sending your boss a presentation, consider including three to five bullet points to summarize the slides. If they want or need all the details, they know to find it in the attachment. But your executive summary email will help them understand the key information, make a decision (if needed), or elicit a response.

This principle extends beyond emails. Some leaders love the sound of their own voice. They will go on and on during meetings or conversations. Don't be this person. And if you are, consider incorporating some basic questions to the audience. Our favorite for those who find themselves rambling on is to stop and ask the audience, "What do you think?" Asking questions gives you an opportunity to pause and listen. You'll hear more about the importance of active listening with Principle #8.

Principle #3: As a leader, communicate early, and often.

In the absence of information in the workplace, people tend to make up stories. Unfortunately, the stories they come up with are typically far from the truth, and they also tend to have a negative tone. For example, you are more likely to hear a rumor from employees talking about anticipating pink slips rather than surprise bonuses. That could be based on something historical (i.e., This company always gives out pink slips at this time of year, so why should this year be any different?) or hearsay. Also, the greater the volatility and uncertainty in the environment, the greater the need for information.

As a leader, it's your job to communicate early, and often. When it comes to performance, values, and objectives, set clear expectations, and provide periodic updates. This applies to both individual and organizational performance. What are the company values? And what happens if someone breaks them? What are the team's objectives? What will I be held accountable for? Clarity matters. None of this should be a guessing game.

Have you ever worked for a leader who doesn't communicate on a regular basis? How about one who communicated the right information at the right time? What was your experience like? What was the company culture like? We've known leaders on both sides of the spectrum—those who communicate rarely and those who communicate often. The difference in results is quite astonishing.

There are rumor mills and a culture of paranoia in the organizations where leaders communicate less. You also see pockets of individualism versus collaboration, because people are looking out for number one. We've heard some describe this as a "toxic culture."

DRIVING ENGAGEMENT

On the other hand, there tends to be more collaboration, focus, and innovation in organizations where leaders have more open, honest, and frequent communication. Engagement is higher because employees feel connected to the leader and to the company. That's not to say these organizations are picture-perfect or have zero challenges. However, there is less energy spent on trying to decipher what's happening or going to happen, and more energy directed toward the work itself.

This is not so much a caveat as what we like to call an "operational reality." There are certainly topics that leaders are privy to that aren't, or shouldn't be, communicated, or they are at least a matter of timing. The essence of leadership is discerning what those topics are and when to share information about the company. It's our job as employees to recognize that not all company topics should be made public. Typical examples include those around organizational changes. Timing matters, but it's still important to factor in time for employees to process any information impacting them. This is a matter of respect.

The bottom line of this principle: Don't leave it to people's imagination, or give them reason to guess; otherwise they will do just that. Besides being the right thing to do, honest and frequent communication prevents some bigger culture, engagement, and trust issues from emerging later. Additionally, it allows you to communicate the message you want delivered and anticipate any questions needing answers. It's unlikely you will have all the answers at the exact right time. That's okay. Don't let that hold you back from providing updates as of that time. An important but often overlooked response is "I don't know" or "Let me look into that."

Principle #4: Don't bury the lede.

What exactly is your main point? Are you providing information or recommendations? If so, what are they? Do you have good news to share? Do you need the recipient(s) to take a specific action? After some brief introductory pleasantries, get to your point.

Sylvia had a task to complete: communicate an update to a wide audience about a new organizational process. The message was a page and a half long (so immediately broke Principle #2, *Be succinct*). We informally surveyed the organization, and, true to form, many had shelved the message because it was just too much to process.

On the positive side, she included many headings and subheadings to enable the reader to move through the content more easily (a good plus for Principle #5, *Be wise—compartmentalize*). But Sylvia buried the lede. For compliance purposes, every employee needed to complete a specific task by a certain date. She included this important fact three-quarters of the way down the first page. Her message was lost, and as a result, compliance was among the lowest levels for any new initiative. It's not that people intentionally shirked their responsibilities; they just didn't know to do it. It wasn't clear.

Besides the low compliance, this resulted in a series of additional messages and delayed implementation of the new processes. This all could have been avoided had Sylvia stated this critical expectation up front.

Principle #5: Be wise—compartmentalize.

This principle is about how you organize your thoughts. We'll first review how this can be applied to your emails, followed by in-person interactions.

Keeping in mind Principle #2, *Be succinct*, your email messages will have space for only one or possibly two main points. That makes this principle straightforward. For emails, compartmentalization may not come from the number of ideas. Instead, it may come from the information you are sharing and what action(s) you are requesting. The last point is critical: Your message and call to action need to be clear.

For example, if you are writing an email to your boss to provide a project update, you could start by noting that this is the report you've been working on, followed by two to four brief highlights, and ending with a request (assuming you have one). The request may be something like "We are looking for your feedback and decisions on our recommendations," or something similar.

You'd be surprised how often we see an email without these important details. As a recipient, what do you want me to do? I shouldn't have to guess. The risk in this case is that I take the wrong action, or no action at all, and your email sits on a virtual shelf somewhere, collecting dust.

Whether you are planning a one-on-one interaction or have a speech or presentation to a larger audience, compartmentalization takes a more important role during in-person communication. It is a critical part of *how* you plan. It will help keep you focused on the key topic(s) at hand and prevent you from wandering off into the proverbial swampland.

For one-on-one interactions, what are the *X* number of topics you want to cover? This may be time- or topic-dependent. If I pass someone in the hallway at work and want to give them a quick update, what I say will be different than if I've scheduled a thirty-minute meeting with them. The hallway conversation may be simply to let them know you've got those findings and recommendations and will be in touch to schedule a time to go over them in more detail. The longer meeting should still be focused on the few things you want to cover.

LESSON

Develop, distribute, and stick to an agenda to keep the flow moving and achieve the intended outcomes.

If planned properly, the agenda for this meeting will include an introduction to set the context of why people are gathering, a small number of topics—findings, recommendations, ideas, decisions—and any action items and next steps. If you expect their input at any point in the meeting, you should specifically call that out and include questions for them to answer. Model the agenda to the time you have and the outcomes you want.

Speeches and presentations follow a similar approach. Have an organized plan based on the time you've been given. How do you know how much time you'll need? Either experience or practice. We've given hundreds of speeches and presentations and we have a good idea of what a thirty-, sixty-, or ninety-minute presentation looks like in terms of content on paper. If you have less experience or are unsure, you will need to put in the time to plan the presentation and do a few dry runs. The planning model still looks the same, though: introduction, a select number of key topics with supporting evidence and/or examples, and a conclusion or call to action.

Do not underestimate the importance of time. Don't try to cram a dozen topics into a thirty-minute meeting. We've all been there—certainly as meeting participants, and possibly as facilitators of the meeting, too. Either schedule more time, or better yet, narrow your topics.

Principle #6: Be honest.

This principle has to do with flat-out, cold lies at one extreme and false promises at the other. The difference between the two is intent. Are you intentionally misleading someone (i.e., lying) or mistakenly providing information that you believe to be true but turns out not to be? In both instances, we are reminded of the emotional bank account and whether you are making more deposits or more withdrawals. All else being equal, intentionally misrepresenting information tends to draw bigger withdrawals, but make no mistake, they both involve withdrawals—including on your credibility and influence.

On the former, this is first and foremost a matter of integrity. Further, the energy that is required to remember and maintain a lie can easily collapse under its own weight. Lying gives people false hope and may cause them to make decisions they otherwise wouldn't make. Lies cause irreparable harm to the individuals as well as the person stating the lie.

One of us recalls that during a values activity at a training session, the topic of integrity came up. George raised his hand and said he strives to always do the right thing, so he can look himself in the mirror. He went on to say that it makes everything else easier from there.

Never, never, never make false promises or those you cannot commit to.

Claire was the CEO of a technology consulting firm. She was very well respected across all levels of the organization. She was regularly lauded for her openness and for keeping the associates informed and up-to-date via town halls and other regular communication. You could say she lived Principle #3 (*As a leader, communicate early, and often*).

During a particularly turbulent time, there was a high degree of uncertainty and fear among employees, including with Claire herself. The market had taken an unprecedented turn for the worse. However, history was on their side. From the day the company was established, all leaders there had prided themselves on never doing a mass layoff. As Claire brought the team together at a town hall to provide an update on the environment and some of the organization's mitigating strategies, she confidently told all of the associates that the company had never done layoffs and did not plan to start doing so now.

Unfortunately for Claire and her associates, this downturn proved to be historic, and six weeks after her town hall, the company had to lay off over 10 percent of the organization. This came as a shock to many associates, both those being laid off and those who remained.

Claire brought the whole organization together in another very somber town hall. Questions were asked. Tears were shed. Claire apologized for having to make such a tough decision to ensure the viability of the company. She wanted everyone to rest assured that the layoffs were done.

In her heart of hearts, Claire truly believed what she had said from the outset, and she had history backing her up. No one doubted her original intentions. However, given the enormity of the situation, it was out of her control. In an unfortunate twist, several weeks later, the company had to make a small number of additional layoffs. Claire continued as a successful, well-liked leader, but her trust and credibility never fully recovered. Had she not built up such a strong emotional bank account prior to this, we're not sure her career would have survived at that company.

LESSON

Intention does not contribute to credibility. Be cautious of—or better yet, avoid altogether—making promises outside of your control. Your credibility depends on it.

This principle holds true at the individual level, too. It is particularly important when providing employee feedback. It's easy to give a simple "Great job!" in passing, or even to go out of your way to tell someone how much you appreciate them going above and beyond on a project. The challenges come when you say that to everyone, all the time. It becomes disingenuous.

If someone did in fact do an excellent job or go above and beyond in their role, it is good and important for you to provide that feedback and for them to feel recognized and appreciated. However, you should only do so when it is true. Also, another tip with providing performance feedback: Do it as close to the activity as possible, and be very clear and specific about what was so great. The timeliness and details go a long way toward reinforcing similar future behaviors.

Honesty extends to two other areas: data and actions. It is important that your actions align with your words. This has to do with being both authentic and transparent. Otherwise, you risk being misunderstood and perceived as lacking credibility.

It's easy to utilize data to reinforce whatever story you want told. One CEO, Sylvia, was fond of saying that for every failed project, there was a spreadsheet that said how successful the project would be. We are not going to assume intent, but the message here is for you to focus on being accurate over being right. Additionally, don't double down on being wrong. In other words, don't be stubborn. It's not about you winning; it's about the organization winning, and accurate data make for better-informed decisions.

Principle #7: Never send anything electronically that will elicit emotions.

This principle is simple and straightforward. Although it applies to all types of emotions, the emphasis is on avoiding those messages that will elicit negative emotions. Basically, don't send an email that is going to make someone angry or sad. This could include messages about someone's job status, negative performance feedback, or anything that oversteps organizational boundaries, to name a few.

What is it about email and other electronic communication that makes this such an important principle? It is sometimes difficult to interpret tone and intention via electronic communication. For that reason, your message is more likely to be misinterpreted when sent electronically. Additionally, an email does not allow for a real-time discussion or the opportunity to ask clarifying questions. It just lands with a thud. The damage to both sender and recipient is done.

But email is quick and it's easy. This makes adhering to this principle challenging, because people often feel more comfortable firing off an email or text rather than having a difficult conversation in person or on the phone. Avoiding the difficult conversations will not make them go away, and electronic messages usually make things worse. It can be uncomfortable to have difficult conversations in person, but it is important.

If you are misaligned with someone's idea, a good tip is to start with a statement such as "Help me understand . . ." and then to really listen to their point of view.

Intention doesn't matter. You've got to imagine the possibility that your message is going to upset someone.

Alternatively, avoid being the person who sends out email with zingers—you know, those witty statements meant to put people in their place. You're better than that. If you know you have a problem with an individual or with one of their ideas, have an in-person conversation. It's okay to disagree. It's not okay to set out to make people feel small.

Ahhh, but what should you do if you receive one of these messages? If there is any substantive content in the message, focus your reply on that. Depending on your relationship with the sender, you could have a conversation about it. This can be risky if they are not open to the feedback.

Notice we didn't say *not* to communicate about these emotion-driven topics; just don't do it electronically. Pick up the phone, walk down the hall, or yes, in our new emerging environment of communications, a videoconference is also okay. What you're trying to avoid is a one-way (often electronic) communication that lands in someone's in-box with a thud, without allowing for any real-time discussion or clarification.

Principle #8: Practice active listening.

Have you ever heard the saying, "The reason we were born with two ears and one mouth is so we can listen more?" It's a good point, and it's the foundation of our active listening principle. Good, clear communication requires active listening. It's a way of connecting with another person, and it helps to reinforce mutual understanding and clarity.

How do you know whether your message is clear? Whether it's received and understood? One way is that time goes by and people have either responded or acted in the way you'd hoped. Keep in mind that hope is not a strategy.

The other way is to look at body language. Some nonverbal signs that your recipients are engaged include nodding (not nodding off), smiling, taking notes, making eye contact, or leaning in. More expressive ways include asking questions, seeking clarification, and reflecting your main points. From a communication standpoint, you've got them right where you want them. They are locked in the moment, and they hear what you are saying.

When you are on the other side of the communication equation, it's your job to practice active listening. Stay engaged. Listen for the key points. Hopefully they're not buried in the message, but even if they are, this is your opportunity to ask clarifying questions. For example, you may say "There's a lot of great information in your discussion. I want to confirm your main points are A, B, and C."

Whether you are the deliverer or the recipient of the message, the more you can maintain a two-way communication via active listening and participation, the more likely your message will be received, understood, and acted upon if necessary.

Principle #9: Be empathetic—and when not to be.

You may have heard the statement that communication is a two-way street. There is a deliverer of the message and a recipient (or recipients). How and when the message is communicated can significantly impact the clarity of your communication and whether your message is heard, received, and if needed, acted upon. Your delivery and timing are essential.

Why would you need to be empathetic? When? And are there any exceptions?

The implications are for how the message is received. If it's not received the way you intended, it may not be because you weren't clear. You may have been succinct. It may very well be because you did not connect with the recipient.

There are also implications for the emotional bank account (i.e., the virtual deposits or withdrawals associated with interpersonal exchanges). With your communication, deposits come from adhering to many of the principles described in this appendix, as well as making positive connections to people outside of requests.

Withdrawals come from areas such as the frequency of the request and the significance. For example, how you ask someone to work on a project over a weekend will have a different interpretation based on when, how, and how often you ask. The result will likely be the same: working over the weekend. Do you ask every other Friday, but wait until after 4:00 or 5:00 p.m.? Do you offer to be available and help? Do you consider the plans they may have that will need to be changed? Do you show appreciation and empathy? All of these and more contribute to how your message lands. The request lands very differently if delivered on a Monday versus a Friday afternoon, because it allows people to plan.

FEEDBACK FATIGUE

Sandra was a leader of a team with four associates. As they worked on a wide variety of projects, she was always the last reviewer. She was known to send people's work back four, five, or more times to be revised. Her comments were vague at best, with the occasional question mark next to a section of text.

Her team had feedback fatigue and lower morale due to the frequency and uncertainty of the feedback. To a person, they all dreaded submitting their work; they lost confidence and excitement for their work; and they couldn't wait to leave her team. Sandra had one of the highest turnover rates in the company. Nobody wants to be continuously beat up.

True, Sandra is the boss, and she is responsible for the work that is put forward. However, this is not about right or wrong. It's about improving clarity and the costs and benefits associated with it. Can you imagine if Sandra took the time up front to set clearer expectations? Or what if she provided clear and detailed feedback at the first submission? Alternatively, the issue could be one of hiring or training her staff appropriately. She could have used the process as a learning and development tool. She could have even had them work with one another prior to submitting their work and reinforced a strong collaborative environment.

Consider how many times you ask someone to go back and redo their work. After the third time—fourth, max—the issue becomes one of clarifying expectations, not having the right skill set, or the reviewer's subjective opinions. Rather than go back a fourth or fifth time, a different approach may be necessary.

There's another statement you may be familiar with: *Timing is everything*. There may be more art than science to determining just the right timing. And, if you have multiple people you're communicating with, it's unlikely that you will get it just right for everyone. This principle is not about getting timing down perfectly; it's about connecting with the recipients.

There are two caveats to this principle. First, sometimes a message cannot wait. In fact, waiting may exacerbate a problem. For example, if you are making organizational changes that affect a particular person or team, you will want to let them know as early as possible, so they don't hear about it through some rumor mill. If done correctly, this can also avoid the issue raised in Principle #3 (*As a leader, communicate early, and often*). On the flip side, be sure you're not just trying to check a box on your to-do list.

The second situation in which you should not be overly empathetic is if you have to let someone go. You should be cautious with how you empathize. Some say not to empathize at all. Don't say "I know how you must feel right now." This is trite, and there's a very strong likelihood you *don't* know how they feel in that moment. We're not suggesting you be cold and callous. Just choose your words carefully in those more sensitive circumstances.

We didn't say these principles would be easy. You need to apply some judgment as to when and how to apply them.

Principle #10: Have an exit strategy.

When giving a presentation, most people spend a significant and disproportionate time preparing for and rehearsing their introduction compared to their ending. The ending is equally important; it's about closure and a call to action. This can be all too painfully obvious during their delivery. This extends beyond presentations to meetings and other forms of communication, as well. The error primarily comes from a lack of planning, or, at least, effective planning.

Another challenge driving this principle is that most people are uncomfortable with silence, so they fill the space. The risk with this is that you will lose your audience, or your main message will get lost. Another by-product is that your personal communication brand is tarnished. People will perceive that you drone on and on or that you don't have a point. Your credibility can be compromised. This is not an ideal reputation to have because you also risk people shutting you and your messages down before they even have a chance to get off the ground. They see you coming, and their guard goes up—or they take their phones out, ready to be distracted.

Plan. Get to the point. And get out. You need to know how and when you are finished—when to exit. How will you know? The proactive way is because you will have gotten your few select points across succinctly, and you will have provided supporting evidence and a call to action, i.e., what you want them to accept or do. You may even see some heads nodding—from agreement as opposed to trying to stay awake.

More reactive ways to know whether you are finished is that you can look at the expressions on your recipients' faces. Do they look dazed and confused? By then, of course, it may be too late. But even in such cases, fear not. If you see your audience dozing off or looking lost or bored, we recommend engaging them with some questions (i.e., What do you think? How would you react to/handle this?).

Summary of Coaching Tips

There are lessons to be learned across each of the ten guiding principles of the Crystal Rule. In addition to the summary below, consider adding any key lessons you learned from this appendix.

- Practice benign neglect with your messaging. If it can wait to check clarity, wait.
- Don't write anything you wouldn't want to appear on the evening news. This is about discoverability and accountability.
- Plan all communications and interactions in advance.
- Identify a writing buddy to review select messages using the Crystal Rule as a guide.
- Practice the four-finger rule for your emails.
- Know the purpose of your communication and stick to it.
- When it comes to performance, values, and objectives, set clear expectations, and provide periodic updates.
- Clearly state your call to action.
- Plan, distribute, and stick to an agenda for meetings, presentations, and speeches.

Summary of the Crystal Rule

Clear communication takes time. It takes practice to hone your skills. However, you need to practice the right things; otherwise, you risk developing bad habits. Follow the Crystal Rule to achieve great clarity with your communications.

The ten guiding principles provide additional context and specificity when it comes to process and execution. They don't operate in isolation from one another. To be clear and effective, you need to have a plan. You need to be succinct and organized. You need to time your messages well and put yourself in the recipient's shoes.

The people who make it look easy have a plan. We don't always see how or when they plan, only the delivery, which makes us feel we should be able to do it just as easily. That's where people get themselves into trouble.

You can avoid trouble with your communications by living the Crystal Rule. Keep your audience, key messages, and call to action crystal clear and top of mind.

The rest of the book provides greater detail about speed bumps to watch out for, how to plan and execute your communications, and the implications for your personal brand and leadership—or, put another way, your credibility and your influence.

Additional Resources

- *Active Listening Techniques: 30 Practical Skills to Hone Your Communication Skills* by Nixaly Leonardo LCSW (New York: Rockridge Press, 2020).
- *Empathy: Why It Matters and How to Get It* by Roman Krznaric (New York: TarcherPerigee, 2015).
- *HBR's 10 Must-Reads on Communication* (with featured article, "The Necessary Art of Persuasion," by Jay Conger) (Cambridge, MA: Harvard Business Review Press, 2013).

Appendix B

Traits Associated with Good Critical Thinking

By David Lapakko, PhD, Associate Professor of Communication Studies, Augsburg University

A good critical thinker thinks in certain ways, and these ways of thinking are also conducive to making good arguments.

Intellectual humility (vs. intellectual arrogance): As you've been told many times, the world is a complicated place; "truth" is elusive, and there are limits to what we know. Anyone who thinks they "know it all" is usually delusional. We must draw conclusions, but we must also be aware of our limitations. A study of argument should force us to realize that we don't have all the answers, and that differing points of view can have merit, even if we disagree with them in the end. Also, intellectual arrogance is not a desirable trait for arguers for purely practical reasons; to be blunt, most audiences don't react well to people who come off as know-it-alls.

Intellectual courage (vs. intellectual cowardice): Sometimes coming to your own conclusions will invite criticism from others, even ridicule. Critical thinkers have the courage of their convictions, and a reluctance to simply follow along because an idea is popular or expressed repeatedly. We live in a world where people like to fit in, but sometimes we need to call it as we see it, even if that means leaving us open to disapproval. We live in an age where once people give themselves a label (e.g., "conservative," "Democrat," "Christian"), they sometimes feel constrained from having an opinion that is at odds with the groups of people to which they feel affiliated. Good critical thinkers are braver than that. On a related note, one fallacy in reasoning, *argumentum ad populum*, is based on the assumption that if most people believe something, then it must necessarily be "right" or "true." Although what the majority believes is worth considering, it should seldom be assumed that such a view is automatically correct.

Intellectual perseverance (vs. intellectual laziness): Good critical thinkers really need to work at what they do. They have to do careful and extensive research. They have to spend time at it. As with physical exercise, good critical thinkers must feel the burn a little bit—"No pain, no gain." These days, with the pace of life being what it is, and people being stressed out in many ways, we all are tempted to take shortcuts. Rather than carefully reading and thinking, we often wind up scanning a few headlines, glancing at a few websites, and consulting with a couple of friends, regarding that as "research."

Fair-mindedness (vs. intellectual unfairness): We must be aware of our biases and be careful not to prejudge an issue based on those biases. We must be willing to consider alternative points of view, even if we end up disagreeing with them. And we must acknowledge that we all have a lot of knee-jerk reactions to opposing ideas that must be kept in check.

Confusing labels with reality: Words are not things—they merely attempt to represent reality. Just because you have a label for something—"victimless crime," for example—does not mean that you have fully captured its real meaning. We use a variety of labels—for example, "terrorist," "Republican," or "tax-and-spend liberal"—as if they are self-evident explanations of people or ideas. But we can be deceived by labels; the world is usually more complex than these labels would suggest.

Giving meaning to unrelated events: Just because your mom sneezed at the moment you opened your textbook doesn't necessarily mean that she's allergic to books. That's a silly example, but consider this one: Just because the economy improved after so-and-so was elected president does not necessarily mean that the president was responsible for the improvement. Just because two things happen together in time, or in space, does not necessarily give them a causal relationship.

Wishful thinking: We all wish that things could be a certain way. Will there be global warming? Will we see World War III? Can I afford that new laptop? In each case, our personal wishes and desires can cloud our judgment—we'd like to think that global warming won't ruin the planet, that World War III is out of the question, and that anything we want to buy will be affordable. But our wishes may conflict with cold, hard reality. A variation of wishful thinking is called the "confirmation bias" in the field of psychology—that is, people often see what they want to see. If you drink coffee, you might only notice articles that say caffeine is harmless and tend to ignore those that raise health concerns.

Either/or thinking: Sometimes called "dualistic" thinking, this approach to looking at the world has a black-and-white orientation. Either you are "good" or "bad"; you either want "war" or "peace"; you are either "liberal" or "conservative"; you are either "part of the problem" or "part of the solution." Such simplistic orientations to the world again ignore the many complexities of an issue. Falsely assuming that something must be either "A" or "B" can lead to the fallacy in reasoning called a "false dilemma."

Unconscious assumptions and biases: Many people are not even aware that they make assumptions or have biases. We are so much a part of our own world—both personally and culturally—that we often cannot see what is right in front of us. As mentioned above, all arguments include assumptions and are based on certain values; therefore, we need to be aware of what these assumptions and biases are. For example, many people in the United States are strongly "individualistic," believe in the value of self-reliance, and think that most anyone can be rich and successful provided that they work hard enough. If that is part of how we view the world, then you can imagine how such a view might influence one's arguments around issues such as poverty, welfare, and homelessness, to name just a few. Similarly, what assumptions one makes about "human nature" will influence how you view teaching or managing other people. If you believe that people are naturally curious and industrious by nature, you will communicate with your students or employees differently than if you see humans as basically dull and lazy.

Overall, it would be tempting to believe that humans are "rational decision-makers" who excel at thinking—after all, it's the ability to think and to symbolize that's supposed to differentiate us from the "animals." However, there is abundant evidence to suggest that we are far from perfect when it comes to reasoned or sensible decision-making. Indeed, if you have never made a "dumb decision" in your life—based on weak evidence, poor reasoning, or limited or careless evaluation of the issues involved—we would all like to meet you!

Additional Resources

- *Argumentation: Critical Thinking in Action*, 4th ed., by David Lapakko (Dubuque, IA: Kendall Hunt, 2016), 18–20.
- *The Miniature Guide to Critical Thinking* by Richard Paul and Linda Elder (Dillon Beach, CA: Foundation for Critical Thinking Press, 2007).

Appendix C

A Five-Step, Hypothesis-Focused Approach to Problem-Solving

Overview and Benefits

- This approach is essential to communicate problems and solutions in a quick and collaborative manner.
- Taking such an approach reinforces your critical thinking and provides clarity of your message.
- This structured approach to problem-solving allows for quicker identification of potential problems and testing of respective solutions.
- Promotes making the right decisions when it is too costly to get them wrong.
- Focuses on efficiency associated with data collection and analysis.
- Allows for increased speed and quality of decisions; starts and stays focused rather than casting a wide net to see what emerges.
- On a personal level, if used effectively it can increase clarity and credibility.
- This is a process not a result, but if followed, the process drives results.

Five Steps

Consider this an iterative process that leverages key experience and expertise to ensure that you have enough insight about a topic to make an informed and strong business decision. One caution: Don't skip any steps.

Step 1: Establish the initial understanding of the problem or challenge.

- Overview and benefits:
  - Provides a snapshot in time and a baseline understanding.
  - Depicts the actual versus the ideal/proposed processes and outcomes.
- Approach tips:
  - Seek input from people with knowledge and/or experience with the subject.

- o Include the initial presenting observations/data that will generate further explanation/possibilities/hypotheses.
- o Consider how it is known to be a problem:
  —Need to consider the presenting data and evidence relative to any number of metrics (e.g., historical performance, industry standards, and competitors, to name a few)
- o From a business standpoint, these data should be reflected as key business outcomes.
  —Why is this a problem for our organization?
  —What is/is not happening regarding key outcomes such as productivity, quality, or other performance-based criteria?

Step 2: Generate and refine hypothesis.

- Overview and benefits:
  - o *Hypothesis* is a statement of belief based on current understanding.
  - o *Objective* is to find and narrow the opportunity.
  - o Helps establish priorities.
  - o Targets root causes
  - o Hypotheses are essential to focus the data collection efforts.
- Approach tips:
  - o Ask the question, "What can be the possible cause of the issue(s)?"
  - o How: leverage expertise of others via brainstorming or discussion
  - o We have included the following guidelines for effective brainstorming:
    —Suspend judgment: No criticism or judgment.
    —Be open to all ideas: Wild is welcome.
    —Quantity is key: The more the better.
    —Combine and improve: Eliminate duplicates, combine similar, and develop potential ideas.
  - o Establish ideas for both the problem and possible solutions.

Step 3: Plan for and gather the data needed to test the hypothesis.

- Overview and benefits:
  - o Data serves to validate, prove, or modify the hypotheses.
  - o Stay focused; only pursue what is absolutely necessary to make a decision and/or take action.
    —Consider something along the lines of MVP (minimal viable product): What is the least amount of data needed to make a strong decision?

- Approach tips:
  - o As a starting point, remember there was likely some presenting data that showed the initial problem (e.g., cycle times, response times, customer satisfaction, revenues and costs, and many others).
  - o Consider all possible sources of data and how to obtain the data.
    —Think in terms of cause and effect plus verification of hypotheses.
    —Who has/where can I find the insight needed for hypotheses?
  - o Identify who will be involved:
    —Note: Always work the key managers involved to ensure that you have their support for any data or people requests.
  - o Consider how the data will be obtained (e.g., interviews, surveys, focus groups, archival performance data, observations).
  - o Validate early and often to ensure the data is representative; multiple sources help with this.
  - o Evolve your work plan as new information is identified.
  - o Consider whether the data will drive action.

Step 4: Analyze the data.

- Overview and benefits:
  - o Provides the explanation and meaning behind the data.
  - o Allows you to further refine hypotheses wherever applicable.
  - o Data provides credibility.
    —The power of data and analysis drives action and transitions you from just a person with an opinion to something more substantive.
- Approach tips:
  - o Look for trends, patterns, and anomalies in the data.
  - o Reformulate any hypothesis proven to be wrong.
  - o Consider what the data means in business terms. We call this the "So what?"

Step 5: Summarize findings and develop recommendations.

- Overview and benefits:
  - o Analysis is about facts. Your job is to draw conclusions by looking for key relationships and insights and determining how the findings fit or do not fit with the hypothesis.

- o The data will facilitate discussion and home in on solutions.
  —Keep in mind there can be multiple perspectives regarding the answer.
- Approach tips:
  - o Consider how you present your findings (e.g., tables, charts, and diagrams) to illustrate key points.
  - o Ask yourself (and the team) whether these changes will drive better/desired results.
  - o Clearly articulate what actions can/should be taken.
    —Ensure that solutions are realistic and feasible (cost, existing processes, timing, ownership of solution, technology, process requirements, legal, staffing).

Acknowledgments

Substantial endeavors require substantial support. I'd like to thank my wife Sara, daughter Chase, and son Finley for their unwavering belief, encouragement, and optimism throughout this project—and frankly, every day.

Thanks to co-author Roger for always being a great writing partner and friend. Your openness to ideas, creativity, and diligence are truly exemplary.

I've been the beneficiary of wisdom and guidance from friends and colleagues throughout this project and my career. Thank you for being available, for listening, and for sharing ideas and feedback. And to my current team: You all are absolutely wonderful people to have the privilege of working with. Thank you for your hard work, energy, and initiative. It is truly inspiring.

—Timothy J. Tobin
Washington, DC

Several of my acquaintances contributed to the development of this book. I thank Dr. David Lapakko of Augsburg University for his appendix on the traits of good critical thinking. Former boss, the late Chuck Ritley, my old Macalester College buddy David Foster, and past writing colleagues Nick Montoya and Cara Hale Alter all offered great, vivid vignettes.

In this book, we recommend that everyone acquire a "writing buddy" to challenge their thinking and logic and clarity. Co-author Tim Tobin has been a great writing buddy. The result is a well-tested book. Thanks, Tim.

Special thanks go to my wife Rita, an avid reader and a fellow veteran of advertising and college textbook publishing. Her edits and comments remain invaluable to me.

We added many quotations from famous people, living and dead. Good websites are available to find quotations for your needs. Our favorites are www.brainyquote.com and Goodreads.com. You can spend hours having fun with their entries.

—Roger S. Peterson
Rocklin, California

INDEX

About the Authors

Timothy J. Tobin, EdD, is a learning and leadership development professional committed to helping individuals and organizations reach their greatest potential. He has worked across multiple industries, including consulting, financial services, education, and hospitality. He has held executive-level learning, leadership, and operations positions in multiple global organizations. Tim has been a leadership speaker, consultant, and coach. In addition to numerous academic and professional blogs and articles, Tim is the author of *Peak Leadership Fitness: Elevating Your Leadership Game* and *Your Leadership Story: Use Your Story to Energize, Inspire, and Motivate.* He holds a bachelor's degree in psychology, a master's degree in organizational management, and a doctorate in human and organizational studies, as well as professional certifications as a senior professional of human resources (SPHR) and a Society for Human Resource Management senior certified professional (SHRM-SCP). On a personal note, Tim is an endurance athlete and has completed thirteen marathons and thirteen Ironman triathlons.

Roger S. Peterson, PCM, is one of the original professional certified marketers (PCM) of the American Marketing Association and past president of AMA/Sacramento. His advertising days were spent at divisions of J. Walter Thompson and Ogilvy & Mather. Roger co-authored the AMA's handbook on managing business-to-business marketing communications after serving in that role for two technology firms. As an acquisitions editor in college textbook publishing, he published forty-five texts on education and psychology. He is the co-author of four business books and served as a developmental editor for seven books. Roger was a columnist for *Tradeshow Week*, a three-time columnist for the *Sacramento Business Journal*, and a five-time guest editorialist for *The Sacramento Bee.* His two hundred published articles cover topics ranging from business to education and history. He served in the US Navy and is a former high school teacher. On a personal note, for exercise Roger just takes long walks.